A VERY
GOOD YEAR

A VERY
GOOD YEAR

*The Journey
of a California Wine
from Vine to Table*

MIKE WEISS

GOTHAM BOOKS

GOTHAM BOOKS
Published by Penguin Group (USA) Inc.
375 Hudson Street, New York, New York 10014, U.S.A.
Penguin Group (Canada), 10 Alcorn Avenue, Toronto, Ontario, Canada M4V 3B2 (a division of Pearson Penguin Canada Inc.); Penguin Books Ltd, 80 Strand, London WC2R 0RL, England; Penguin Ireland, 25 St Stephen's Green, Dublin 2, Ireland (a division of Penguin Books Ltd); Penguin Group (Australia), 250 Camberwell Road, Camberwell, Victoria 3124, Australia (a division of Pearson Australia Group Pty Ltd); Penguin Books India Pvt Ltd, 11 Community Centre, Panchsheel Park, New Delhi - 110 017, India; Penguin Group (NZ), Cnr Airborne and Rosedale Roads, Albany, Auckland, New Zealand (a division of Pearson New Zealand Ltd); Penguin Books (South Africa) (Pty) Ltd, 24 Sturdee Avenue, Rosebank, Johannesburg 2196, South Africa

Penguin Books Ltd, Registered Offices: 80 Strand, London WC2R 0RL, England

Published by Gotham Books, a division of Penguin Group (USA) Inc.

First printing, June 2005
10   9   8   7   6   5   4   3   2   1

Copyright © Mike Weiss, 2005
All rights reserved
Portions of this book were originally published as a series in the *San Francisco Chronicle*.

Gotham Books and the skyscraper logo are trademarks of Penguin Group (USA) Inc.

LIBRARY OF CONGRESS CATALOGING-IN-PUBLICATION DATA

Weiss, Mike
    A very good year : the journey of a California wine from vine to table / Mike Weiss.
        p.   cm.
    Includes bibliographical references and index.
    ISBN 1-592-40129-5 (alk. paper)
        1. Wine and wine making—California.   2. Viticulture—California.   I. Title.

    TP557.W447   2005
    663'.2'09794—dc22   2004027995

Printed in the United States of America
Set in Perpetua
Designed by Lynn Newmark

For Carole

"Businessmen they drink my wine
Plowmen dig my earth,
None of them along the line
Know what any of it is worth."
—Bob Dylan, "All Along the Watchtower"

"Everyone thinks winemaking is the great romance of the agricultural industry. You pick grapes once a year, nothing else to it. Yeah——your mutha."
—Hoss Milone

A VERY
GOOD YEAR

Prologue

April 21, 2003: The Villa Fiore

IT WAS COLD and damp on Easter Monday morning, 2003. During the night it had snowed high in the Donner Pass, just as it had two decades earlier when Don and Rhonda Carano, seeking the knowledge they would need to succeed in the wine business, had driven across the mountains to attend viticulture classes at U.C. Davis. At the time, Rhonda had thought they were nuts. But twenty years on, their success was more than sufficient justification—among the hundreds of wineries in Napa and Sonoma counties, only four sold more wine in restaurants than Ferrari-Carano.

This morning four people sat at a circular table in a private tasting room on the second floor of the Villa Fiore, where the never-opened leather bindings of the world's classics on the bookshelves stuck together when you tried to remove one. A twenty-two-thousand-square-foot hospitality center for Ferrari-Carano Vineyards and Winery, with two thousand more feet of wine cellar, the splendiferous villa was the icon of their brand, and a testament to Don and Rhonda's marketing acumen. Joining the Caranos were two longtime employees, their winemaker George Bursick, and the man who grew their grapes, Steve Domenichelli. At thirty-eight, Steve was the youngest person at the table, and the best-looking man. Everybody was in jeans. Steve and George's were inexpensive and well-worn. Rhonda's unfaded designer jeans were sharply creased.

At the center of the table stood the reason for this gathering—two flint-green bottles of Ferrari-Carano 2002 Fumé Blanc. The question before them was whether this just-bottled vintage was ready to be released to market. The deeper question was whether they had failed, or succeeded. Beneath that lurked unarticulated fears and anxieties. About the wine. About the economy. About their own well-being. The mood was self-consciously festive, animated by those anxieties.

When I had approached them in November 2001, the grapes that would be transformed into the wine in the bottles in front of us had not yet appeared on the dormant vines, winter vines that Steve Domenichelli had said were asleep. Now, if they had succeeded, the wine, made from Sauvignon Blanc grapes, would, in George Bursick's words, "jump out of the frigging glass." They had agreed to let me witness every step in the process of making a single bottle of this afford- able, premium California wine. I had come to know these four, and many others who worked for and with them—had become familiar with their accomplishments, their rivalries, their joys and sorrows, their losses. In the past seventeen months people they loved, who had worked with them side by side, had died. Children had been born. Mortality had asserted its unbreakable grip.

Their Fumé Blanc was among the best-selling white wines made from Sauvignon Blanc grapes in America's premier restaurants, and the anchor of their business. If they gave the thumbs-up this morning, there were eighty thousand cases of it—the most they had ever pro- duced, a dozen bottles to a case, the white cardboard cases stacked and bound on pallets in a warehouse—ready to be launched into the world. For every bottle, untold gallons of precious Western water had been expended, and unmeasured amounts of potentially danger-ous sulfur had been sprayed. Many other parts of the California story had touched the making of the wine held within these Burgundy-style bottles, with their slender, sloping shoulders. To begin with, the im-migration, both legal and illegal, of the Mexican workers who tended the Caranos' vines and harvested their grapes, most of them from the same drought-parched village of El Charco; like their employers, they dreamt a California dream. There was the matter of the threatened health of the Russian River, whose breezes cooled their vineyards, but whose water could not legally be siphoned off to irrigate them. Most of all, perhaps, what they did at Ferrari-Carano seemed to em-blemize the flamboyant, high-rolling, self-assured, sun-kissed, risk-taking earnestness that characterized California at its best and worst, and drove people on the East Coast and in Europe mad with contempt and envy.

The bucolic land surrounding the Villa Fiore could have served as a poster for California wine country. Rhonda Carano had chosen to build the villa on this particular site in the Dry Creek Valley because of that view. Outside the French doors in the room where we were sitting, contoured rows of vines swathed in lingering morning tule fog rolled gently down the distant hillside toward the creek, with its forested banks. Closer to the villa were acres of vines with pale-green young tendrils and still-dormant buds—it was a new growing year, 2003, and the ceaseless cycle that had produced the wine on the table was repeating itself. Closer yet was a pool. Don, who had made a for-tune in casino/hotels in Reno, Nevada, and invested "umpteen million"—his phrase—in this winery, had wanted the pool to have a waterfall; but Rhonda, who at forty-eight was two decades younger than her husband of twenty-two years, had wanted a reflecting pool, and that was what she got. At night, the fiber-optic steps changed colors. She had also overruled some suggestions from her design consultant and friend, Raul Rodriguez. Rodriguez's claim to fame was designing the gaudy floats for the Rose Day Parade in Pasadena. At the far end of the pool were four sculptural columns, the kind you'd see in Roman ruins. But these, in the words of the architectural writer John King, were ruins of things that never were. Raul had wanted heroic statues between the columns, and urns on top. Flash. Rhonda had said, "We don't want Caesars Palace."

Rhonda was petite with a pretty, oval face and lots of dark hair, a woman who gave the impression of being competent, energetic, and eager. But there was something more, an underlying toughness and resiliency. Rhonda had another agenda, as well, this Monday morning. She wanted to get the Fumé Blanc to *Wine Spectator* magazine, whose ratings could be crucial to the success of a wine. The deadline was looming, and she didn't want to miss it the way they had to their detriment once before.

Out on the street, in the marketplace, the drumbeat of failure threatening people in the restaurant, wine, and hospitality industries since the attacks of 9/11 was relentless. It was amazing how far the unintended damage reached, wreaked by those nineteen young Muslims who forswore alcohol, and whose dreams were dreams of hatred and destruction. Just a few months ago, George Bursick's friend Mike Mondavi had lost the business that had been in his family for generations. A depressed restaurant industry, where Ferrari-Carano was accustomed to selling the greater share of its line of wines, had forced them to offer incentives to large chains and discounters—for the first time the wine was widely available at a reduced retail price. Steve Meisner, Ferrari-Carano's hard-driving, speed-rapping director of sales and marketing, was impatient to bring their 2002 Fumé Blanc to market no later than the day before yesterday. It was their cash cow.

Don Carano, a courtly man whose ambition was not banked by success, had prospered first as a gaming lawyer in Nevada, and then twice over as an entrepreneur. His dreams were dreams of pleasure—the small-minded would say of sin—of gambling and drink. And of a legacy. Don was the patriarch of a large clan. His vineyards were spread across four fertile valleys.

George Bursick was making his way around the table, pouring wines from both bottles of the 2002 Fumé Blanc into the stemware in front of each of us. One bottle had been refrigerated and was being served cold, the way most of us are accustomed to drinking white wines; the other bottle had been in the fridge for just one hour because, as George had taught me, the aromas were more evident at the slightly higher temperature.

"Our purpose here," Don said, "we're tasting if there's sufficient bottle aging before release. In part, because of Steve Meisner's demands—we're losing placements, and so on." Meisner always pushed to move product into the pipeline: Sometimes his salesman's urgency had to be resisted. Because of his goading, the 2000 vintage had been scheduled for release too early and subsequently had to be yanked back to be given more time to age in the bottle. "Now," Don said, "we've worked our way back into sufficient bottle aging."

The four of them were now swirling the wine and plunging their noses into their glasses to sniff the pale golden liquid, the color of California hillsides in May before they fade from gold to straw. Was I supposed to swirl clockwise or counterclockwise? It was one of those things I could never remember, like how many r's and s's in "embarrassed." To play it safe, I alternated directions. I had always drunk wine, as I suppose many people do, without giving much thought to what had gone into making it. When I first approached the Caranos, I had proposed looking deeply into a bottle of California wine in order to find the whole epic of contemporary California in a single bottle of its symbolic product, its face to the world. Tourism and globalism, the environment and sustainability, immigration and glamour, drought and dammed rivers. Along the way my attention had been seduced by the particulars—by these people and their coworkers, and by the complex process that produced the simple pleasure of a bottle of wine. So I had set out to do one thing, and ended up caring more about another. It was Hemingway, who seemed to do everything a man could do, who said, "We never do the things we want to do; those are the things we never do."

"This is a fruit-driven wine," said George Bursick, swirling. "This is pretty much the style we're known for. This is why people buy us. So the question is—is this acceptable just now in its fruit-forwardness?"

George had been with the Caranos since the beginning, had been their first employee, and his early wines had put them on the map. He was paid a handsome salary, and treated with respect. Yet around the Caranos he was nervous—jumpy in his eagerness to please. I wondered what made him so insecure. But the personal was always off-limits for the forty-eight-year-old winemaker, with his round, bland face and straight brown hair streaked with gray.

"Steve's pruning did a lot to bring this wine back into our style," George said. "Steve massaged Storey Ranch Vineyard to bring us back into more melon flavors."

For the first time, Steve Domenichelli spoke up. These dog-and-pony shows made him antsy—he wanted to be back in his truck, hurtling along the back roads of Sonoma County from vineyard to vineyard, tending to his vines and his men. "You can take each individual vine"—1,360,000 in all, grown by Ferrari-Carano—"and through careful pruning get just the right sunlight." Steve knew I knew this—I had spent months at his side. Normally the most casual of men, he had picked up on the anxiety and formality of the occasion.

6

"We worked backwards," George continued, "trying to induce the vineyards to produce the style of wine that's already popular. We really started making this style in 1986. In 1985 we used some Sémillon; it tended to mute the Sauvignon Blanc flavors . . ."

"He made me sell the vineyard, by the way," Don interjected, smiling indulgently.

". . . So when we dropped the Sémillon," George continued, "that left two sources for Sauvignon Blanc, one right outside here, the other one above Don and Rhonda's house in the Alexander Valley." The Villa Fiore—where we were sitting—was for show. When the Caranos were in residence, flying in from Reno aboard their Beechcraft King Air 350 turbo jet, they bedded down in a restored turn-of-the-century farmhouse. "Those two vineyards made our style," George continued. "Grassy Dry Creek, with melon from Alexander Valley. Boom! Out of the blue, immensely popular. It's always been a challenge to make this wine with the components of each." Since then, the Caranos had acquired additional vineyards, and now needed to maintain that balance of elements among many hundreds of tons of additional grapes, tens of thousands more bottles.

Steve Domenichelli had drifted away again as George continued to talk. A fourth-generation California grape farmer, he was boyishly handsome in the way of a Tom Cruise, with brown eyes that were turned inward. A lock of his thick, dark hair had fallen over his pale forehead. His nails were gnawed at.

"When we picked these grapes, when we tasted 'em, we could taste where we want to go," George continued. "A couple of blocks, we were concerned, they were too aggressively herbaceous. We barrel fermented them"—as opposed to fermenting them in a stainless steel tank—"so we could temper those aggressive herbal components. And that's why you get a little bit of oak in here, because the oak's job is to rein in those aggressive tendencies. And everything fits in, fits into the framework."

George meant his own framework. If you read between the lines of what he was saying, it was that Steve's fruit was slightly out of control, and it took George's ministrations to put it right. To restore balance. To guarantee future success. That brought Steve—who was swirling his wine faster than anybody else—right back to what was going on. He spoke of Don's land, Don's grapes, and his own husbandry. The winter of 2003 had been colder than winter of 2002, he said, recounting how his crews had been out at midnight, turning on heat machines, anticipating a frost, saving crop. A small amount of Chardonnay growing at upper elevations had been lost to frost, but much that might have been lost had been saved.

Enough talk. The moment of truth was at hand. What had begun with dormant vines had unfolded through bloom and bud break and veraison; through the dropping of crop and harvest; through barreling and fermenting, blending and bottling. It was time to find out how well they had done. Don stepped between his warring princes.

"Very good, Steve, George," Don said. "The biggest thing is to taste those component parts, what you're doing in the vineyard, and how it relates to the wine. So. Let's taste."

They lifted their wine to their lips.

1
VINE

November 2001–March 2002

THE CARANOS

IN THE BEGINNING was The Story.

To succeed in the California wine business you strategize back-to-front: You need good wine in the bottle, yes, but there's plenty of that around; and for good wine you need good technique in the winery; and before that, good grapes, which come from fecund land, well tended. All those exist in abundance, but not everybody has a good Story. A friend of mine whose small winery produces expensive, highly praised wines once had a top-end New York retailer explain why he would not stock his wines by saying, "Frankly, your story isn't good enough."

The feuds and the dynasties of the Mondavis and Gallos are well known, and it is no coincidence that they are giants in the industry. Their stories are writ large. Robert Mondavi was the master storyteller. It was he, for instance, who in the 1960s took a workaday Sauvignon Blanc, not a glamorous grape, and rechristened it Fumé Blanc, which sounded French and smoky and exotic. He still produces one of the best, and today so do the Caranos.

The Ferrari-Carano Story has the same generic elements as the Gallo and Mondavi Stories. Italian. Family. Wine. And unique elements as well. "No other vintners also are casino owners," says Michael Ouellette, a Napa Valley winemaker and restaurateur. "And that's an interesting story." But Don Carano preferred to downplay that he made his fortune in gambling, the fortune that allowed him to buy into the fine-wine game. Didn't want that to detract from The Story.

"There's a tremendous number of people who've come here and failed miserably," Ouellette continued. "Clos Pegase, to this day is mediocre at best. You know who messed up for the longest time? Francis Coppola. He made absolutely dreadful wine for the longest time, and nobody could tell him anything—he thought he knew it all.

"This is like the Aspen of the last decade—they've got their ski chalet, or two, or three, now they've got to have a winery," says Ouellette. "So they all come here with their twenty million dollars, which is what it takes, and build the winery, and most of them fail miserably. So what was Don Carano able to do that others weren't able to do?"

I first met the Caranos in late November 2001. The first storm of winter was about a week in the past when I drove up the Dry Creek Valley past dormant vineyards with a ridge of low-slung hillsides to the west. The fields and slopes were showing more shades of green than Crayola ever imagined. The sun was shining, but there were ominous clouds above the hills.

When I turned into Ferrari-Carano Vineyards and Winery nine miles northwest of Highway 101, and a mile and a half short of Lake Sonoma, what I saw was the Villa Fiore, the house of flowers. Tourists and tasters got to drive past its imposing faux Mediterranean facade, shut away behind a heavy locked gate. The hoi polloi were allowed only at the tasting room and gift shop around to the side, where they were welcome to leave their money, but the Villa's real hospitality was for the trade only. The Villa was massively impressive, and massively out of place in the bucolic valley. One thought immediately of Nevada, of themed hotels and casinos, and of the suites, the privileges, the comps reserved for high-rollers. Rhonda Carano, who helped design it and whose domain it was, thought the Villa was "stately"; in the working partnership of husband and wife, she was the artist and Don the businessman. Not an unusual division of labor in wine country, or elsewhere. At the Eldorado, in Reno, she directed the advertising and public relations. The Villa was designed to reflect their brand. A popular wine aficionado Web site called it "the most spectacular hospitality site ever built." I was not inclined to disagree.

My initial impressions of the interior of the Villa were fleeting. There was a two-story-high entrance hall floored in green marble that rose to a painted dome a là the Sistine Chapel. Above a huge fireplace what appeared to be a Ferrari-Carano coat of arms was topped with a grape cluster; it was pseudo-heraldic but also Californian, because a similar cluster appears on the state seal as a symbol of agriculture. There was a grand staircase. Don and Rhonda led me through to a large, open-plan dining room and kitchen—not the formal dining room, but a place for more intimate entertaining—overlooking vineyards. Don was not physically imposing, but he was comfortable entertaining and selling.

We were going to eat lunch. Normally, Rhonda did not eat much lunch, and to keep fit she ran. At forty-eight, she was a picture of attractive good health. When there were no guests, the Caranos didn't drink wine with lunch but iced tea or water. But hospitality is an essential component of The Story, and unlike the software multimillionaires and developers who were buying wineries in the eighties and nineties, the Caranos had the advantage of already being successful hoteliers in Reno, where their major holding, the Eldorado, was famous for its restaurants. "Good food," a family friend once said, "is their Frank Sinatra." They were also partners in the Silver Legacy, and proprietors of some smaller holdings as well. In the Villa Fiore's state-of-the-art kitchen the executive chef, Joey Costanzo, and a staff of assistants and servers were preparing a three-course lunch with a tomato-based pork and hominy stew as the entrée. It was a recipe of Rhonda's, and right on Story—Italian, homey, delicious, authentic.

"Few people could build an Italian chateau like they did," I had been told by Eileen Fredrikson, of Gomberg, Fredrikson & Associates, an influential wine consultancy. "But they didn't just build their Story, the story of an Italian family . . . their personal entertaining style is clearly not phony. They are what they seem to be. So the wine and The Story are totally congruent." Rhonda had even played the accordion for five hundred guests at her fortieth birthday party.

The same people sat down to eat who would be there again, seventeen months later, when we gathered to see if they had failed or succeeded. The Caranos; George Bursick, their winemaker; and Steve Domenichelli, their director of vineyard operations. I had come here shopping for a winery that was neither too large nor too small to write about. An eight-hundred-pound gorilla like Gallo was atypical. A boutique winery, on the other hand, surprisingly *was* typical because 70 percent of California wineries produced a mere three thousand cases a year or less, but because of the economies of scale, their wines usually sold for high prices. What I was seeking was a winery that would serve as a stand-in for the entire industry. Its wines had to be well received, and they had to be affordable. I didn't want to write about a sixty-five-dollar bottle of Chardonnay, or a hundred-dollar Cabernet Sauvignon, something that was out of reach for most people. I wanted to write about a bottle of wine that I might buy.

According to Eileen Fredrikson—Gomberg-Fredrikson's numbers are gospel throughout the industry—Ferrari-Carano produced

185,000 total cases in 2001, a number that would rise in 2002. About fifty thousand of those had been Fumé Blanc, their best-seller, with a suggested retail price of fourteen dollars—affordable for most people who drink wine. Ferrari-Carano had come a long way in a short time. "We just evolved big thanks to the quality of our wines," said George Bursick when we sat down to lunch. Of course, every winemaker claims that his wines are products of the highest quality.

Rhonda Carano segued easily from Bursick's remark into The Story. "You've got to understand," she said, smiling, "Don's an Italian, and his grandfather always told him to buy land." The Caranos were from Genoa, and Don's grandfather had arrived near the turn of the century, working as a janitor and clerk for the Central Pacific. Soon he bought a small dairy ranch outside Reno. The Ferraris were Don's mother's people. Rhonda's family, the Bevilacquas, were also Genovese. Her grandfather was a bricklayer, and her dad worked as a house mover until he hurt his back and Don hired him to be the pasta maker for the Eldorado.

Both Don and Rhonda grew up in Reno, one of the least attractive cities in the West, in neighborhoods near the Truckee River. Rhonda's uncle Joe was the best home winemaker in her family. Everybody drank wine with meals, although the kids' was cut with 7-Up or water. For Italians wine was like water, Rhonda said, and we all laughed dutifully. It certainly had been true in the fifteenth century when the Romans were having more than a few problems with their water supply.

Salami. Head cheese. Sausage. "My family made that stuff when I was growing up," Rhonda said.

"When you butchered a pig," Don said, "you never threw anything away." Don spoke softly, but everybody at the table deferred when he said something. There was something appealingly avuncular about him—I got the feeling immediately that he was a nice man.

From Reno, Don moved to San Francisco to attend law school at the University of San Francisco, served in the armed forces, returned to Reno to work for the state legislative council, and then joined the law firm headed by the late U.S. senator Alan Bible. In his telling, he did not mention that virtually all Democratic politics in Nevada runs through that law office to this day. Nor did he mention at this juncture that his father, Louis, died when Don was seventeen and that he was raised by his late mother, Millie, said to be one of the most beautiful women in northern Nevada. She supported her only child by selling at upscale clothiers—Joseph Magnin in Reno, and later at I. Magnin on Geary Street in San Francisco, where she moved to be with her second husband. Eventually Don specialized in real estate and gambling law, and, he said, "That's how I got into the gaming business." One of his sons would later amplify that: When Don learned how much money casino owners made, it was motivation enough to abandon a lucrative law practice.

At his first opportunity, George Bursick, who looked to be about fifty and had an eager-to-please, nearly pleading face, interjected: "Don's name is now on the front door of that law firm." George had been with the Caranos since the beginning, and his longevity lent their wines a consistency that was an important element in their success.

Don himself projected a certain modesty. If you met him in Safeway—and you might, because he does the family shopping and enjoys being told at checkout how much he saved by using his red Safeway card—you would not guess that he's fabulously rich and one of the truly powerful men in Nevada. Today he was wearing blue jeans, loafers, and a powder-blue sweatshirt with a Ferrari-Carano logo, more or less the uniform of California's mega-wealthy winery owners, who tool around Napa and Sonoma counties in their pickups or SUVs, dressed the same way they did in high school.

The talk at lunch turned to their Fumé Blanc. The Bureau of Alcohol, Tobacco and Firearms considers Mondavi's invention to be a "fanciful varietal," that is to say, an imaginary kind of grape. The Caranos said their use of Fumé—for a wine made entirely with Sauvignon Blanc grapes—connotes the fact that the wine is held in oak barrels for a few months, or, as they say in the trade, they throw some oak on it. But there was more to it. Once again Mondavi seemed to be their model. Mondavi had demonstrated, as James Conaway put it in *The Far Side of Eden,* that "fine wine moves best through channels lubricated by the personality of the creator and . . . 'family values.'"

George Bursick explained that their Fumé Blanc was blended from the produce of five different vineyards, some contributing melonlike characteristics and others, like Keegan Ranch, adding what he called "big herbaceous, grassy" elements. Alas, the subtleties of wine tastes and aromas went in one of my ears and out the other. I was a novice, the extent of my involvement in the industry entirely on the consuming end. It would take months before I began to understand the urgency of Ferrari-Carano's attempts in the year ahead to bring the taste of their Fumé Blanc back to its origins, for fear that if they didn't, they would lose market share.

What I did know was that the wine was well reviewed, and that it tasted good to me. "Undiscerning" would be a charitable way of describing my palate. "We make it user-friendly," said George. "We always had a real strong following for it . . . but we have so many resources, we should nail it every time. It's a fun wine. I drink it every night."

"Me, too," said Steve Domenichelli, who had not said much.

"It's not rocket science," said George. "You have a moving target but you have an idea where you're going. It's important to follow the trends, see what people want. But it's also important to stay on track, important to stay with the style people have been buying for fifteen or twenty years."

Three quarters of their production, Don said, had traditionally been sold to restaurants and hotels, "on-premises" in the lingo of the trade. Ferrari-Carano was, according to a 2002 survey conducted by *Wine & Spirits* magazine, the fifth most popular restaurant brand in the country, ahead of such well-known rivals as Robert Mondavi, Sterling, Beringer, and Silver Oak. Their Fumé Blanc ranked third among Sauvignon Blancs, behind only the cultishly desirable Cloudy Bay from New Zealand, and California's Frog's Leap. The remaining quarter of their production had gone mostly to fine-wine shops. But as we sat there eating Joey's delicious stew and sipping our wine, that sales balance was shifting seismically. With many restaurants failing in the aftermath of 9/11, and others struggling, Ferrari-Carano was forced to change its marketing strategy. In a few weeks their sales reps would convene at the Villa for their annual meeting, and the urgency of shifting toward 60 percent restaurant sales and 40 percent retail sales would be emphasized. The falloff in restaurant trade, especially in the Northeast—the second-biggest market after California— meant "everyone moved," Don said. "It's going to take us a long time to come back."

But greater retail sales also had its dangers. Off-premises sales brought greater direct exposure to consumers, and Ferrari-Carano had always dealt primarily with the trade, and let the trade sell their brand to the public. It had been a marketing-driven rather than a sales-driven business. That was the importance of being served in restaurants like the Four Seasons in New York or Boulevard in San Francisco; those restaurants were trendsetters and created a market.

"One of the amazing things Ferrari-Carano has been able to do is create the illusion that they are a small family owned and operated winery," says Pat Kuleto, who designed and owns Boulevard, and became a close friend of the Caranos in the last few years. Before he knew Don and Rhonda, and even though he was in the business and Ferrari-Carano Chardonnay was a personal favorite of his, Kuleto had bought into The Story. "I thought of them as a little family winery becoming well known. They keep the quality way up. They keep the price accessible. Even though they've gotten big in scale. I'll let Don give you the numbers, but pretty huge."

In a year of conversations, some of them personal and intimate, Don would speak about many things, but about his production he was always coy, and he would never disclose his profit margin. Nonetheless, it was an open secret that the winery produced a tad more than two hundred thousand cases in 2002, which made it nearly twice the size of Murphy Goode and one-tenth the size of Beringer. Big but not giant. After a year of hectoring him about it, I got Don to reluctantly acknowledge revenue of about $25 million, but only after the number had been published in a local newspaper. And he hastened to point out that that was before costs, in an industry that was both labor- and cash-intensive.

"One of the things I hope you don't spill the beans on is we're as large as we are," Steve Meisner, Ferrari-Carano's chain-smoking marketing and sales director would eventually say to me. "Although it's your prerogative. A lot of people who buy our wines think we're a twenty-five-thousand-case winery. Every winery wants to be perceived as small; it's kind of nose-against-the-candy-store-window syndrome. I have a saying," said Meisner (who often had a saying): "The only thing better than the image of scarcity is scarcity itself."

As the luncheon wound down I learned why Steve Domenichelli, the man responsible for the quantity and quality of grapes on Don and Rhonda's properties, had been so quiet. Rhonda asked after his wife, Stephanie—she, too, had once worked in the Villa Fiore—and he told me that his fourth child, his first with Stephanie, and his first girl, was due any moment.

We were drinking a Ferrari-Carano El Dorado Gold, a Sauternes-like sweet wine, and drinking coffee, as the talk turned to the weather. George Bursick had read in *The Old Farmer's Almanac* that there wouldn't be much rainfall until January, but that later in 2002, El Niño was supposed to roar back in.

Two days later, as Thanksgiving weekend began, the second storm of the winter of 2001 drenched Northern California. By then I had decided to write about a bottle of Ferrari-Carano Fumé Blanc. The winery was a good size, neither huge nor tiny, and produced reasonably priced wines that experts said were very good and popular. It grew virtually all of its own grapes, and so controlled the entire process of producing a bottle of wine. It had succeeded in making itself a fair stand-in for the California wine business. On the surface, the winery presented an incomparable picture of graciousness and good living, the very image of what someone once called California's second most glamorous industry. Just below the surface, though, I sensed tension, and perhaps secrets. Although one person alone seemed immune—the courtly Don Carano himself.

THE GROWER AND
THE WINEMAKER

STEVE DOMENICHELLI (pronounced doe-men-uh-KEL-ly) took hold of a woody Sauvignon Blanc cane with the gentle firmness of a pediatrician percussing a child's chest, and swiftly cracked it. In the hush of a January morning in the soggy vineyard you could hear the crack, yet the vine was not broken.

"It's an old trick," he said, looking up from where he was leaning into the vine. "It wakes 'em up. Gets 'em all the same size when they wake up, that's what my grandfather used to say."

He bounded away walking like a farmer, with loping, arm-swinging strides no city dweller can duplicate, strides that seemed too long for his height. There was a bounce to his step, and it was not hard to imagine what he had once looked like with a basketball in those confident hands, leading his Cloverdale High School team to three straight Division III state championships. He was wearing jeans, work boots, a long-sleeved white thermal shirt, and a baseball cap.

Steve whipped a pruning shears out of its holster. You could prune, he said, for as long as the vines were dormant. "You have to have a great eye," he explained over his shoulder, as I trailed behind scribbling notes, "to make everything consistent. It looks real simple but it's a real crucial time.

"That's a nice sun cane right there," he said, halting. "Fertile. Medium buds. These clusters," pointing at the tiny, tightly closed buds, "they're made the year prior to harvest, last year. You could see them under a microscope. Your farming practices the year before dictate the fruit the following year, your crop loads." I had a sudden sense of endlessly looping three-year cycles, a helixlike continuum. "You want to keep the vines healthy, balanced, and consistent, so I give George uniform grapes and sugar content."

His crews had been pruning for several weeks, leaving three to five canes on each plant, with fifteen to twenty buds on each cane, and were close to being finished. "A lot of people don't like to prune until there's full flowering," he continued. "I like to see ten percent flowers, go in and remove my leaves. You have to have enough people"—as Ferrari-Carano did, employing about 120 vineyard workers full time, although many of them had returned home to Mexico for the winter—"work seven days a week to catch it. Sunlight and shade, it's huge. If you get big, massive vines you have no fruit. Then it takes three, four years to get back in balance. You want a balance out there, get the vines perfect for next year, all green and lush."

He reached for a vine and began to prune fast, instinctively. As he pruned he talked, the words as fast as the hands but less precise, less under his control. He was good with words but they were not his true means of expression—these vines were; they expressed his vision of life. At some deeper level he was entirely in synch with the slow, steady annual cycle of the vineyard, but everything he did was rapid-fire: talk, walk, prune. You could imagine him pushing up the court, a point guard leading a fast break, at top speed and under control.

"You want to make a small umbrella," he said, making a hemispheric motion with his arms, which were long for his torso. "Eliminates bunch rot, so when you do spray chemicals you get good coverage. You spray Sauvignon Blanc with sulfur to keep mildew out. This takes a long time, to learn how to prune. Kind of got to get an eye for it, y'know?" Not all his field hands were allowed to prune, only those who showed an aptitude.

We kept walking, and his thoughts turned momentarily toward his family. His first daughter had been born at Thanksgiving time. "Ava," he said. "Ava Sophia Domenichelli. She slept through the night the last two nights." He beamed with pride and the relief of a father who finally had a full night's sleep. Then his mind spun on.

"At fourteen dollars, sixteen dollars a bottle," he said, referring to the Fumé Blanc that would be made from the fruit of these vines, "you want to get some crop." You added or subtracted value from the vines according to how you pruned; these vines were producers. "We get probably seven, eight tons per acre off Keegan. Before, there was apple here, Golden Delicious. Got fifty tons to an acre. We pulled it in '95," the year Don Carano bought this land. "First crop was '98. Five tons an acre. Unheard-of; I don't know why we've always had good luck on first crops," he said. Perhaps to avoid my reading the pride in his face he knelt and grabbed a handful of reddish-brown soil that was damp from days of hard rain rolling in over the hills to the northwest. At ten-thirty in the morning a dense fog was just beginning to lift off the vineyard. Overnight temperatures had been in the forties. "This is beautiful soil," Steve said. "Gorgeous. You could plant tomatoes down here."

The Dry Creek Valley was old, 225 million years old. It had been formed several hundred feet beneath the surface of the Pacific Ocean, beyond the marine shelf, when the Pacific plate and the North American plate slammed together, creating a gigantic mountain range running from Alaska to Chile. This valley was the result of an undersea

23

landslide, and geomorphologists identified it as part of the Franciscan Complex—"complex" because of the many different types of marine sediment that comprised it. When the Dry Creek appellation, or growing region, was designated in 1983, the soils in its eighty thousand acres varied considerably from vineyard to vineyard, and much was still wooded hillside. There were blue and black oaks and pines on the eastern slopes, redwood and Douglas fir on the western. It was about eighty miles from the Golden Gate Bridge to where we were standing in Keegan Ranch, and thirty miles west over the hills to the ocean. Mission grapes for wine had been grown in the valley as early as 1860 by a transplanted Brooklynite named Davenport Cozzens, who apparently thought it was a good way of avoiding further trouble after he was released from San Quentin following a spot of bother with a neighbor.

Despite the variations in composition, the soil was uniformly deep and vigorous throughout. That vigor meant that whatever you planted grew like all get out. City slicker that I am, I assumed that that was always a good thing. I would learn better.

Keegan Ranch was a near rectangle at the southern end of the valley angled from northwest to southeast, except for a bit that stuck out from its northwest corner like a bird's beak. The ranch sloped from Kinley Drive, a service road parallel to southbound Highway 101, down toward Dry Creek, flowing along its short western edge. Just off Kinley Drive were a shop, a semi-outdoor shed, and a house for one of the Caranos' most senior and trusted fieldworkers, Robby Bodalla, and his family. Keegan's 70.97 acres were laid out from road to creek in eleven demarcated blocks. Malbec grapes were planted closest to the road, to be used in some of the red blends that Ferrari-Carano made. Then there were six blocks of Merlot. The remaining blocks—7, 8, 9, and 10, totaling 25.38 acres—were planted in Sauvignon Blanc. Thanks to the vigor of the soil, those twenty-five acres contributed more grapes for Ferrari-Carano Sonoma County Fumé Blanc than any of their other vineyards, which was why I was going to follow Keegan Ranch during the growing year. It was the backbone of the operation. I had originally hoped to follow a wine made entirely from a single vineyard, but had learned, to my regret, that designated vineyard wines, those from a single vineyard, tended to be much more expensive.

To the north, Geyser Peak could be seen in the distance, and Mount St. Helena even farther away to the east. About a mile and a half south of Keegan, the Dry Creek emptied into the Russian River, marking the point at which the Dry Creek appellation ended and the Russian River appellation began. The grapes that went into the Fumé Blanc came from both those valleys and from the Alexander Valley, east of Dry Creek Valley, as well. Here in Keegan cool breezes off the Russian River mitigated the vigor of the soil, but only slightly. Keegan was usually a few degrees cooler than the vineyards planted nine miles up-valley at the Villa Fiore.

Steve showed me a shed where he was growing experimental root-stocks and grafting Sauvignon Blanc (and other) clones to them in dif-ferent combinations. Vines are not genetically stable but mutate over time so that every grape variety has many subtypes, or clones. The root-stock is no more than a bearer, chosen because of its adaptability to the soil conditions in a specific vineyard, or because it will withstand partic-ular pests; the flavors and textures are imparted from the grafted grape clones, the scions. Winemakers are forever manipulating different combinations of stock and scion to achieve different effects. In looking for the best rootstock Steve took into account not only the soil and the variety, or kind of grape, but such other factors as how closely the vines were planted, how they were trellised, and the angle of the sun.

The sun was the key to photosynthesis, to the rate of growth, and much more. "It's a huge deal where the sun sets," Steve said, "because they're sun-worshipping gods. The rows are laid out north by north-west, by south by southeast, so there's some afternoon exposure but not a lot. I want to let 'em get nice, good morning sun. Down here where it's cooler, I want a little more afternoon sun. George likes it a little herbaceous," a connection I did not yet grasp, but would come to see was essential to everything that would happen in the year ahead.

Steve was currently using three rootstocks for the Sauvignon Blanc in Keegan. Most of the rootstocks in use in California today are French in origin, and were bred to combat iron deficiency, because French soil is generally short on iron compared to the land in Sonoma and Napa counties. The one called 10114, he explained, liked water, and since these vines were prolifically irrigated to produce a heavy crop, their 10114 roots were unlikely to rot. The 5C, used farther away from the creek, where the soil was less sandy and had more clay, held moisture better, as did its sister rootstock SO4, which was the fastest grower.

The mind spun to contemplate all his myriad responsibilities. Sixteen vineyards, fifteen varieties, fourteen hundred acres in three valleys with their varying soils and climates. All told, 1,360,000 vines and each and every plant needed, he said, to be touched by human hands—Mexican hands, for the most part—three or four times a year. "It's crazy," he said. "There's so much to think about. That's why I never think, I just do it."

In 2002, the wine business was taking its first battering after a decade of giddy growth and prosperity. There were a number of contributing factors. Good, inexpensive imports from other wine-producing countries, especially Chile, Australia, New Zealand, and South Africa, were capturing an ever-larger market share. Meanwhile, during the booming nineties, when wealthy entrepreneurs, dot-comers, and investment bankers absolutely needed to have a winery with their name on it, the number of California wineries had increased from six hundred to nine hundred; between 1995 and 2001, 177,000 new acres were planted in premium wine grapes. Taken together, the imports plus the increased domestic production created what everybody described as a wine glut, too much of a good thing. That might not have been the problem it was becoming if more premium wine was being drunk, but it was not: Consumption had flattened out in 2001, and would stay flat in 2002. Only about one in nine Americans drank wine with any regularity. Add to that the aftereffects of the 9/11 terrorist attacks: People were dining out less often and restaurants were failing at an alarming rate. The *San Francisco Chronicle* found 168 restaurant closures between December 2001 and February 2003. In New York, Windows on the World at the top of the Twin Towers was simply no more, and it had been a good customer. The cumulative effect was forcing some wineries out of business altogether. Quail Ridge in Napa Valley was gone, Seven Peaks was dissolving, Belvedere in Healdsburg was facing foreclosure, Bridlewood and Sonoma Creek would soon be filing for Chapter 11 protection. And before the year was out, De Loach, which had its headquarters in Santa Rosa and produced about the same number of cases as Ferrari-Carano, would declare bankruptcy after amassing debts of $30 million. One of the state's largest brokers of bulk wine told the *Los Angeles Times* that he thought two hundred California wineries could shut down or be gobbled up by larger competitors as the industry consolidated. "We are going to lose scores of wineries to bankruptcy," Joe Ciatti told the newspaper. The mood in the industry was gloomy; the future appeared to be perilous. Even on the seventy-one acres of Keegan Ranch, just north of Healdsburg, population 9,750, three time zones and many states of mind removed from the Twin Towers and the Pentagon, the impact of those hijacked planes was being felt in the way they farmed.

Meanwhile Ferrari-Carano was on track to increase production significantly. Don Carano had launched an ambitious new hillside program in the Alexander Valley for red wines. The Sauvignon Blanc vines on Keegan and Storey Creek ranches were coming into full production now, a few years after they were purchased. Sauvignon Blanc captures a relatively tiny share, only 3 percent of the $20 billion domestic wine industry. But for Ferrari-Carano, it was the core product.

Steve's rootstock experiments had another, bottom-line benefit. By spring, he would be producing most of the rootstock replacements he would need as some vines grew old and new blocks were planted. "It works out good," he said, hurrying along. "It saves Don seventy, eighty cents a plant and keeps the guys busy. Don lets us do everything, we don't have to go through a corporate structure, just give him a bottom line. I love making Don money," he said, enthusiastically. When he was growing up, Steve continued "Squeezing every dollar out, that was our dinner-table conversation. When I go to courses at U.C. Davis"—where the viticulture department produces many of the leading lights of the industry—"they're talking about things we've already done. We're cutting-edge," he said, laughing to conceal his obvious pride at knowing all that he knew without having attended Davis, as George Bursick had. "It's just gut instinct, Mother Nature, and experience."

Back at his truck, Steve paused for a moment to chatter and tease in Spanish with two vineyard workers who were pruning in Block 8. As we drove back to the winery and villa, which were side by side, Steve talked about his own roots. Unguarded thoughts and associations tumbled out of him helter-skelter. His hands on the steering wheel were square with small palms but long fingers.

"My great-grandfather came out at the turn of the century," he said. The first American Domenichelli had earned his living working at Italian Swiss Colony but made some wine at home to sell. "During Prohibition," Steve told me, "he dumped all his wine down the creek. All the other guys were bootlegging it, making a fortune. He was an honest guy, I guess. I'm a fourth-generation farmer. My grandfather, he was more a salesman. I don't think he was a true farmer. He'd really get pissed off if he heard me, and I think he did too because he's Upstairs.

"My dad, he always said never to count on anything until it's in the crusher. My brothers and me, we'd work all the way to Thanksgiving and not get paid for it. But if it didn't rain," and the crop was intact, "we'd get good school shoes that year."

A sudden thought turned his usually sunny mien cloudy. "I'm a little worried," Steve said. "Bass are biting real early, that's not good. Could be an early bud break."

NOW THAT pruning was completed, winter in Keegan was a time for waiting and watching. Steve Domenichelli liked to say the dormant vines were asleep. Through most of January 2002, the temperatures dipped into the high twenties and low thirties overnight, but rose as high as the mid-fifties on days when the sun shone. When the temperature dropped low enough, the starch in the wood was converted to sugar to act as a natural antifreeze (only to be reconverted at the start of the growing season). There was a weather station in the vineyard, and both Steve and Ferrari-Carano's other self-styled weather geek, Jeffrey Gould, tracked the data from the station and read multiple forecasts obsessively. Steve was happy about the cold nights; the only problem would come if things warmed up too early, you got bud break, and *then* you had a late frost. That could mean big trouble, potentially the loss of a significant portion of the crop. But by the beginning of the third week of the month Steve was starting to

worry that one more week of cold nights might mean a late spring after all, whether the bass were biting and the willows budding early or
not. Nothing in nature was ever certain. He did his best to keep his
anxiety in check, and continued to predict an early spring and thus an
early bud break.

Because it was a slow time in the vineyard, I made an appointment
to get better acquainted with the winemaker, George Bursick. George
was so private that when a Ferrari-Carano employee preparing a
newsletter asked him for a biography, he balked—but he finally re-
lented, acknowledging that he was raised in Santa Rosa, where his
mother still lived, though his father was deceased; had studied music
and botany in college; was a member of the much-celebrated enology
and viticulture class of 1976 at U.C. Davis; and had two young sons,
John and Dylan.

"Just a lot of things going through my mind," he said when I asked
him casually how it was going. "Are the pieces all fitting? Today I'm
working on blending a 2000 red that needs to be put together because it needs to be put back and aged in the barrel. I need to know
how much Merlot I need for the blend to know how much I have for
the 2000 Merlot, and at the same time, the crew is pulling out the
1999 Cabernet. I need to look at fine-tuning because it needs to be
bottled next month. Plus the 2001 Sauvignon Blanc needs to be bottled next month, too, and all that impacts the sales department,"
which was pressing him to get those bottles into the marketplace to
distributors on time and as promised. "The last weekend in January
and the first week in February are going to be just hell," George
groaned. "Today I've been going since eight-thirty. I tasted probably
forty different blend variables, different combinations, and we're
still not there. I never taste in the afternoon; from eight-thirty to
eleven, that's when your taste is most acute." George had exquisite
sensitivity to wine. His master's thesis at U.C. Davis had been on

sensory perceptions of wine—tastes, aromas, and especially body—and he regularly returned to his alma mater to lecture on the subject. "After lunch, forget it," George said, taking a bite of Joey Costanzo's famous meatloaf. The Caranos called Joey their chef, which was consistent with The Story, but I'd call him a cook, a darn good cook. Every Wednesday he made a meatloaf lunch on a patio behind the winery for the eighty-five or so people who worked in the winery and the villa. Today, George was joined by Marlene Ing, Ferrari-Carano's purchasing manager, and a close friend of his. Marlene's appearance was dramatic: She was wearing a navy beret pulled low, and had apparently plucked her eyebrows and penciled in more exciting versions.

George's other great passion was rock 'n' roll; he was the drummer for a band made up of wine industry people called Private Reserve, and he had helped Marlene get her job because he played with her husband. But today his mind was on his work. "Did I make the right choices?" he continued. He was deep into his winemaker's soliloquy. "Doesn't even bother me anymore—did I make the right choices? You go as far as you can, then move on. I never second-guess myself. You stand by the decisions you made today, but you learn from the decisions you made five years ago. I won't know if I made a mistake today until next year, or the year after. As we take this journey, we'll be making hundreds of decisions," he said, and I understood that he was thinking now about the 2002 Fumé Blanc, the wine that eventually would be made from Steve Domenichelli's "sleeping" buds. "And we won't know until that guy in that restaurant pulls that cork." He sighed. "It isn't like fixing a car—if it doesn't run, you know you made a mistake. It isn't that immediate, it's a prolonged thing and you don't realize you made a mistake until down the road and you can't do anything about it. It's kind of fun," he said. He laughed at himself. "My wife just knows, Sunday night I don't sleep."

He looked up at the sky. George had nervous eyes. "All this cloud cover," he said. "We could have an early bud break."

I remarked that Steve had predicted the same thing, based in part on how the bass were biting. George nodded. His straight brown hair had gray streaks—he was fifty-four—and he wore it long over his ears and collar. "Steve's sharp," he said. "A sharp kid. You get a lot of people who grow up in Pittsburgh, Pennsylvania, and go to viticulture school. Steve's done this his whole life. He can read the antlers on a deer, and they don't teach you that in viticulture school. You grow up as a farmer, you learn from your mistakes or you don't succeed. I have tremendous respect for him; he's just so motivated to deliver quality. In the industry there's usually an adversarial relationship between the grower and the winery. As a grower, you want to maximize your investment, that means you have to maximize your crop. But the winery is interested in the best quality. Quantity never relates to quality. But Steve's just the opposite. He's always willing to take that extra step. Everybody can get to eighty percent, and that takes so much energy, but to go that extra ten percent or twenty percent, that takes as much energy, that extra increment takes a huge amount of money and time to get super-super-premium quality fruit. So it's rare to find a guy who'll do that instead of go home and watch football on TV.

"Wines are made in the vineyard," George said, an industry cliché. "My job is just not to screw up great grapes. Steve came to us as an assistant, as a ranch foreman. Quite frankly," he said—in my experience nobody ever began a sentence with the words "quite frankly" without following them with an evasion, a half-truth, or an obfuscation, so I had to wonder what it was about Steve's rise that made George evasive—"when our former vineyard manager retired, he was the natural choice, and as our vineyard holdings grew and the distances between them grew, Steve just rose to the occasion."

The meatloaf was gone, and so were the mashed potatoes, the salad, the brownies, and the lemonade.

"Don Carano," George concluded, with the fulsomeness he displayed when talking about his boss, "has an uncanny ability to encourage talent. He can read people. For him, it's all about the chemistry. It's an art. That's why everybody who works for Don never leaves, because it's a good fit right to begin with."

Without being conscious of it, George was conveying an attitude toward Steve that was more complicated than what he was saying: calling him "a sharp kid," or making it sound almost as if he rather than Don Carano had tapped Steve to become vineyard manager. If George truly believed that wines were made in the vineyard, would his attitude have been so subtly defensive?

Someone at Ferrari-Carano in a position to observe the most powerful people on its team—Don and Rhonda, George and Steve, the marketing and sales director Steve Meisner, and the finance guy Dave James—shared insights with me on the condition that I not reveal his or her identity. Let's call this person Deep Cork.

"George gets a lot of respect from Don," Deep Cork told me, "but he's under the gun all the time to produce better wines. I doubt there are many nights when George gets a good night's sleep. If there's a problem, George's the whipping boy. Many times he says, 'Don's upset' or 'Don wants me to do this or that.' I just get a tremendous sense of frustration and powerlessness from George. At the same time, he has an ego. And he's the only one at this winery who has a big name.

"But Steve Domenichelli is so obviously a favorite of Don's," Deep Cork continued. "He always praises Steve to the skies. It's blatant favoritism. I always wonder, is this just Don playing one against the other?"

FAMILY MATTERS

THERE WAS A soft, steady rain falling when Don Carano put on a yellow slicker, grabbed the keys to his Jeep, and took me on a tour of his vineyards. He didn't bring along a cell phone—he doesn't carry one—nor was there a car phone.

"I just feel a lot more comfortable in property than in the stock market," he said, as we started off. "If I was going to do a winery—this is good hindsight thinking, anyway—I wanted to own and control the grapes going into the bottle. From a quality standpoint, and a price standpoint." Before they made the decision to go into the wine business in a serious way in 1983, Don and Rhonda had acquired two vineyards—the forty-eight acres at their new home in Geyserville that they bought soon after they were married, and another ninety-one acres nearby. They returned from a trip to Italy and France, and found they were approaching winemaking not as dilettantes or tourists but as passionate students. Land prices in Sonoma County were still reasonable then—their early purchases didn't exceed eleven thousand dollars an acre, about a third of what they would have to pay Tim

Keegan in 1995. Maybe just as important, the wine business would be theirs and theirs alone. It had been awkward for everybody when Rhonda married a man with five grown children near her own age.

When Don talked about land, his family was never far from his thoughts. As his friend, the restaurateur Pat Kuleto, says: "We Italians, we think generationally. You have to when you think vineyards. It takes fourteen years from the time you plant your first grape until you see black ink," although Don had achieved that in just eight years. "It's not a typical American thing," Kuleto says. "Great vineyards don't come out of lifestyle, and you don't have corporations able to think long-term like that. Like Piero Antinori said—he's the Robert Mondavi of Italy—'This is a wonderful property, I think we will get our wines right in about four hundred years.' You largely do it from family focus."

So it was natural that as we set out to look at the portions of California wine country that belonged to him, Don would talk about his family first. "My mother passed away eleven years ago," he said. Don talks softly, and hardly moves his lips, so you have to pay attention not to miss anything. "My father passed away when I was seventeen. He had a heart problem that today could be resolved with a valve, but in those days couldn't." His father's death thrust him into adult responsibilities.

"I was an only child. My mother and I, she and I were very, very close. I was born and raised a Catholic but I guess I'm one of those Catholics who don't spend enough time in church. I have a good relationship, though, with the monsignor in Reno, but nah, I don't go to church. My mother always said, 'You're religious within yourself.'"

In everything he did, Don was quick. As a star running back at Reno High School he was known as Fast Don Carano. His oldest pal, Ben Akert, says he was fast with the girls back then, too.

The Eldorado, which Don built as a 262-room, ten-story high-rise in 1973, is run by two of his five children with his first wife, four boys and a girl, all now earning their living in the family casino/hotels. "My oldest son," he said, with the windshield wipers slapping time, "he went to Vegas, dealt and everything, became very qualified, and then he came back. The boys are really the experts in gaming," he said, "gaming" being what people who run casinos prefer to call gambling.

There was more to the story of the Eldorado than Don volunteered. Before 1973, Reno's casinos were on the south side of the Central Pacific tracks; everybody knew there was a red line—that gambling ceased at the railroad tracks. Don Carano changed that, and Reno has never been the same. Quicker than anybody else, he saw an opportunity when an exit off I-80 was opened north of the tracks in 1970. Don had a little piece of property on the near north side from his grandfather, and he was able to persuade his family, some reluctant bankers who not incidentally were old family friends, and the gaming and zoning boards before which he had practiced law and where he also had good relationships, to back his play. Within three years he had opened his casino/hotel.

Today the Eldorado has 811 rooms, and where it stands has become downtown Reno. Don anticipated that the world would follow him, and he bought every nearby parcel he could. The Eldorado and the Silver Legacy, a second, newer hotel and casino he owns in partnership with Circus Circus, occupy the better part of three square blocks, and the Legacy is run by two Carano sons as well. In Reno, Don has the political and economic influence that wealth combined with vision commands. "He's sort of the head Italian in northern Nevada," says Don Cox, a reporter for the *Reno Gazette-Journal*.

Don's friend Ben Akert sees Don's achievement as having built "a dynasty, no question about it; all five of those kids are tall, good-looking, their names are in the paper every day." There are also eleven grandchildren. "He's feeding five, six families out of there, and they're all making big money," says the man Don calls Suds, because of Ben's youthful fondness for beer.

Don met Rhonda when he hired her at the Eldorado. He had known the Bevilacqua family and found a job for Rhonda straight out of college in 1976 as a trainee in sales and marketing. Rhonda majored in nutrition and photojournalism and was thinking about becoming a food stylist. She was also a high school classmate of Don's fraternal twin boys, Glenn and Gene. There was tittering around town about Don's pretty, young third wife. "Don and his three wives is a topic of endless chuckling and speculation," says the reporter Don Cox.

Don's first marriage, to a gorgeous high school sweetheart named Patty Creek, had produced all four of his children. His second, short-lived marriage was described to me by his friends as, variously, "to a beautiful blonde," and "an awful mistake." When he and Rhonda were married, there was jealousy and unease at first within the blended family. Just like the Carano children, all of whom were athletes, Rhonda was intensely competitive. One can easily imagine the suspicions, with a huge fortune at stake. But that was twenty-two years ago. "Rhonda has made Dad so happy over the years," says Gregg Carano, the general manager of the Eldorado.

Now Don and Rhonda were growing older together, and though they didn't know it yet, the year ahead held some terrible reminders of their mortality. No matter what was going on, though, nothing calmed Don like touring his vineyards. He would do it alone when he was having a bad day.

Don eased the Jeep down the short, steep slope from the road onto Keegan Ranch, and drove slowly around the long southern perimeter road toward the creek. When Don bought Keegan in 1995, Ferrari-Carano Fumé Blanc was an established success, sought after not for its quality alone but for its quality at the price, or as they say in the wine business, the "price point." "The Caranos were ahead of the curve," says Pat Kuleto, who has made a huge investment in his own winery, and is able to appreciate what went into the Caranos' success.

"They were asking twelve, fourteen years ago, what do we want to be? To who? Where is our market niche and what can we do to accomplish that? They were aiming for a concept of perceived value. When you drink their wine you feel, 'You know what? This wine is great, it's worth way more than we're paying.' And they absolutely hit the target." Kuleto thought so much of their Chardonnay—this was before he had met them—that he kept a bottle for himself in the refrigerator at his flagship restaurant, Boulevard, and his staff knew to pour him a glass when he showed up.

Typically, Chardonnay is more expensive than Sauvignon Blanc: Ferrari-Carano Chardonnays, for instance, cost more than twice as much. There are a number of reasons why this is so. Sauvignon Blanc grapes give much higher yields. You can press every last drop out of the grapes, but if you do that with Chardonnay the skins impart a bitterness, so to make a premium Chardonnay you rely on what's called the free-run juice. You can squeeze about twenty gallons more juice per ton from Sauvignon Blanc grapes. Because it develops its full flavors rapidly, Sauvignon Blanc spends less time in the barrel and the tank before it's bottled. Sauvignon Blanc, in other words, gives you more product that moves from vine to market faster, and with less expense, allowing you to recapture your costs more rapidly. Ferrari-Carano's other wines are far pricier, and they position their Fumé Blanc as an introductory wine, making money on volume. But the success of this strategy depends on a plentiful supply of cheap grapes. In the mid-1990s, Sauvignon Blancs from New Zealand, led by Cloudy Bay, became the rage. Their desirability drove up the price of premium Sauvignon Blanc grapes in California. Reacting to these changes, Don knew that if he had to buy additional grapes in an inflated market there was no way he could take advantage of the Sauvignon Blanc boom by increasing production, and still hold the price that made his wine so attractive to white-tablecloth restaurants. He needed more vines. Buying Keegan Ranch and Storey Creek was the solution.

Photographer Eric Luse, who was along on the tour, wanted to take a portrait of Don on Keegan Ranch, so we piled out of the Jeep into a light drizzle, and found ourselves beside the five acres of Tim Keegan's apples, which Steve Domenichelli kept as a buffer between the creek and the vineyard. Don looked over at the orchard. The apples make Don some money—one year he sold them to San Quentin prison—and they supply the Eldorado as well. He began to chuckle at Steve's innovation.

"Steve. George," he said. "You know these are remarkable guys. I just love the way they love their jobs, their lives. They're so fortunate."

Luse had Don kneel amid the still-dormant vines, one arm draped over the trellising. Before he was photographed, though, Don took off the eyeglasses he usually wears—a small vanity. His face came into focus as he did, a certain fleshiness and sensuality, with small, twinkling eyes.

"It's nice," he said. "It's nice, God's country."

And then, a moment later: "These valley-floor vineyards, they're flat. Seen one, seen 'em all. But the hillsides—you want to see the caves?"

THE MAN who made Reno follow him north of the railroad tracks now wants to change the way the world of wine thinks about Sonoma County, especially his patch of it. Cabernet Sauvignon, the best-selling, and in some instances most expensive, of the California red wines, is inextricably associated with Napa County, and in particular the vineyards around Oakville.

Ferrari-Carano's own attempts to make an outstanding Cabernet have been less than successful. So Don decided to storm the hillsides. Nobody has ever thrown the kind of resources—money, men, machinery—Don Carano has into making great red wines from Sonoma County hillside vineyards. Ferrari-Carano is building a second winery on its land in the Alexander Valley, this one to operate on a gravity-flow system, a purist's benchmark because the wine is moved around so gently during fermentation. Wine is notoriously sensitive to movement, and this winery would operate vertically, with the grapes brought in at the topmost level, and, ultimately, the bottling at the bottom. The new winery would have all the bells and whistles winemakers could dream of and money could buy.

A pitched battle had been fought in Sonoma County between environmentalists and some wineries and developers over preventing erosion on the hillsides, but the industry-friendly regulations finally enacted were not standing in the way of Don's new dream. Don had started to buy hillside acreage fifteen years ago, well before he was fully able to exploit it. But that is an aspect of his genius—seeing the future and assembling the pieces that turn what he imagines into reality.

"We feel quite strongly," he said, driving toward the hillside vineyards, "that to have a world-class Cabernet program, we need to do it on the hillside. As I see it, this area has not been explored. Up until recently there were very few hillside vineyards in this part of Sonoma—Cabernet has not come from the hillsides—and the Cabernet is not the quality that this area is capable of producing. With that in mind, and what my grandfather told me long ago"—one sensed The Story of Ferrari-Carano Cabernet Sauvignon taking shape—" 'You want good grapes, go to the hillside,' fifteen years ago we purchased our first hillside vineyard. We were able," he said, "to react," thanks to his wealth.

Don waxed enthusiastic for a long time about volcanic soils, trellising systems, exposures to the sun, and the countless tons of rock that had to be removed and crushed in a rock crusher he brought up from Nevada. "By the time you drink one of our red wines, you'll say, 'Man, this better be good for a guy to go through all of this.' So it's a challenge," he concluded. "Every winery should have a superb red. And a superb Chardonnay. And caves. There's just certain things that are absolutely required." Required, that is, if you want to be mentioned in the same breath with California's great wine producers, with the Mondavis of this world. For all that he is unassuming and down to earth—and he is—nobody thinks bigger than Don Carano does. His friend Kuleto says, "He never brags, I never heard him tell a story about what he accomplished. He sees himself as a minimum guy. But the truth is, he can see the big picture on a scale that's pretty dynamic. I'm a pretty big thinker but this guy makes me think I'm Donald Duck going around with Walt Disney."

Thinking big in the fad-driven wine industry means doing what others do but bigger and better. Take caves. They serve three purposes. They let you store large quantities of aging wine under optimum conditions. They create an atmospheric setting for tastings and business entertaining, a kind of Villa Fiore underground. And they are a mark of prestige.

"First we had guys come up here, buy a nice piece of ground, build a nice cave—that was pretty cool," says Michael Ouellette, the Napa wine grower and restaurateur. "Then came guys who wanted to build bigger caves, and added the finest olive oils. Then we had guys—'Okay, we do olives, we do a vineyard, we do caves. Let's raise Scottish cattle.' Now the latest is Leslie Rudd," the owner of Standard Beverage Company, who hails from Kansas City. "He bought the old Martini property, renovated it to one hundred years ago, and farmed it with horses to take it up another notch. His cave's got oriental rugs; it's got an elevator from his office straight down into his cave, like the Bat Cave. He's out-caved everybody."

When it was completed, Don and Rhonda's cave would store six thousand barrels of red wine, though it would take years after its completion to produce enough to fill all that space. While Don was walking me through the not-yet-completed cave—only about thirteen feet a day can be carved out beneath the hillside—I begin to think, Ferrari-Carano is going to be *big,* a thought I made the mistake of expressing, agitating him to no end.

"Large is *large!*" Don shouted, exasperated. "Four or five million cases. K-J! Gallo! When you're talking about four hundred thousand, five hundred thousand cases, that's how large we have the potential to be. We're not huge. Where we're considered larger is the amount of Fumé Blanc we make. Everything is so hands-on here, because we *are* involved personally. It's not corporate, it's personal. The garden, food, and wine—that's us, that's how people are perceiving us." I had, without thinking, contradicted The Story, and Don was not happy.

When the first of his hillside reds is rolled out, Don will get an industry report card. What matters most is what *Wine Spectator* magazine says.

"Don, by the time he dies," says Kuleto, "if he doesn't have ninety-nine points, or one hundred points on his tombstone, he's not going to be happy."

"He wants it desperately," agrees Deep Cork, who has heard Don yell at George Bursick and others when *Wine Spectator* has given Ferrari-Carano wine a rating that displeases him. "Don's whole ego is so tied up in those vineyards. And he's waiting. How long has he got to wait? The guy's seventy years old." And his father had died at forty-nine.

So what began with a small piece of property from his grandfather that Don transmogrified into downtown Reno has culminated, in a sense, in these hillside vineyards, the gravity-flow winery, and the cave where he hopes to leave an enduring mark again—this time on a far bigger canvas. Don Carano is trying to rewrite the California wine story. All he needs is time.

"Don's created enough financial magnitude," says Kuleto, "so that when he says let's become the best, he doesn't want to become the most expensive, he wants to create fantastic wine that's the most incredible value. He's made the commitment and has the wherewithal to back it up. He realizes it's in the vineyards, and in the vineyards you have to think like a tree, season after season."

Maybe lightning will strike twice. It is human nature, wisely or unwisely, to try to replicate early success. Don and Rhonda were only in their second year of production when *Wine Spectator* put George Bursick's "Sophisticated Chardonnay" on its cover. It put them on the map and assured their subsequent success, so that a little more than a decade after they began by producing twenty-five hundred cases, they were generating revenue of close to $25 million. Michael Ouellette remembers that when *Wine Spectator* came out in July 1988, he was driving cross-country and went hundreds of miles out of his way, over the Rockies from Denver to Reno, to the Eldorado, just to try the Chardonnay. That is the length that oenophiles will go to taste the hot new thing. *Oenopoetic*—the poetry of wine—is the classical word for anything pertaining to winemaking. In Greek mythology, Oeneus was the first to cultivate grapes. He neglected to make a sacrifice to the virgin huntress Artemis, Apollo's sister, who punished him by sending a wild boar to ravage his land.

Every rose has its thorns, though. In such an ephemeral and faddish industry, perceptions tend to become frozen, and wines, like Hollywood stars, have their moment in the sun, after which they may be typecast forevermore. Fairly or unfairly, for better or for worse, Ferrari-Carano has been thought of primarily as a white wine house ever since.

TIM KEEGAN was drinking tap water from thick tumblers, sitting at his daughter's kitchen counter in a pleasant tract home no more than a mile from Keegan Ranch, and considerably less than that as the crow flies. Highway 101 lay between.

"My grandfather bought that piece of property, 1927. Just an excellent piece of ground," he said. "Freeway came through in the mid-sixties, cut right through our land. Left five acres this side of the freeway." When another interstate would reach Reno a few years later, Don Carano would see before anybody else that it represented a golden opportunity, and by seizing that moment would create a family dynasty. Not so the Keegan clan. "When my grandfather died, we sold that five acres," Keegan said.

"We started apples, 1972, because there was a bust in the grape market at that time. I had seven different varieties of apple I fresh marketed. Ten acres of Golden Delicious. I got fifty tons an acre, which nobody would believe because the county average was twelve. Fertilize them hard, water them pretty constantly from June on. Used to stick a pipe in the creek and irrigate out of that." Plenty of farmers did it, laws or no laws. It's still going on today at certain places in Dry Creek Valley.

By the mid-nineties, Keegan had a large amount of acreage in need of replanting—he farmed grapes, too—and experience had taught him that if you worked on borrowed money, as he did, "it seemed like it took ten years to get your money back. I didn't want to be working for trash dollars. That seemed like a pretty good reason for selling. My sons didn't want to go into the business. I put it up for sale, not advertising it real hard, letting some people know."

This was 1995, when there was a land rush on. "Three, four months later, Carano came in," said Keegan. With a thoroughness and attention to detail that characterizes everything he does, Don Carano's people, including George Bursick and Steve Domenichelli's predecessor Barney Fernandez, brought in backhoes, did extensive soil testing, and monitored the drainage, the well reports, and the weather. What they found was consistently deep, rich, loamy soil and huge fertility in a relatively cool climate, land that would produce an abundance of the Sauvignon Blanc grapes with characteristics they craved.

"They made a very fair offer. I believe it was thirty thousand dollars an acre. We did a little haggling," Keegan said. "They wanted to buy, so I sold it to them. I met Don after most of the negotiations were over. He struck me as a fair man, an honest man. He actually offered me full-time work. I didn't want it. At that time. I was tired. I ran the ranch as a one-man show. Too much for one person.

"I stayed on a year consulting on the apples," even though Steve Domenichelli was raised on apples. Retaining Keegan's services showed something about Don Carano's sensitivity.

For about a year Keegan hunted and fished; he played too much golf. Gradually he began to miss his work, the life he had always known. "I don't miss the seven-day-a-week, twenty-four-hour part. But I miss the ranch, I miss the farming. I'd have liked to keep twenty acres, keep me busy." He called Steve Domenichelli. Could he hire back on? He was only fifty-two, but he wasn't needed.

"In two years they planted about sixty acres," Tim Keegan said. "They got a lot of people working and he's got a lot of money behind him. Amazing what you can do when you've got money."

RENÉ RUIZ

THE FIRST THING I learned about René Ruiz, as he is called in the United States, was that he had a neat hand. It was a Wednesday, the day when Joey Costanzo served lunch on the outdoor patio for the eighty-five people who worked in the winery and the villa—virtually all of them Anglos. René borrowed my pen and pad and wrote the name of his village as well as the larger market town nearby where I would stay when I visited. EL CHARCO. URIANGATO. All small capital letters.

To reach El Charco you drive southeast from Guadalajara about seventy-five miles along a new federal toll road nearly devoid of other cars; the tolls are too expensive for local people, and there were no tourists in sight. Along much of the way, small farms with rich black soil are sectioned off with low stone walls. In the distance, fog shrouded the mountains. Once past the city of Morelia, though, as you leave 15D and turn north off the tourist trail and into the mountains, the landscape becomes ever drier and grayer. You enter a parched, neglected land.

The Caranos had asked René to be my guide. He had been home in El Charco for weeks, and came with Rafael Gonzales to meet me at my hotel, one of two in Uriangato (the next morning I would discover that there was no running water). We drove the six or seven miles uphill to his village. "El Charco" means "watering hole," René said, but he calls it The Bathtub. And like the taps in my hotel room, The Bathtub had no water.

"Because we don't have wells, if it stops raining you don't get the kind of harvest you expect, so nobody likes to farm anymore," René said in his accented, fluent English. "Only a few, they got their own land, got their own wells. My village, pretty much everybody depends on their families in the United States."

There were five hundred homes in El Charco, and about seventy men from the village and surrounding areas, including Uriangato, spend seven, eight, nine months of the year tilling Don and Rhonda Carano's land. El Charco is a classic company town. In the new global economy a bone-dry Mexican village where farming has died because of drought and government neglect sends its workers some two thousand miles north to cultivate what is by any measure a luxury product. And all along the way everybody makes money. But the sacrifice is entirely El Charco's.

The Mexican government, René said, turns its back on the plight of the *campesinos*. The only contact the people of El Charco have with the central authorities is visits by gun-toting *federales,* who, when the mood strikes them, assess fines immediately payable in cash against anyone caught committing infractions such as walking, talking, or driving in a way displeasing to the federal cops.

"Here I make one thousand pesos a week, maybe one hundred and fifty dollars, doing welding, which is not too much because here everything is pretty expensive," René said. "Welding is hard work, y'know, because everything is by weight. I had another brother in

California, he asked me and I said, yeah, I want to go over and make better money."

In 1984, his brother paid a coyote three hundred dollars to smuggle René across the border and deposit him near Sebastopol, in Sonoma County. His first year in California, René picked apples, but the money was better in grapes; as soon as possible he caught on at Domaine Saint George, in the hills above the Russian River Valley, where his brother worked, and where he was taught to prune. He first met Steve Domenichelli there while Steve was still working for his old man, and came by looking for temporary workers. At that time René was content to stay put. In 1989, when René was twenty-five and just married, he agreed to go to work for Steve Domenichelli at Ferrari-Carano.

René continued with his story as we rolled into El Charco. We passed a dry creek bed, a telephone exchange for the people in the village who cannot afford their own phones, a one-room schoolhouse, and a tiny ancient church. Crimson and violet bougainvillea grew over old stone walls and up the sides of brick and adobe houses.

"After five years in Domaine Saint George," René said, "I come back to my village and got married. They give me a month vacation and I took, like, three. Actually, I fired myself. Then I went to Steve and he hired me right away."

The street in front of René's house, in the more prosperous lower part of the village, was one of a handful in El Charco that was paved. We pulled up in front of an imposing metal gate, painted bright yellow, that René had fabricated himself.

"Steve," he said fondly, "we call him The Coyote. He's sneaky, y'know? He likes to get out in the morning early and look around, see what's going on. And we call him Loco, too. Because he's like a fuckin' rabbit, he never stops. One time he took us to pick mushrooms, he keeps you fuckin' working, we say, let him go all he fuckin' wants, we stop following him." Steve has never visited El Charco, though he is fluent in Spanish, and would be treated like a king—probably the very reason he doesn't come.

Nor was Steve the only one with a nickname—all the men had them. Rafael Gonzales, who was driving, was called Boa. René was Canseco, because he played and coached baseball, his passion. He owned a slew of different New York Yankees caps, and the one he was wearing today was white and spotless.

Pretty much the first thing Steve asked about a potential new hire was, Does he know how to prune? "Because," René said, "that's the most important thing, pruning and harvesting."

René himself had been too ambitious to stay any longer in the vineyard than he had to. By the time he began at Ferrari-Carano he had taught himself English, swapping words with an Anglo winery worker at Domaine Saint George. At Ferrari-Carano he rose rapidly from laborer, to tractor driver, to foreman. In 1994, "Steve needed somebody in the office, because he didn't have any secretary. That's when I start. I'm pretty much in payroll. I keep track of the hours everybody works." His bilingual literacy, and that neat hand, were paying dividends.

René Ruiz Lopez—in El Charco he used his full name—was a powerful man, perhaps the most powerful Mexican working at Ferrari-Carano. He was not only the payroll master but also a man who, with a judicious word or two, could determine which El Charco men would be hired and which would not. He wore a heavy gold bracelet, an expensive gold watch, floppy, golden Shaq-style shorts, and Nikes that looked like they just came out of the box. He was a powerfully built man with a big hard belly and calves the size of a young girl's waist. He didn't walk through El Charco, he swaggered.

In California he and his wife, the Caranos' housekeeper, occupied a house next to the restored 1904 farmhouse in Geyserville where

Don and Rhonda lived. "He's my neighbor, Don Carano," René said. "The Caranos are paying my rent. It's nice there, quiet. No traffic, no *cholos*."

Here, in his village, other men attended him. As René showed me through his house, a solid one-story home with a big front porch, other guys drifted up to wait outside the gate, laughing, talking, and having a morning beer. But mostly they were waiting, as René showed me his new fridge. His new stove. The new mattress still wrapped in heavy plastic. A plumber was installing a heater. "I'm still working on my house, trying to make it nice," René said as we climbed onto the flat roof to have a look around. "It takes time and I don't have time because I'm over there all the time. I can't find somebody here to really rely on." Every winter René returned for a month or less, although other men with fewer responsibilities came home from November through January. "We pretty much sleep, eat, drink, have fun," René said. "Look for the *chicas*. When you come, you come to relax."

Finally, René went out to the waiting *campesinos*, the country boys of El Charco, and grabbed a seven-ounce Coronanita from a nearly empty case. "These are the best," he said. "You can't get them in the United States." The men were shooting the breeze in Spanish, a language I speak haltingly and understand fitfully. Because I could not comprehend most of the colorful, double entendre–loaded Spanish these men spoke, I would probably never win their confidence. And I was seen, however wrongly, as an emissary of their Anglo bosses. The little bit I did understand included talk of rabbit hunting, of girls, of baseball. A man approached with some tomato seeds for René, a strain similar to Romas but not commonly found in California. "To keep Rhonda happy," René said.

The midday sun was directly above us in a robin's-egg-blue sky. A second case of Coronanitas had magically appeared. There was a gentle, cooling breeze. A woman dressed in a long black dress with a black shawl over her head passed by with her eyes averted; nobody seemed to notice her, and certainly nobody greeted her the way they did other men. When I asked René why she was in mourning he explained that it was the second of nine days during which the women of the village were praying for a villager who had died. "Just the women. The men don't like to pray." He paused. "I like to pray. I go to church."

During three days in El Charco I was introduced to a woman only once, when I asked to meet the wife of a young man who worked at Ferrari-Carano named Jaime Ruiz; nor did a woman ever join the sociable knots of men who gathered in the streets outside the scantily stocked *tiendas,* knocking back the Coronanitas and shots of tequila that are sold by the tiny grocery shops. In the evenings, the women, young and old, all in black, passed by silently on their way to and from the home of the recent widow. It put me in mind of the deep-reaching gender segregation I had experienced in the rural areas of Islamic Pakistan. In the States, I had tended to think of machismo as male posturing; but here I saw how complex and culturally entrenched machismo was.

One evening we went up to the top of the hill, passing from the lower village where each house was sheltered by a wall or a gate, and the streets were paved to the upper village. The way up was rocky and rutted, goats and chickens wandered the front yards, and the homes—mostly made of cinder blocks—were almost all unfinished, projects that may have run out of money or were a tax dodge; no increase in property taxes was imposed until building improvements were completed, an incentive to leave projects permanently unfinished. In a garage with no door a mariachi band was playing. At the summit it was easy to see why the village is called El Charco. It sits in a trough created by three hills: Lagunia, or big lagoon; El Cerro de

Don Jesus, or Jesus' heel; and El Carnal, the flat oven where you warm a tortilla.

The sun had set and the sky was turning purple over El Cerro de Don Jesus. All around us were brown, stubbly, uncultivated fields. Nobody had planted beans or corn. "You spend a lot of time and money, and then if the rain don't come," as it hadn't in three years, "you get nothing," René said. "Nobody wants to risk it. We have two wells to supply the town, and one is dry. By the time it's May, June, the other one doesn't do too good. The people all depend on the United States. It's cheaper, y'know, buying the tortillas already made than planting the corn and waiting for harvesting."

I recalled, though, something René had told me earlier when we were standing on the roof of his house looking out at the crimson and violet bougainvillea while a rooster was crowing at midday, one of the most evocative and haunting sounds on earth.

"It's nice here," René said. "I love it here, man. I wouldn't change nothing in this place. Someday I'm going to retire here."

How good is the almighty dollar, and how cruel.

I'd Take a Bullet

"I'M REALLY, *REALLY* stressed," Steve Domenichelli said in early March, balling his fist and pressing a knuckle against his lip. He was driving us in his truck over to Geyserville, where he had grown up, to eat lunch at the Smoke House. "If I don't think too much it doesn't scare me. It's mostly in bed. The anxiety to get things done—I've got so many places to hit on time."

Take, for example, the Sauvignon Blanc. It could be finicky. He had made mistakes with it, and he recalled his mistakes, too, awake in his bed in the middle of the night with tasks that took on added urgency in the predawn darkness tumbling through his mind like clothes in a dryer. That first year on Keegan he hadn't taken sufficient account of the cool temperatures, approaching the vineyard like the warmer Alexander Valley vineyards; by the time he recognized his mistake, the canopy had become so aggressive he had to whack it back. Too much leaf cover meant too little sun, and too little sun made the grapes more herbal in taste than George Bursick wanted.

"We can change the flavors in the vineyard," Steve said. "Isn't that crazy?" Now he knew better than to repeat that same mistake, but others lurked, because there were so many variables. You regulated your soil and subsoil, the water and drainage; you reacted to temperature and sunlight, and all that contributed to, or detracted from, the quality of the wine. Where, precisely, within your vineyard did you choose to plant? What rootstock did you use? Which clones? How far apart should the rows be? And the vines? What trellis system to use? What kind of irrigation system? How much water was enough but not too much? Was that amount available to you? How were you going to prune, and when, to regulate sunlight and air circulation? When should you spray and when shouldn't you, and what kinds of sprays and fertilizers should you use? There were infestations of mildew or of blue-green sharpshooters or, God forbid, glassy-winged sharpshooters, to worry about. Not to mention the hundred-plus laborers and five vineyard managers under his command. It was always good to get up in the morning. Once he was up and moving he felt strong.

The buds were still tightly closed in Keegan, which was how Steve wanted them. He had his crews prune as late as possible, trying to delay bud break until the threat of frost was past. Despite every precaution, though, Mother Nature would have her way. Frost had taken some Chardonnay vines at higher elevations: The loss wasn't serious, but it reinforced the need for vigilance.

I had assumed that farmers growing a luxury crop in some of the most beautiful valleys west of Tuscany would be bucolic in nature. But Steve Domenichelli was rapidly disabusing me of that notion. Steve and his first wife had been divorced for years, but they still fought over custody of their three sons, who were now fifteen, twelve, and ten. The oldest boy lived with Steve and his second wife, Stephanie. The younger two moved back and forth between his house and their mother's, but Steve wanted full custody. On the other hand, he didn't want their mom not to be in their lives. There was bitter-ness and emotional exhaustion. Now he and his ex-wife had agreed to counseling. That was there, too, disturbing his sleep.

His daughter Ava was now three months old, and had begun to laugh. It was the most beautiful sound.

"It's so different," he said, "being a father at thirty-eight than at twenty-two. Know what's great? I can teach the boys to be a great fa-ther. They're changing diapers and everything. My wife's really happy." There was a light in his brown eyes, and the furrows in his broad brow smoothed as the muscles in his face relaxed. Yet he was still coiled, he was always coiled, his gestures alive with kinetic en-ergy. There was a glow to Steve Domenichelli that would embarrass him half to death to be told about.

I asked him if the twin pressures of the vineyard and the demands of his family weren't a conflict.

"Nobody knows that," he said, catching my eye. "I try to tell my wife. She says, 'How can that be? You've got enough time.' I'll tell you who understands—Don. He's the only one. He's taught me a tremendous amount. Shit, I've gone to him with my divorce—I can go to him with anything. He's a brilliant guy; I'm just lucky to have the one-on-one time with him alone. A lot of guys don't get that." Af-ter Steve's first marriage broke up, Don made a house available on Magnolia Ranch to help Steve remain stable, so he could keep his kids with him as often as possible.

"Yesterday," Steve continued, "I went on a field trip with my kids, I had a great day. But I put it on my calendar and told Don two weeks ago. It was the middle of the week but he understood—he let me do that. Last night my son didn't have any homework. I said, 'Jared, why don't you write about how many newts we saw and everything?' I read it before I went to bed. The last line was, 'I had the greatest time of my life.' I got goose bumps.

"So if the vines need water Christmas Eve, I'll be there. There's no boundary here. He's the most understanding guy in the world. I'd take a bullet for him. I would."

Once Steve almost did.

Driving home to Cloverdale a few years ago he stopped at one of the several help-houses, as they call the bunkhouses that Ferrari-Carano provides rent-free to their unmarried vineyard workers or those whose wives were not allowed to join them in the United States. Men lived two and three to a dormitory room, with shared communal baths and a kitchen. Steve was close to many of his "Hispanic guys"—that was what he and the foremen called them. He had hired them personally one at a time, and had known some of them since his childhood. That afternoon, though, a man they called Winky, a holdover from before Steve's time, got in his face, screaming that Steve was too young to be telling people what to do. What a joke that was. Steve had become fluent in Spanish in his father's vineyards, where he had been bossing crews since he was twelve.

So he told Winky to go fuck himself.

Winky drew a pistol. *What about this,* he screamed in Spanish.

Pull the trigger, coward. That's what Steve said. He looked Winky right in the eye. Everybody waited.

Hey, man, Winky said, *I'm just kidding.*

The next day Steve returned to tell Winky to pack his bags and get out. Steve knew enough to give him time to save face. He sighed with relief when he finally departed, three weeks later.

Steve knew his men; he had slept beside them, eaten with them, worked among them. "Listen," he said, when we arrived at the restaurant, "they've been lied to by their people and their government so much they can't trust anybody. And there are guys around here who exploit them. But they're the nicest people in the world, really. I don't want to come off like a big hard-ass either, but there are certain times you've got to be." It was something he learned from his father. René Ruiz, who had also worked for Steve's dad, says he was "kind of mean." René told me Steve's dad was short but had huge muscles, that Steve's father and brother were both bulky. Coming from René, with his calf muscles like bowling balls, that was a hoot.

I asked Steve if he got along with his father. Steve had the gregarious youthfulness of many men whose relationships with their fathers remained unresolved, which can be both charming and suspect.

"Yes and no," Steve said. "You know, I worked for him my whole life. I started working out in the field when I was eight years old, until he made me the best I could be; he really pushed me hard. Which is fine. He's a great farmer; I always idolized him in that respect. I get along with him better now that I don't work for him. He's a good dad. I love him."

When he was seventeen, Steve came to drive a tractor for Ferrari-Carano, which was just getting started. Soon he was promoted to vineyard manager under Barney Fernandez, a huge man with an abrasive side who occupied the job Steve held now as Don Carano's chief farmer. Steve had a knack with the men that Barney lacked. "Most guys around here," Steve said, "know I've been in every ditch. There's a little bit different respect. You can't just come in and give orders in your sunglasses, or something."

Steve was attacking his barbecue with gusto. I always had the strange feeling that his body should have been twice the size it was.

Eliseo Martinez had been the first El Charco man Steve got to know. Eliseo came across the border with a coyote back when Reagan was president, and the passage cost three hundred and fifty dollars, not the one thousand dollars it costs today. A quiet man with a black mustache, Eliseo was a hard worker and a natural leader who Steve's father helped get his papers. Eliseo was grateful and loyal to the Domenichellis. The moment Steve was in a position to hire for Ferrari-Carano, he lured Eliseo away from his dad.

It was easy, Steve said. "My dad is a control guy. He wants their hair short, he won't let them have cars." When the old man heard that his own son had hired away his top hand, he went berserk. He even called Don Carano, which made Don ask Steve what the hell was going on.

Don't worry, he answered, *typical Italian family opera, I'll deal with it.* The Domenichellis, Steve says, put the incident behind them. But Steve had been at Ferrari-Carano for fifteen years, drawing a substantial salary for overseeing some of the best vineyards in Sonoma County, before his dad had consented in 2000 to come look at what his son had accomplished.

"He had never seen what I do. It was really neat," Steve said.

Over those fifteen years, many El Charco men had followed Eliseo Martinez to work for Steve at Ferrari-Carano. One of the first was Eliseo's best friend, Rafael Gonzales.

BOA

ALL THE MEN from El Charco called Rafael Gonzales "Boa," and seemed to hold him in special affection. He was a little guy, Boa, maybe five feet four, but bouncy like a gymnast, and with a big, friendly smile that revealed all the gold in his mouth. His hair was buzz cut, and there was a scar in his scalp. Other men rubbed his head, the way you would a child's, although he was thirty years old and a remarried widower.

His father had been a farmer raising beans and corn when there was enough water for a crop. Boa told me he was fifteen when he left El Charco for El Norte the first time, alone, off to make his own way. Steve Domenichelli hired him at Ferrari-Carano five years later, by which time Boa had his working papers. In 1999, he became a citizen of the United States.

Steve took an instant shine to Boa, maybe because, like Steve, he had manic energy and high spirits. Boa's walk was virtually a trot, and he was always on the go, driving when he wasn't walking. He was associated with his vehicle. It was his thing.

The first time he got some dollars saved up, that's what he had wanted, a car. That first car was destroyed in a crash. Boa had had more than one scrape behind the wheel—and with the ladies. Steve said Boa was a laugher and a lover, a prankster and a pint-sized Romeo.

In January 2002, Boa had come with René Ruiz to meet me when I arrived in Uriangato. "I came back in October," Boa told me. "I been here three months." Men like Boa, whose wives do not have papers and are not able to follow them north, are given more time off than guys like René, whose wife lived with him in California. René flew back and forth, but Boa drove. One thousand, eight hundred seventy miles from El Charco to the help-house near Jimtown Corner where he shared a room with his brother-in-law. As many as a dozen men would pile into Boa's truck, and they made the trip in forty or forty-five hours.

"It's time to go back," he said. We were standing on René's roof, enjoying the view and the sunshine.

"He spent all his money," René said, making Boa laugh. It was true, Boa said. In three months he had spent maybe seven thousand dollars—*chingón de lana,* he called it, a shitload of money. Some of it had gone into his house, which like most of the homes in El Charco would never be entirely finished. But his nature was to live for today.

At Ferrari-Carano, Boa worked his way up to field boss. Or, as he explained it to me, "I don't pick, I'm just watching." In fact he worked hard; the hardest thing, *más duro,* he said, was breaking up rocks when they had planted the hillside vineyards at Michalek Ranch, where the cave and the gravity-flow winery were being built. He made $10.25 an hour, he said, $1.25 more than an ordinary vineyard worker, and he worked a nine- or ten-hour day, six days a week, seven days at harvest. That translated to nearly twenty-five thousand dollars, several times what he could make trying to farm in the drought-stricken state of Guanajuato. If true, it was fabulous money. But to make it, he had to spend nine months a year away from his wife and children. In the two years he had been married, he had been home for only six months. Partings were the defining characteristic of life in El Charco, Ferrari-Carano's unintentional and distant company town.

"Leaving your house is the hardest part," René agreed. "But then at the airport everybody's happy, taking a couple of shots."

Boa grinned. He's a hospitable guy. For three days he would spend most of his time, as would René, shepherding me around El Charco, Uriangato, and Moroleón. One afternoon Boa took me up to his new house in the upper part of El Charco, where the road is rutted. There was a burro in the front yard. The house was concrete, with vertical rebars still visible above the roofline. There was a lot of volcanic rock in El Charco, no doubt thousands of years old, and that suggestion of upheaval, combined with the slender rebars intended to keep concrete from breaking apart in an earthquake, gave the village an aura of physical instability. Boa's house was painted a jolly red and green, and the sides were faced with locally made brick, *tabique*. The house, Boa said, cost forty thousand dollars to build, and the land another twenty thousand dollars. It seemed a lot to me, an exaggeration, but I was beginning to grasp that Boa and the other guys from El Charco had a relaxed attitude about truth-telling when they talked to me. No doubt it stemmed from their initial need to confuse the authorities about their status. And in addition, it was important to remember that these were village people whose world was very small. Their stimulation came from the church, *telenovelas,* and gossip among friends and family. Their formal education was virtually nonexistent. The average number of books read in Mexico per capita is one, and I never saw a newspaper in El Charco. Why should education be valued, when there was no immediate use for it? The guys like Boa working in the vineyards of California, or painting houses in Chicago, or working in slaughterhouses in Nebraska, were making far more than the teachers who tried to keep them in school. About 80 percent of Mexico's recent university graduates were unemployed.

Boa's house had four rooms, all with bare concrete floors, and by American standards the furnishings were sparse. There was a refrigerator and a TV.

His wife, who was holding their daughter in her arms, was shy. She spoke no English and was understandably uncomfortable to have two tall Americans, one of them—photographer John Storey—snapping pictures, in her home. René had explained to me that Boa's wife was a widow, and thus had few choices of a husband. Without a husband she would have been unable to support herself, and a burden to her family. Though she was no more than thirty herself, she had a teenage daughter, a girl even shyer than her mother, who kept her eyes averted during the few minutes we stayed. Later, I would wish that I had paid closer attention to this girl.

Boa did not introduce us. He'd come home for his car keys because he and René were taking us out for the evening. El Charco had no restaurants; in fact it had no shops except for the tiny *tiendas* with their half-empty shelves selling rice and matches, flour and detergent along with Coronanitas and shots of tequila. We were going, they said, to the club. But first we stopped for tacos in Uriangato. While we ate I asked a question I had been wondering about: Why was Rafael called Boa?

By way of an answer, René put both his meaty hands in front of his deep chest, palms far apart.

"But," I said to Rafael, who was laughing, and had dressed for this night in a gold lamé shirt worn outside his jeans, "you're just a little guy."

"Nine inches," said René—which was an occasion for another round of beers before we headed to the edge of town where the sign above the stucco arch by the roadside told us that we had arrived at El

Club Extreme. A strip joint. But that was a euphemism. The place was a bordello. There was no way of saying no to this gesture of hospitality. René was boasting that it was the finest in all Mexico.

El Club Extreme was a warehouse-like room, big and square with high ceilings, painted black and lit by spotlights and strobes. The air was cold, the design simple. In the middle of the floor was a raised, kidney-shaped stage bathed in light, with a fireman's pole in the smaller end. We were seated at a small table just beneath the pole, the best table in the house. The decibel level of the music being played by a disc jockey on a strobe-washed balcony was distressingly loud, and not encouraging of conversation except of the simplest sort—shouted remarks, laughs, gestures. Around three walls of the club, raised perhaps a foot above floor level by a low platform, were booths, some open and some obscured by heavy black drapes. There were parties going on in most, but those with drawn drapes were places where a man could take one of the dancers if he bought a sufficient number of tickets.

One of the girls performing onstage, a blonde, was striking. She looked to be twenty-two, or twenty-three, and unlike most of the other girls, her dance was not so much explicit as it was suggestive.

Shouting, I said to Boa in my pidgin Spanish, *Muy bonita.*

¡Estúpido! The moment she left the stage, Boa approached her, and a minute later she arrived at our table naked, climbed up, and performed a dance. Boa leaned close to ask me, "You want to take her back there?" gesturing with his head toward the booths with the drawn black drapes.

I declined.

He shrugged. When she finished her dance he leapt to his feet and helped her down. She stepped into her high heels. He came to about her shoulder. Boa whispered into her ear, and they headed off, she towering above him. As they passed one of the open, raised booths, Boa hopped up with a nimble gesture and without breaking stride, so that he was still walking beside her, but was now taller than she. He put an arm around her naked shoulder, talking to her. He looked so happy.

MOST EVERY day that he was home Boa drove his Chevy Silverado down the hill from El Charco to Uriangato, where all the stores and services were located. Boa's truck, only four years old, represented so many things. Freedom. Status. Money. An immigrant's dream of America fulfilled. There ought to be a law against burning Chevys, not flags.

The grass on the hillside was brown, with scant vegetation on the slopes, and the road snaked around sharp curves. Just before the road reached the valley floor it leveled out and right there was a small burial plot. It contained a black crucifix and many burned candles. Flowers long dead and dried out were scattered within the neglected, wrought-iron enclosure. The place was below road level, in a gully where boulders that had broken off the mountain had come to rest.

One night after dark as we were approaching the place, Boa said to me, in the intimacy of the cab, the dashboard lights glowing, "The first car I bring from California, I crash. Because it was the first time they make the road, there was a lot of gravel. I go into big rock. My wife died and my little kid, too. My son Arturo, he was seven."

That was all he said. He did not tell me, as René would later, that Boa had been drinking, as usual, and driving his car too fast, which caused his wife Gloria to ask him to slow down just before they crashed.

"Rafael," René said, "he gets sad sometime."

I thought about Boa, the joker and lover, driving past there every day, that scar in his scalp, and how the men of El Charco liked to pat him on the head.

JET-SET BAG LADY

RHONDA CARANO WAS in her domain—at a round table in a sitting room on the second floor of the Villa Fiore—the executive suite, where Don and Rhonda both had spacious, light-filled offices.

"Don and I," Rhonda was saying, "work more as a team. I'm more the creative side, he's more the business side. He didn't even know what the Villa was going to look like," she said, and laughed—a short, sharp laugh. "I had free rein on the interior. He didn't care."

The room—the same room where a year later the Caranos would decide whether or not their 2002 Fumé Blanc was market-ready—had a small couch in one corner, in front of the bookcases stocked with leather-bound Great Books. Marlene Ing was with us. I loved her flamboyant hats, that Hedda Hopper look. Today's was soft and round on top with a rolled-up brim, a bright red that the red piping in her sweater picked up.

Marlene was the purchasing manager for the winery. But she was more important to the Caranos than that title suggested. She worked closely with Rhonda, but Don also relied on her, and for more than purchasing bottles and corks and the like. Don was accustomed to people telling him what he wanted to hear—the culture of Ferrari-Carano was yes-ish. Marlene was a breath of fresh air; she would always tell Don what was what, and as a consequence Don not only liked her but also trusted her. Marlene reported to Rhonda, though.

The division of responsibility between Don and Rhonda was about more than a difference of temperament. Something like eighty-five people worked in administration, in the labs, maintenance, landscaping, marketing and public relations, hospitality, housekeeping, the tasting room, shipping, and the cellar. Heaven help you, says Deep Cork, if you reported to Don and went to Rhonda with something, or vice versa. But the Caranos made an exception for Marlene, whose status seemed unique.

There was something crisp about Rhonda, who had sharper edges than her husband. She wasn't the schmoozer he was, but then a rich and powerful woman could choose not to be.

Amy Kelsey was a young enologist—a wine scientist—who worked for George Bursick, and Kelsey thought Rhonda seemed almost lonely; she was surprised to find herself feeling sorry for this rich, successful, and attractive woman. It seemed to her that everybody Rhonda came into contact with either worked for her or was kissing her ass. And while everybody else, even Don, would hang around in worn jeans and T-shirts, Rhonda was always dressed to the nines. Today she was wearing a tailored blouse and slacks set off with heavy, expensive jewelry. Like a movie star, she was always on.

We were overlooking the pool and the faux ruins, about which Rhonda had instructed her design consultant, "We don't want Caesar's Palace." Indeed not. If Ferrari-Carano Vineyards and Winery was any one thing, it was *not* Nevada, *not* Reno, *not* where the Caranos still spent a considerable portion of their time maintaining the casino empire that Don had built. They were forever rushing back and forth. "I'm like a bag lady," Rhonda said. "I bring my desk in boxes from there to here."

Not unlike the men of El Charco, they lived and worked in two worlds, each quite different, each demanding different responses. Of course, it helped to have a private jet with white leather upholstery.

"The hardest part," Rhonda said, "is to slow down. There, it's twenty-four hours, you can get anything done at any time. That was hard for me, just to slow down and go with the flow of Mother Nature. But the older I get the more I appreciate it. Don, here, can live well and don't have the day-to-day stress." Don used to be a good-sized Scotch drinker but he cut that out after Rhonda came into his life. Rhonda made sure he looked after himself; she watched over his diet and got him up onto the stationary bike.

Don had said some similar things during our vineyard tour, but with a slightly different emphasis. "The gaming business, your commodity is money, winning or losing, twenty-four-hours, seven days a week," he said. "It's very competitive. I'm not saying the wine business is not competitive, but it's a product with an emphasis on quality, and how you control that quality. At five o'clock you go home. At my age, at my stage of life, I like this lifestyle better. By eight o'clock you're thinking about going to sleep."

Rhonda was more ambivalent. "I think I like it here better, too. I miss Reno at times. I miss my family. I miss that energy of the casino business. I get sort of jazzed."

It took two years, Rhonda said, just to decide on what they would call their winery. Two years! But if you have invested as much as they had in a venture as capital intensive as a winery—its investment-to-sales ratio is higher than the automobile industry's—you had better get the details right. When I had asked Don how much buying into the wine game had required, he had chuckled and said, "Umpteen million."

WHEN THEY decided to commit to the wine business in a serious way in 1983—Don was the motivator, he was the one who got the bug—they hired as their consultant the late Justin Meyer, whose Silver Oak Cabernet Sauvignon many knowledgeable people considered California's best. Meyer advised them to put their own name on their label because, he said, wine was personal. It is that kind of pretentiousness (*personal?*) that gives the fine-wine business an off-putting snobbishness and preciousness. But to some people with a fortune to invest it has an irresistible lure. The Caranos lapped it up. As James Conaway points out in his book *The Far Side of Eden,* a wine label is the twenty-first-century equivalent of a coat of arms.

"We didn't want it to be Carano," Rhonda said. "Very old-fashioned, like Pedroncelli, Gallo, Louis Martini. We went over all our names. My name was Bevilacqua; it means drink of water. Out of the question." She laughed her abrupt laugh again. "Sorry, Dad.

"Don's mother's family name was Ferrari. It had a nice flow. As well as marketability." Because of the renowned Italian automaker, Ferrari said luxury. "You look down the wine list, people could say it. As opposed to Carano, which has a hard 'C'—people have trouble pronouncing it. It took us a long time."

Don is a big-picture guy who surrounds himself with capable people, expert in their own areas, and inspires effort and loyalty. Rhonda is by nature a detail person. "Rhonda could be sitting still and look like she's doing something," says Deep Cork. "Rhonda wants her finger in every pie, she makes decisions about everything rather than delegating. You have to check with her first on *everything*. And that level of involvement is bound to be stressful. Don is much more laid-back."

So their baby winery had a name. Now they needed a label. Rhonda believed in the importance of packaging in providing an iden-

tity that established your brand. In retail in particular, where a shop-
per can choose among dozens of Napa County Cabernets or Sonoma
County Chardonnays, packaging can be decisive. The Caranos had already made a fundamental marketing decision that they were going to
focus on wine lists at white-tablecloth restaurants, places of the cal-
iber of Le Cirque in New York, Spago's in Los Angeles, the Zuni Café
in San Francisco. The thought was to establish their brand identity at a
certain quality level that was implied by their inclusion on those wine
lists. That would translate to retail desirability, but retail was their
secondary market.

For Rhonda, designing the label was exciting, a creative
challenge—and her chance to make her mark. In Reno it was all
about Don and his wife—his third wife—Rhonda. Here, it was the
Caranos. Rhonda played around with four-color gardens. She didn't
want a creek or a tree—too commonplace. They hadn't yet built
the Villa—no image there. Eventually she envisioned what she
wanted: a label that would look like an invitation to a wedding or
bar mitzvah, but this would be an invitation to drink their wine. After that breakthrough, the font style for their name seemed apparent. It had to be art deco, very 1920s. First they tried gold on
white, but that didn't work. So they added silver. Then platinum.
"That really popped," Rhonda said. "Really invited you to drink the
wine."

But still, it wasn't good enough. They changed printers. Eventually she got it to where she wanted it to be: with black art deco let-
tering on a chalky white background, and tri-color borders of varying
widths in silver, platinum, and gold. Over the years, they made some
modifications. They went, for instance, to a thicker, richer paper, and
changed glues, but the fundamental design used on all their white
wines remains unchanged. "My god, it took so long," Rhonda said.
"Don't change it!"

"I've done a lot of labels," said Marlene Ing, "and this is the trickiest I've ever done." It was also expensive, adding about a dollar a case to the cost of the Fumé Blanc.

"Silver and gold is tough," Rhonda agreed. "It only looks easy."

Most importantly, it works. Eileen Fredrikson of Gomberg, Fredrikson & Associates, the wine consultants, was discussing the Caranos one day several months later, when she said: "Everything about them says, 'I'm a classic product produced by people who care about the land, who care about the classic table, so we invite you to try our wine.'" When I told her that was precisely Rhonda's intention, she nodded. "I had no idea. But subliminally, she accomplished what she set out to do."

Rhonda left the conference room to fetch a bottle, and while she was gone Marlene gestured at the room where we were sitting and said: "Rhonda, she could be an interior decorator. Look at this. Look how nice this is. It's just so beautiful." Marlene was sweet and sincere. Rhonda returned with a bottle of Fumé Blanc. She put it down in front of us on the polished tabletop. We all stared at it.

Finally, Rhonda said: "We made a choice a long time ago about the color of the bottle. We didn't do dead-leaf green. We specifically went to a flint-color bottle to complement the label. We tried this label on all colors of bottles. We started out with a Canadian company. The color of this bottle was unique to Ferrari-Carano. You didn't see too many flint-color bottles in 1987, when we released this wine." The current bottle manufacturer, Oakland Glass, calls the color smoky quartz.

"People said, the color is going to affect the flavor," Rhonda continued. "But George said, 'Forget about it. People drink it before that.'" Fumé Blanc is not a wine for laying down; after a year or two it will lose its freshness of flavor. It's a wine to be drunk when new.

The Burgundy-style bottle, Marlene explained, was not traditional for Sauvignon Blanc, which usually came in a wider Bordeaux-style bottle. The slim-shouldered Burgundian bottles cost them $5.82 a case.

Rhonda ran her hand over the bottle, from the short neck over the narrow shoulders that slid into the body. "It doesn't bulge," she said. "It's just nice and sleek."

It had taken yet more time to select a Spanish foil capsule, to write and edit the label copy, to decide where to position the label. When all that was done, they carried a sample bottle to a liquor store owned by Don's oldest friend, Ben Akert. Before he left the liquor business, "Suds" had boasted that he sold enough booze in his nine retail stores to keep every man and woman in Nevada soused around the clock. The Caranos put their bottle on a shelf and determined that, yes, it stood out.

But they didn't stop there. Steve Meisner, the Caranos' sales and marketing director from day one, remembers they set up a simulated white-tablecloth restaurant, with the lights dimmed, to see how it looked on the table. "And the next week," he said, "they built a shelf with one hundred of our competing wines, to see if it was visually stunning. They are very, very meticulous."

Rhonda and Marlene and I had been talking for hours and it was almost time for lunch. Joey was preparing a nonfat lentil, vegetable, and brown-rice soup, as well as a Chinese noodle salad with duck. As we waited for Don to join us, Rhonda talked about the direction of the wine business, and what Ferrari-Carano would have to do to grow—"elegantly," she emphasized—in a global market. Its wines were now sold in seventeen countries on three continents. It was promoted on the Ferrari-Carano Web site. The barrels were French, the corks Portuguese, the foil capsules Spanish, the workers Mexican.

She told me about flying with Don from Milan to London and finding their Fumé Blanc on the wine list; before you knew it, she said with delight, Don was conducting a seminar on winemaking in the first-class cabin. In a climate where consolidation among wholesalers as well as producers was accelerating, she said, "We need global brand recognition not to get swallowed up by the big guys. It's scary in a lot of respects. And sort of exciting, too."

The consequences of the 9/11 attacks for their restaurant sales came up briefly, and Rhonda was adamant, her striking blue eyes flashing. "We'll come back. That's number one. We will never lose our name on wine lists." She chopped the tabletop to make her point. "Never."

Creativity may be her life, but business is business.

To Go Unnoticed

HERE IS HOW you produce the cork that fits precisely into the neck of the Burgundy-style, smoky quartz bottle with its invitationlike label that will contain the 2002 Ferrari-Carano Fumé Blanc.

You begin in the Algarve, in southern Portugal, when the Silva family had planted a cork oak forest before Manuel Silva Jr., their current commercial director, was born. It's going to take a minimum of fifty-two years, or three harvests, for the longitudinal growth rings in the second or outer bark of the cork trees—*Quercus suber*—to be useful. The outer bark is dead, but the inner bark is not, and great care must be taken not to damage it when removing the dead bark. This slow growth and concomitant patience is essential to develop the density you need to impart the inimitable characteristics of cork. It is lightweight, moisture-resistant, and compressible, has natural wet suction, compensates for imperfections in glass, and ages without deteriorating. That it is also biodegradable is simply a bonus.

The long wait, the fact that you plant a cork oak forest for your grandchildren—the Silva family has been in cork for eight generations, though Manuel's father struck out on his own only thirty years ago when political upheaval in Portugal brought about a restructuring of the industry—gives cork families a philosophical outlook. "Wine is a trinity," said a farmer named João Posser de Andrade, explaining to the *New York Times* why he believes synthetics will never replace his cork. "The bottle is the skeleton, the wine is the blood, and the cork is the lung. Can you imagine a lung made of by-products of the petroleum industry?"

So you've waited generations before you strip the outer bark in early summer, when the humidity is high near the sea and the bark is at its least brittle. As quickly as possible you truck it north to the region around Oporto, where you disinfect it, then stack it on cement bars the same way it came off the tree, in long hemispheric strips. After a year of aging, you boil it for two hours in reconstituted fresh water to eliminate tannins that have the potential to flavor a wine. You are just getting started.

You dry the cork for two weeks until it reaches about 15 percent humidity, then lay it out on plastic pallets—not wood—for grading of its visual qualities and thickness. You strip sections of the required depth, in the case of this Fumé Blanc, forty-four millimeters. You convey the strips into punchers, and for these high-quality corks the punchers are manually operated, a job that takes five years to master and has cost many a finger. There are families of punchers who pass the skills of the trade down from generation to generation. You must get every possible cork out of the strips, so it is tight, demanding work, and the leftovers will be used for champagne corks or flooring. You hand sand the new corks to be as perfect as possible until, as Manuel Silva says, you have "the clean end, the beautiful sides, and few pores. Nobody can imagine how much work."

You wash the corks in a sterile ozone solution to eliminate dust, mold, and the dread 2,4,6-trichloroanisole, or TCA, a compound formed in the cork by the interaction of moisture, chlorine, and mold, the slightest taint of which can impart the odor of wet dog and onion, and ruin an otherwise superb bottle of wine. You rinse the corks again, delicately, so there is no residual chlorine. You leave zero residuals, or try to. The first shipments Ferrari-Carano bought from the Silvas had some problems in this regard, but Marlene Ing got very tough indeed with Manuel Silva, and there have been no such problems since.

You dry the corks again, usually to a level of six to eight degrees of humidity, and then inject ozone to sterilize them. Now you sort. You put them on a roller table and select the higher-quality corks that go to houses such as Rothschild, Château Margaux, Robert Mondavi, and Ferrari-Carano. The Caranos send a representative to Oporto, to inspect the corks before you ship them—the first of four inspections—something few wineries have the knowledge and resources to do. You airfreight the corks, which costs more than ocean shipping but is quicker and safer.

At a plant in Napa you firebrand the ends of the cork with the Ferrari-Carano logo. Then you ink-dye the brand, the Villa Fiore, onto the side of the cork because firebranding is not fine enough for the image. You apply de-dusters that are somewhat harsh and can add pores to the cork, and finally you treat them with a paraffin and silicon sealant. You pack them in bags of one thousand and add sulfur dioxide gas for sterility, and now they are ready to be trucked to the winery in the Dry Creek Valley. You are careful about choosing your trucker, avoiding for instance the firm that had once planned to transport them with a load of cod.

At the winery they undergo their ultimate visual and sensory inspections. Ferrari-Carano, which is paying thirty-nine cents a cork, not much less than the forty-eight cents it is paying for bottles, will not accept a shipment with more than two bad corks in every fifty, and even that will cause them to be skeptical of the overall quality of the lot. All this effort you expend is to ensure that in the end the consumer removing the cork will not notice it at all.

Like so much in America, even the usual relationship between their cork makers and the Caranos had been subtly affected by the 9/11 terror attacks. In the past, the Portuguese had put a few cases of vintage port in with the cork shipment; now the Department of Homeland Security had ordered the practice stopped. It was difficult to know what effect the port had on security against terror attacks, but then again, Tom Ridge's people were also seizing Cuban cigars imported from Canada. I feel infinitely safer to think of the agents, their feet up, drinking the best port, smoking those Cohibas.

On the day the corks for the 2002 Fumé Blanc underwent their final inspection, Manuel Silva and an associate met with Ferrari-Carano's assistant winemaker, Andrew Levi, who conducted visual, aural, and chemical tests, and with Marlene Ing. When the Silva corks passed muster everybody in the room was pleased. Manuel Silva, a pudgy man with a five o'clock shadow and the face of a landed aristocrat, albeit a working aristocrat, stood and shook Marlene's hand.

"We have a partnership," she said. "It's a mutual respect. We know the Silvas are in it heart and soul."

"We never close at five, Marlene," said a wry Silva.

But I was hardly listening to him. Months after I should have, I grasped why Marlene always wore the low-slung hats and penciled eyebrows I thought were marks of flamboyance. How could I have been so dumb? Her hair had fallen out. Chemotherapy.

2

FRUIT

March 2002–September 2002

Bud Break

THE PACE OF life in the vineyards was beginning to accelerate.

On March 26 the Sauvignon Blanc buds on Keegan Ranch began to open. One by one by one they unfurled tiny, fresh, pale-green leaves and revealed their densely packed, moist, pink centers. Within a few days the growing year began in a uniform, balanced way throughout the 25.38 acres. Pink-white blossoms soon appeared on the apple trees that stood between the vineyard and Dry Creek.

As winter waned and temperatures rose, more daylight and greater warmth released the buds from their sleep. The dormant cells became the flowers they were meant to be. Almost overnight, the shoots grew a meter long; it was the fastest growth they would experience in the entire reproductive process. This would be Keegan's sixth season since Don had bought it from Tim Keegan for $29,487 an acre. It had cost about another $12,000 an acre to develop it: to pull out the apple orchard, bring the soil into balance, adjust the pH levels, drive the stakes, set up the two-wire, seven-foot T-arm trellis system laid out in rows eleven feet apart, and plant rootstock with its grafted Sauvignon Blanc clones, 14,362 vines on Keegan Ranch. Every dime, and every drop of sweat, lay behind the journey that was now beginning from vine to table.

From now until harvest, the men who tended this vineyard would watch and intervene as needed, twenty-four hours a day, seven days a week. If all went well, each of the slowly opening buds would pro-duce two clusters of grapes—but not yet. For now, the weather was still cool, reaching the low sixties at the warmest part of the day at the southern end of the Dry Creek Valley, where the Russian River breezes stirred. At night, temperatures were falling close to frost point. Nothing was more crucial to the quality of the grapes that would come off these vines than the weather; as it grew warmer, their growth would accelerate to a point in high summer when the vines added as much as an inch a day. But their vigor and abundance came mostly from the soil. The ancient slide that had created this val-ley had left behind soil with good drainage. The vines spread their roots several feet deep into the rich earth, feeding off its nutrients.

Everything was ready for bringing in a tractor and plowing. That work began on April 1 and lasted four days. Crimson clover and brome had been encouraged to grow between the rows, and as the tractor blades churned them into the soil, circulation around the root systems was enhanced, organic sources of nutrients were built up, and most important of all—at a time of year when anxiety about a crop-killing frost ran high—the color of the earth was changed. Pale green turned to a rich burnt red-brown as the tractor rumbled be-tween rows. The brown absorbed more heat than green, and then re-leased it at night, grabbing perhaps two or three critical degrees of warmth.

What was best for the vines was not necessarily best for the health of the ecosystem, though. Environmentalists frowned upon disking because maintaining a year-round cover crop of clover and brome would protect the creek in the winter of 2002, during winter rains. It would take several storms the next winter before the cover crop reemerged, and until then, environmentalists said, topsoil washing into the creek would hurt its health.

True, but only if Steve Domenichelli farmed irresponsibly—that was his view. He believed he cared more deeply about the well-being of this place than any outsider, no matter how well-intentioned. I have heard the same conviction from lumberjacks and fishermen, as well as farmers; they are the stewards of the forests, the sea, the vineyard, and care far more deeply about them than any outsider can appreciate. Steve took pride that he left the environment as he found it. He thought Dry Creek was special, teeming with salmon and steelhead, and he understood fully that soil running off into its waters would damage the spawning beds. That was one reason he stuck to the letter of the law requiring him to stop farming fifty feet back from the creek bank. He would do nothing in that protected riparian zone.

There were some large-scale producers, such as Fetzer Vineyards, in Mendocino County, that practiced sustainable farming: They composted their vineyards exclusively with the residue of harvested grapes, or pomace; they spurned pesticides and herbicides; they irrigated only with recycled water; they even used chickens to scratch the soil rather than employ a tiller. Steve wanted to be responsible, but the emphasis at Ferrari-Carano was not on the environment, it was focused on the quality of grapes and the bottom line.

On the afternoon of April 3, a Wednesday, Steve came to Keegan along with its manager Dave Bacci, one of the five Ferrari-Carano vineyard managers. Eliseo Martinez, the chief foreman and the original El Charco hand, the first man Steve had stolen away from his dad, was there, too.

There was a racial hierarchy at Ferrari-Carano, the same one that generally prevailed throughout the Napa and Sonoma valleys. The white guys were management and the Mexican guys were laborers. As a rule of thumb, the Mexicans could become foremen but rise no higher. In the mostly nonunionized wine industry, that hierarchy goes unchallenged and unquestioned, treated as if it were as natural as the weather, but of less concern.

Dave Bacci, a tall, lean Anglo with a cleft chin, had started to work for Steve as a manager two days after he graduated from Cal Poly San Luis Obispo in 1995. Steve found that Dave needed a lot of propping up at first. "His self-esteem was broken down; he didn't think much of himself," Steve told me when Dave was out of earshot. "I worked really close with him for fourteen months. Now he does so much for me."

One requirement of Bacci's job was to learn Spanish. "A white guy has to speak Spanish in one year," Steve said. "If you don't make the effort to converse with these guys in the field, you better order an airline ticket. I put them next to guys who don't speak any English. You start to talk all day—the weather, the vines, the river. You play cards, drink beer. The Hispanic guys are such great teachers because they're so patient, not many of them get excited. They try so hard to speak English when they come here, it shows them these American guys are making the effort, too. The Hispanic boys are where it all starts and you've got to be there."

Eliseo had been there longer than Bacci and understood English perfectly, but he would never be more than a foreman. Steve had told me Eliseo spoke very little English, and he knew Eliseo inside out; yet when I talked to Eliseo myself, I found his English to be easily understood—and I realized how high Steve's standards were for fluency when it came to the Mexican hands. Eliseo's job kept him in the vineyards, where English was needed only when conversing with his bosses, all of whom also spoke Spanish. In this he was different from the other big man from El Charco, René Ruiz, who took English classes and read the newspaper, and who had been able to escape the vineyards, not for a manager's job like Dave Bacci's, though for easier indoor work that paid better.

There are 11 million Latinos in California out of a total of 36 million people—Anglos are no longer a majority, but the largest plurality—many of them working in agriculture, and a fair portion of those in the vineyards. Eliseo told me that his son, a first-grader, was in a bilingual program in Healdsburg. The boy spent a couple of hours learning English, and the rest of the day being taught in Spanish. "That way he doesn't forget his culture," Eliseo said, "and it's better to know English for the money." The program, one upshot of a state struggling with a multilingual, multicultural population, would continue through third grade.

Eliseo had four brothers already working at Ferrari-Carano. Now he began to tell Steve about his youngest brother, who was having a problem down in Mexico with his boss. Eliseo, who was only thirty-four himself, wanted the kid to come north, too.

"Tell him to give the guy notice," Steve said, "and come on up." Eliseo was pleased, and so was Steve, who knew that any brother of Eliseo's would be a hard worker and no trouble.

After Eliseo went back to work, Dave Bacci and Steve took me to look at the three wells in Keegan. Grapes need a lot of water, and planting them in rows makes irrigation easy. Drawing water from the Russian River and its tributaries was tightly restricted, so the wells were a necessity. Two older wells were dug in mid-vineyard to a depth of 170 feet, and a more recent one closer to the creek was eighty feet deep. In Sonoma County it is legal to sink wells if your property is adjacent to a creek. Your rights along the riverbank, or riparian rights, are weighed by county officials against the rights of other landowners on the creek. Nine million acres of California are artificially watered, and there is a looming catastrophe that everyone knows about, but nobody can figure out how to prevent, over the conflicting demands for water by farmers and the other millions of Californians, most of them crowded into sprawling urban centers. What happens when the next drought arrives, as it surely will? In Sonoma County, where water is plentiful for now, thousands of acres of vines have been planted in the last decade, and a day of reckoning is sure to come.

"We only turn on the water as we have to," Steve said, "whereas there are other guys who turn it on and go back to bed." Steve had a habit of favorably comparing his practices to the "other guys," a habit I was all but certain he had picked up from his father. His drive to achieve perfection, and the judgmental quality that accompanied it, had once almost caused Steve to leave Ferrari-Carano. Working under Barney Fernandez had driven Steve crazy because he believed as an article of faith he could bring in better fruit at a lower cost. Just as he was reaching his breaking point, Don had made Steve his director of vineyard operations.

The wells, Steve explained, provided water for a drip-irrigation system, and right now they were supplying every vine in Keegan with an average six gallons every ten days, but that volume would increase later in the growing cycle. If you overirrigated now, the vines would grow too fast, and there was the danger of their becoming out of balance with grape development. But if you did not provide enough water, the vegetative characteristics—that "herbaceousness" that George craved—would be diminished. So Steve's watering strategy had to vary block by block, depending on what he knew about the characteristics of the grapes in each patch of land, and his overall design.

If the temperature dropped below freezing, misting the vines could coat them with a thin layer of ice that, strangely enough, kept the green tissue within from being destroyed. It worked because when water freezes, heat is released. In addition, as long as the solution on the surface of the plant included water as well as ice it would remain at precisely thirty-two degrees, just high enough to avoid disaster. But the wells in Keegan lacked the capacity to provide overhead frost protection, so Steve kept wind machines on standby to suck cold air upward and allow warmer air from above to flood the inversion. So far in 2002, they had not needed the wind machines here on the valley floor.

"We've been lucky," Dave Bacci said. "Springtime is an anxious time of year, everything pushing out, the operation starting to roll again."

Frost was one reason to worry. Another was the cutworm that emerged when the soil was disked, and fed on the roots of the vines. If you put poison bait out for them they didn't last long. The possibility of rain was of greater concern. Rain could bring phylloxera, and there was absolutely nothing, except perhaps for the glassy-winged sharpshooter or the reemergence of Prohibition, that wine growers feared more.

"A tiny yellow aphid one thirtieth of an inch long and one sixtieth of an inch wide," Karen MacNeil writes in *The Wine Bible,* "phylloxera feeds on a vine's roots, ultimately sucking life out of the vine. . . . Growers watched in desperate frustration as their vines yellowed, shriveled and then slowly perished." There was a first onslaught of phylloxera in California about one hundred years ago that almost destroyed what was becoming a thriving industry. For a long time there was no known cure, but then it was discovered that the roots of certain American varieties seemed to render the pest powerless. In the 1980s phylloxera erupted again, and the new strain thrived on the very rootstock—the AxR1—that had been urged on growers as resistant by researchers and bankers during the planting frenzy of the 1960s and 1970s. The cure had contained the seeds of future destruction, and the bitterness and anger persists. All you could do if your vines were attacked by phylloxera was pull them and replant. Mac-Neil estimates that replanting has cost California growers $1.2 billion, and others estimate the potential damage at several times that. After the 2001 harvest, Ferrari-Carano had had to pull out a phylloxera-infested Sauvignon Blanc vineyard near Don and Rhonda's home in Geyserville that had provided grapes whose honeysuckle flavor none of their other vines could duplicate.

So rather than coaxing the vines toward faster growth, which he could do, Steve was happy to hang back and let the cool weather dictate a slow, balanced progress. "Rain or cold weather," he said, "then you're fucked." For once he was in no hurry; he seemed to operate at two speeds simultaneously, one driven by anxiety and the other by what he called Mother Nature.

Steve wanted me to see some of the experiments he was doing with clones and rootstocks on a hillside in the Russian River Valley. We drove up there, talking about our kids, the difficulties of divorce, sports. He was good company because he seemed to have no censors; everything spilled out of him with an appealing openness.

From the hilltop we looked down on the rain-swollen Russian River charting its sinuous course through the geometrically cultivated valley, a Mondrian canvas in green and brown. The sky was a deep blue with piles of white, fluffy clouds riding a strong breeze. The landscape was lush, rolling, and sensuous—Mother Nature indeed. At the small experimental vineyard Steve dropped to his knees, pruning shears gripped in his long, bony fingers. Six months earlier he had grafted a French Cabernet Sauvignon vine, a scion, onto a wild rootstock. Scion and budwood might have been incompatible, or the graft might have been bad and killed the vine. But the graft had taken hold, and here again was fresh, densely packed new life. As he pruned off the top of the vine to encourage all the vigor of the root system into growing the baby buds, he looked up and said: "This is one of my favorite things." There was a timbre I had not heard from him before; it was different from the joyfulness when he talked about Ava, or the humble gratitude when he recalled his outing with his son Jared. It sounded—and this effect was heightened by his posture on his knees—spiritual. "This is like birth to me," he said. "It's like a match made in heaven."

Finally I grasped the full depth of Steve Domenichelli's connection to Don Carano's land, and the grapes he grew on it.

Dangers

THE STORM BLEW out of Alaska, but then had snuck up on Keegan Ranch from the south when a low-pressure front swirled it around and through the back door. Near Dixon, to the east, there was a rare baby tornado. A little more than an inch of rain fell on Keegan on Sunday and Monday, and they began to spray to save their crop.

On Tuesday, May 22, there were five tractors pulling three-hundred-gallon sprayers through the vineyard, misting the vines with a mixture of sulfur and the fungicides called Rally and Vanguard. They were also spraying a fertilizer called 2BK. The fertilizer had short- and long-term benefits. It helped goose the vines to set—the point at which berries would appear—as quickly as possible; it also balanced deficiencies in the micronutrients needed for a healthy plant (magnesium, boron, and zinc), or in macronutrients (nitrogen, phosphorus, and potassium) that could adversely affect set. Later, these same nutrients in the grapes would be required by the yeast during fermentation.

For now, only about 5 percent of the clusters were open, exposing their anthers and pistil. Most still looked like green caviar. Until they had set, the clusters were vulnerable to powdery mildew, caused by moisture, which made the capsules sticky; if they remained stuck, they would not pollinate. You could easily lose half or more of your crop. Sulfur was the remedy—nasty stuff, but nowhere near as awful as the fumigant methyl bromide, which had been banned from vineyards when it was shown to be toxic and to cause birth defects.

According to the Pesticide Action Network North America, 60 million pounds of fumigants and pesticides a year are used by California farmers, some 6 to 10 million of them sulfur, depending on how wet the year is. In a report called "Fields of Poison 2002: California Farmworkers and Pesticides," the network, along with California Rural Legal Assistance and the United Farm Workers, concluded that: "Agricultural workers face greater risks of suffering from pesticide-related illnesses—including acute poisonings and long-term effects such as cancer and birth defects—than any other sector of society. . . . Grapes continue to rank first in reported illnesses, attributed in part to frequent high level applications of sulfur." The ill effects of sulfur exposure are not, however, life-threatening.

Steve's crew would be spraying sulfur in Keegan every ten days, and Rally every sixteen days, until the end of June, after which they had to stop to be sure the stinky-egg smell of hydrogen sulfide on the harvested grapes wouldn't linger. They sprayed all day, and then would dry spray, or dust, again at night, working from midnight on, after the wind died down and you could control your coverage without its blowing all over creation. That blow was what made sulfur unpleasant for humans in the vicinity. People who lived near vineyards told the Pesticide Action Network the sulfur gave them headaches, sore throats, and respiratory and skin irritations. Nobody had studied these long-term, low-dose exposures, says the network's Susan Kegley. "They *are* doing experiments on humans, there's just no one to look at the results," she says. The Environmental Protection Agency has imposed many regulations covering the use of sulfur. You have to, for example, clean and flush your equipment every day, and provide workers with protective garb; and you are not supposed to apply sulfur within three days of anyone entering the vineyard. Nevertheless, the EPA considers sulfur to be organic.

This Tuesday morning, Dave Bacci was leaning against the fender of his pickup truck and watching the sprayers as they moved through the vineyard he supervised, the three-wheel tractors making tight turns at the wide, packed-earth avenues that bordered the rows. The men operating the tractors wore white jumpsuits and goggles. "It's just another form of protection," Bacci said. "Cheap. Effective. Can do it fast, three hundred and fifty to four hundred acres in eight hours, so labor costs are low. We do try to spray as little as possible, be as environmentally protective as possible, but still, we have a crop to protect."

Just then, Steve Domenichelli roared up and leapt out of his four-wheel drive, talking on his cell phone, waving at us, scanning the vineyard as he hurried toward us with his big-man strides. "I love it," Steve said exuberantly, putting away his phone. "Love it. Just perfect.

"Right now, these guys," he said, waving toward the men aboard the tractors, "are working seven days a week," moving from vineyard to vineyard. "I'm hoping to do the entire bloom cycle in no more than ten or twelve days, if we get some mild weather seven or eight. That would be beautiful. Ten or twelve days to set. It's not like last year, when all the varieties bloomed within fifteen days. Cabernet's way behind, Chardonnays and Pinot Noirs are way ahead."

Steve rushed partway up a row and stood in it with his arms spread-eagled. The leaf canopies were about three feet now, with the lower leaves a dark green and the newer growth the color of lime pulp. "These canes will grow out to here," he said. "Right now is the most important time with Sauvignon Blanc. Right now. Because we have such freaky storms in California." Something caught his attention, and he scowled. "I don't really like to see that," he said, looking at a grayish puddle left in the wake of a sprayer.

His cell phone rang and he dashed a few yards away to have a brief conversation. In the rows the ground was littered with what looked like recently fallen leaves, and when he came back I asked about that.

"We pulled those leaves off, knowing it was going to rain," Steve said. "To give [the vines] ample air movement and sunlight." The leaves had come off on the morning-sun side, facing the road rather than the creek, and for the most part from the middle of the vines. That way the weaker morning light would penetrate while the hotter afternoon sun continued to be filtered. The leaves had been carefully removed individually from the stem, not ripped free. It was painstaking work, a mind-boggling amount of work when you remembered there were 14,362 vines in Keegan alone.

"We worked Wednesday night and again Friday and then we worked seventy-five guys on Sunday," Steve said. "Some guys were saying, let's wait and see. But these are protectants, not eradicants. I said to these guys, do all you can do, then sleep when it rains.

"You want everything the same. But you can't get it the same unless you open it up like this and get it uniform sunlight, and you won't have that unless the clusters are the same. So if I keep it in balance now the glass of Fumé will be about as uniform as you can get."

But how did he know to pull more leaves than he had anticipated, and at just the right moment before the storm hit?

"It was just a gut feeling on the rain," Steve said. "I read the weather really well. I'm not blowing my own horn—I knew, with the storm coming in from Alaska. It was a lot of overtime. But if we hadn't, the fruit would be infested, and we're done."

JAIME RUIZ is a boyish twenty-six. He is a pale, slender young man, quiet by nature but given to laughter, especially with a few beers in him. He's a lot like his father, Carlos, who worked for Steve Domenichelli's dad. He lives with his parents and three brothers in a house they bought in Cloverdale. I had first met Jaime in El Charco in January when he was home with his bride Milagros.

René Ruiz led us to Jaime's place—the two men were not related although they were next-door neighbors. "Every year they come down, they make one," René joked. "Most of the guys come down and next year they have a baby." René had no children.

Jaime greeted us at his sky-blue gate and invited us to sit in his kitchen, where there was a poured concrete floor, a plastic tablecloth covering a Formica table, and a large shrine to the Virgin Mary strung with Christmas lights. Although he had worked nine years at Ferrari-Carano, Jaime spoke little English, so René translated.

Last year, Jaime said, he worked from February to November and earned about sixteen thousand dollars. "Everything over there is better," he said, but coming home meant returning to Milagros. She was somewhere in the house but had not joined her husband in the kitchen. Jaime met Milagros at a dance, and they were married in January 2001, a month before he had to leave her to go back to work in California. He rubbed his arm when he said this and emitted a low sound: "Ooooh. I felt very sad." *Muy triste*. He called her all the time from California, and wrote letters, and once in a while she'd say, "Hurry up. Come home." He was studying to become a citizen so he could begin the years-long process of bringing Milagros to the family home in Cloverdale.

Jaime went up to their bedroom via an external staircase to bring Milagros down to introduce us. After a long delay, Milagros and her husband came and sat on the tattered plastic chairs at the kitchen table. She was very pretty with a broad, butterscotch-colored face and apple cheeks. She clasped her hands between her thighs. I asked her questions and René translated, but her answers required no translation. Did she want to join her husband in California? "*Sí,*" she said, and laughed. Was she sad when her man was gone so long? "*Sí, mucho.*"

Milagros blushingly consented to have her picture taken. Jaime stood beside her, a slim youngster, dressed like many other American youth in baggy calf-length shorts and a sports logo polo shirt. He put his arm protectively around her shoulders. They both composed their faces into formal expressions, her hip leaning into his.

Someday Jaime hoped that he and Milagros could buy a little shop in California, something easier than working in the vineyards. So if Steve Domenichelli wanted him to work all night spraying sulfur, or in the rain and mud, and would pay overtime for it, Jaime was grateful.

IT IS taken as an article of faith among oenophiles that more is less: that there comes a point in the vineyard, and in the winery, where quantity overwhelms quality. If you are staking your business reputation on the quality of your product, then the perception that you may have passed beyond this point is a constant concern. But if, on the other hand, you were in a capital-intensive business, and, furthermore, as Don Carano had, you had made a huge investment in producing great Sonoma County hillside reds, you were going to have to run the risk that by producing more of your best-selling wine you might jeopardize your reputation—then you might undermine your own meticulously constructed Story.

In 2001, Ferrari-Carano had sold about fifty thousand cases of Fumé Blanc—more than ever before. In 2002, if all their vineyards produced the bountiful crop they were hoping for, they would greatly exceed that. This was the first element in a delicate equation that was testing Steve Domenichelli and George Bursick, the winemaker.

Back in 1999, the top people at Ferrari-Carano had sat down with Don Carano and concluded that their Fumé Blanc, the backbone of their operation, was drifting toward a herbaceous, vegetative style. There was nothing inherently wrong with such a style; in fact, many purists considered it the most authentic expression of the Sauvignon Blanc grape. It was not, however, the Ferrari-Carano style. They had produced their first Fumé Blanc in 1986 by blending grapes from two vineyards, with two different flavors. In 1983, when Don bought the Estate Vineyard where the Villa and the winery now stood, its grapes tended toward the grassy, herbaceous flavors you get from Sauvignon Blancs in Bordeaux. But Home Vineyard, above Don and Rhonda's home in the Russian River Valley, gave a more golden berry that produced the melon flavors you might find in the Loire Valley. George blended them and created a style of wine immensely popular with most critics and consumers alike. In those early days it was as if Ferrari-Carano could do no wrong. This was when their Chardonnay had landed on the cover of *Wine Spectator*. And suddenly their Fumé Blanc was in demand by restaurants and distributors everywhere. But it was always a challenge for George to keep those two flavors, the grassy and the melon, in the characteristic balance that denoted Ferrari-Carano.

Over the years, as they acquired more vineyards and increased production, the problem that emerged had an element of irony: Some of their newer holdings, Keegan in particular, were so fertile they were overwhelmingly abundant. The vines loved Keegan's deep, loamy soil. A winemaker looks at soil in terms of how it translates into the wine he will ultimately get, and the dense, luxuriant canopy of leaves the vines put out in parts of Keegan developed into grapes with aggressively herbaceous flavors. Or would, if they were left unchecked. Since 1999, Steve and his crew had been manipulating those vines to rein them in, battling against the natural inclination of the plants to reproduce in the rich soil of the alluvial flood plain that was the Dry Creek Valley. Meanwhile, Storey Ranch Vineyard, acquired a year before Keegan, had soil that was both shallower and rockier. In Storey the vines produced fewer leaves. The more leaves the vines put out in the shallow, rocky soil, the less vigor there was for the grapes, through which the vines reproduced. Grapevines are hermaphrodites, pollinating themselves. Taken altogether, the nature of the soil, the warmer climate, and the modest leafiness translated to a more melon-like flavor.

So Steve and George were trying to do two things simultaneously. First they wanted to nudge the blend back toward the characteristic Ferrari-Carano balance. Second, they were trying to get all the Sauvignon Blanc they could off Don's land without undermining the quality, and thus the desirability, of the wine. Because they had also realized that to hold that fourteen-dollar price, which made it such a value, they had better maximize production. Nothing more or less was at stake than the success or failure of Ferrari-Carano.

It made George testy to hear people say that if you got too big it was always at the expense of quality. "I think that there's, at least for us, there's this misperception that as you grow quality suffers," he told me one day in early spring. "I'll never forget, seventeen years ago when Don and I first talked he asked me: 'How big do you envision we can grow?'"

George had replied that there was no limit. "As long as you play by the rules for quality," George said, "the same rules a little thousand-case producer plays by. Often as a winery grows the bottom line be-comes more the issue, they begin to listen more to accountants—grow more grapes, reduce the quality of your barrels, cut corners. When you start doing that, the end is in sight." But Ferrari-Carano resisted that temptation. "Today, we're using the same percentage of new barrels we did seventeen years ago," he continued. "Today, we're growing thirty percent to forty percent less crop per vine than we did seventeen years ago. It's getting *better*. If we had slipped into mediocrity . . . but we're still getting the same quality of wine in the bottle. So people aren't saying, They're getting so big, they can't con-trol it. Certain critics feel smaller is better—two thousand cases can be a great wine, twenty thousand cases can't be. I take exception to that—if you're *not* cutting corners. That's one of the most frustrating things to me."

Wine Spectator had described the 2001 Ferrari-Carano Fumé Blanc this way: "Ripe and fleshy. With plenty of richness to the floral, sweet pea, fig and melon flavors that fold into vanilla and cream tones." Such preciousness may help Ferrari-Carano market its product, but is also a not-so-subtle form of class snobbery. Nonetheless this stuff counts, as much as anything external. *Wine Spectator* can make or break a brand.

But the very balance that denoted George's Fumé Blanc, the bal-ance that Steve Domenichelli was striving to readjust in the vineyard, did have its critics. One small producer who didn't want to be quoted by name said that the Ferrari-Carano approach of "consistency above all is not unlike the Big Mac. There's nothing daring, innovative or even distinctive about it."

In her highly regarded *The Wine Bible,* Karen MacNeil does not mention Ferrari-Carano among her list of wines to know. She does say, however: "On first consideration, viticulture might seem like a subset of agriculture, but at their philosophical cores, the two are quite different. Agriculture tends to seek standardization, uniformity, high yield, and consistency on as large a scale as possible. . . . What makes fine wines compelling, however, are quirks of individuality."

What Ferrari-Carano seeks is for its Fumé Blanc to straddle both worlds, existing in the is-it-art or is-it-commerce zone where Clint Eastwood movies and John le Carré novels also reside.

THE SHARPSHOOTER AND THE KID

IN THE LAST week of May, following pollination, some-where between three-quarters and three-fifths of the blos-soms dropped off, their life cycle at an end. The remaining blossoms were going to become berries. This was set, and how you thought about it touched not just on farming practices, but on your approach to the philosophy of botanical science. A strict botanical construc-tionist, noting that plants lack a central nervous system, knew that they were incapable of formulating a plan. Nor were they likely to have instincts. Plant scientists, for the most part, would reject the Aristotelian idea that all life is moving toward a certain end. Not so for Steve Domenichelli, whose vines were his friends, and who an-thropomorphized as naturally as he breathed: His vines were asleep or awake, happy or unhappy. For him, at set, the plant was making a de-cision on how many flowers to retain, how many berries to produce, and thus grapes—the crop it would eventually produce. He could see that the plant had a strategy—a strategy he understood as surely, and yet, every bit as obscurely, as he understood the arc of growth experienced by his sons as they matured. The purpose of his every gesture in the vineyard was to influence that strategy and direct it toward his desired goals.

On May 31, just as the clusters in Keegan were fully set with only a minimum amount of stuck pollination caused by the storm, Steve found a new cause for worry.

It was a sunny Friday morning with temperatures headed into the seventies when he put his left hand under a cluster and tapped it with the fingers of his right. What Steve wanted was for the caps to fall loose and the berries to stay in place, "so that when the wind comes up," he said, "Mother Nature can do her job," blowing the caps away and leaving the set berries. Instead, a few unopened caviar-sized berries fell, indicating the presence of bunch stem necrosis, or sticky cap. He had his fingers crossed and still anticipated a good crop, but maybe not as consistent a crop as he wished. It got him a little down but thank goodness he'd had the foresight to pull those leaves before the rain or he'd be as bad off as a neighboring grower who lost half his crop to sticky cap. Steve went on his gut feelings and right now his gut told him this crop was not going to be perfect. "It's kind of a Steve Domenichelli rating," he said, poking fun at himself. "Most people would think it was just fine."

A potentially more threatening trouble was an outbreak of the glassy-winged sharpshooter in Cupertino, about 160 miles south. The sharpshooter was a voracious insect that spread the deadly Pierce's disease. State agriculturists warned that a sizable outbreak would deal the state's $27 billion agriculture industry its worst blow since the Medfly invasion twenty years ago. There was about $20 million in the state budget to fight the sharpshooter and Pierce's disease, which kills grapevines by infesting them with a bacterium,

Xylella fastidiosa. The brown, half-inch-long insect has a large proboscis that it uses to drill into a plant's tissue and suck out fluid, while the bacteria it leaves behind eventually chokes off water and nutrients. Only three of the sharpshooters had been found in Cupertino, but two were adults and one a nymph. Steve knew what that meant—they were breeding.

It was enough to send him down to the bright-yellow sticky traps dangling from tree limbs in what remained of Tim Keegan's apple orchard, the five acres of Golden Delicious Steve had kept between the creek and the vines. The sharpshooter—and this was true of the less lethal but nonetheless dangerous blue-green sharpshooter as well— bred in riparian zones. Steve had noticed that the blue-greens liked apples as much as Don did. And unlike grapes, apples weren't harmed by their presence. So the sliver of remaining orchard was actually an ingenious ecological buffer, and the traps he hung in February were an early warning system.

He found a few scattered blue-green sharpshooters amidst the medley of dead insects on the sticky traps, but he expected to see a few from time to time. Had there been even one glassy-winged sharpshooter, he'd have reported it immediately. But there was none. A few weeks later Don asked about it, and Steve was glad to tell him the apple trees were doing their job.

ON MY last morning in El Charco, Boa had driven eight men to the airport in Guadalajara for the flight back to California. Everybody met on the bridge across from the church at 5:30 a.m. The sky was shading from black toward midnight blue, and the crystalline stars were fading from the sky when I got there. The men arrived in one and twos, without their women, carrying suitcases or duffel bags. Except for the kid, who was empty-handed and looked to be about fifteen.

He spoke not a word, and I never learned his name. Looking at him, I could imagine René, and Boa, years ago, striking out on their own for El Norte, where riches and dangers awaited in equal measure. This was to be this kid's first trip, his first departure from his mother's home. He was on his way to Tijuana to meet a coyote his family had paid one thousand dollars to get him to Chicago, where he had relatives. It was a perilous passage, and some people never made it; they lost their lives or were arrested and returned. And this kid carried only his toothbrush, in his shirt pocket.

But he had made it. That's what René Ruiz told me in mid-June as we were driving up to Michalek Ranch. René pulled up at a hillside Cabernet vineyard. The men in the vineyard wore caps or hats to shade them from the relentless sun and worked silently, the vines rustling as they sorted through them, pruning small young canes, tying others to the wires with short lengths of orange twine they pulled loose from spools slung over their shoulders. They tied square knots, *nudos de hombres*, René called them. Up here on the Alexander Valley hillside, the north wind made a steady whoosh—a constant rhythmic presence, like waves striking a beach, and the pines at the higher elevations swayed restlessly. It was close to quitting time and the moon was a ghostly shadow in the eastern sky.

Grinning, Boa waved. He was full of the spirit of mischief and life, a joker dogged by tragic errors. He came over, wiping his hands on his jeans before shaking hands. His shirt was stained with soil and sweat, and the gold shimmered in his mouth as he smiled. René, of course, was immaculate, with dazzling white running shoes and a brand-new L.A. Dodgers cap.

Some of these vines, Boa said, pointing, "are getting sick. They are not getting strong." He demonstrated by loosening the razor-sharp, scimitar-shaped knife carried on their belts by all the men, the *cuchillo*, and swiftly dispatching a cluster of grapes, *huvas*. The steep, rocky rows were littered with dead clusters drying under the afternoon sun.

The *cuchillo* reminded me of a story Steve once told about a sit-down strike by the men. It was during harvest and word had spread that another grower was paying twenty-five cents more for a full forty-pound lug, a *bandeja*. So the men, most of them from El Charco, sat and began pounding on their *bandejas* with their *cuchillos,* demanding more money. Steve had been with Don Carano when he was called, and Don went with him but kept silent as Steve marched into the middle of the men and demanded in Spanish that anybody with a problem should get up and tell him about it. His strategy was simple: He couldn't deal with ninety guys at once, but three or four, the "troublemakers" as he put it, he could handle. He was always willing, Steve told them, to listen to a legitimate beef. He had known many of these El Charco workers since they were boys. But now they were men. If this was about jerking him around, he wouldn't tolerate it. In the end, the men went back to work, Steve isolated the strike leaders, and ran them off after harvest. Don came away impressed. "He's a tough kid," he told me, when we talked about the incident.

THE $8.50 to $10.25 an hour Ferrari-Carano paid its men, depending on their experience and duties, was a competitive wage, and the winery also provided some full-time workers with health insurance and a pension plan, as well as vineyard housing. At Steve's suggestion, they were also maintaining a small herd of cattle, to provide the men with beef. But they were not unionized. In fact, only five wineries in Napa and Sonoma counties had union contracts, although that may be changing.

Sensing an opportunity, the United Farm Workers were moving organizers to Santa Rosa—their earlier, most famous work had taken place among table grape growers in the Central Valley—and targeting the fine-wine industry. In 1999 they made their first breakthrough at Gallo of Sonoma, like Ferrari-Carano based in the Dry Creek Valley, where the UFW now represented five hundred workers. Then in April 2001, they won a certification election at Sonoma-Cutrer Vineyards in Windsor, a winery whose Chardonnay competed with Ferrari-Carano's, especially in the fine-restaurant market. But contract negotiations were proceeding at a snail's pace, said the UFW, complaining that delaying tactics by growers were both unfair and all too common. They were sponsoring a bill introduced into the state legislature by Senate Majority Leader John Burton of San Francisco to force binding arbitration on growers. Growers hated the bill, and before the year was out, the conflict would cause Governor Gray Davis a good deal of grief.

I asked Don Carano what he paid his workers, but he refused to say. "You could get the unions on our ass and that would kill us," he said. "From our standpoint we're very competitive, and at the same time, I think a major thing is, we provide good housing. I think the fact that we have such long-term employees tells us what we're doing is right."

He is a lifelong Democrat, and the law firm where he is still of-counsel is the powerhouse Democratic firm in Nevada. But his reputation with organized labor is not good. "Don Carano is a Neanderthal," says Dee Taylor, the secretary/treasurer of the hotel and restaurant employees local in Las Vegas. "He fought every union attempt viciously at the Eldorado. It's commonplace in the industry and in northern Nevada particularly. It's very dominated by these single owners worth about fifty trillion dollars." There are certain similarities in the composition of the labor forces in the vineyards and in Reno, where the higher-paid casino workers are mostly white, says

Taylor, and the housekeeping and kitchen staffs, who are paid less, are mainly Hispanic and Filipino.

Unions are a subject that gets under Don's skin. Don Cox, a reporter for the *Reno Gazette-Journal*, told me that Don yelled at him when questioned about unionization efforts in the casinos. Don is famously personable and interested in other people, but in private his temper is also notorious, says Deep Cork. "If Don doesn't hear what he wants he gets angry. He's not nasty, he's just a man who lives in fear and trembling. Don's whole ego is so tied up in those vineyards. He's got to have put upwards of twenty million dollars into it." His refusal to tell me what he paid his workers was hard to understand, because he surely knew I could find out directly from the men. But he is instinctively secretive, and Deep Cork called Don and Rhonda "the most secretive people I ever knew."

"I just know from our standpoint," Don said to me, "when you get outside people, running your business can be very difficult, very expensive. Union or otherwise, when my employees need an outside person to represent them, then you're doing something wrong."

I repeated Don's words to Sergio Guzman, the principal UFW organizer for the wine industry, and he laughed. "Oh yeah," he said. "We hear that all the time. In my opinion the wine industry is one of the most richest in the United States. But they do not provide good salaries and benefits for the workers. Now we will focus on the wine industry."

But these disputes were taking place at a great remove from the gorgeous hillside vineyard where Boa and the other El Charco men were tying cane. At precisely 4:30, as if a whistle had blown, they laid down their spools of string, fetched their empty lunch coolers, piled into Boa's Chevy Suburban, and waited. Boa, however, paused to talk. He had news.

"My wife is going to have a kid," he said proudly. "In August." Just like René had said, every winter the men went home and made a baby. Last year Boa made a daughter, and he also had a teenage step-daughter. After the accident that killed his wife and son Arturo, his other son went to live with Boa's mother and father.

"I hope you have a son," I said, thinking of the boy he lost.

He nodded. Yes, he also wished for another son.

THINK LIKE A TREE

HAD THE MOMENT come to drop crop?

The temperature hit 105 degrees in Keegan at noon, July 10. As long as the vines had enough water they leaped forward in the heat. So before the temperatures soared, Dave Bacci gave them a good soaking and then began to drip a steady six gallons every ten days through the emitters beneath each vine. You had to regulate your drip carefully: Too much water would drown out flavors; on the other hand, you didn't want your vines to fall on their faces. As with so much in the vineyard, balance was your mantra.

For the most part, he would shut down the drip system at night when you couldn't see if you had sprung a leak. They employed a man whose job it was to go from vineyard to vineyard, looking for irrigation system problems. No detail was too picayune for Steve Domenichelli, and if you worked for him that had better be your attitude as well.

As the temperatures rose to above one hundred degrees on Tuesday and Wednesday, and then again on Thursday, the relentless heat began to take a toll on the men. They were in Keegan removing more leaves to allow as much air circulation as possible; Steve was not going to repeat his early mistake with leaving a voluptuous canopy unchecked. But a few men began to bleed from the nose, and others simply succumbed, passing out in the rows. He had no choice but to get the men out of the vineyards during the unsparing heat of the afternoon, so he started them working at six a.m. and had them knock off at noon. It just killed him to give up part of the workday, with so much to be done, but he had to do it for their well-being.

The vines were maturing along with the season. What had been green and luscious in May was now dark and woody. What was happening was that the epidermis was dying and being replaced by bark. The vines needed that extra, woody strength to support the increasing weight of the ripening berries. The same process—called lignification—would also take place in the stems and the seeds. Lignin was a large molecule, impermeable to water, and resistant to breakdown that also had the effect of keeping the seeds dormant while the berries ripened. And they were still berries, still in their adolescence, on the cusp of becoming grapes once they began to soften and develop sugars. That moment of passage was called veraison, and it was perhaps two weeks away. The crop you had now was the crop you were going to get. You could thin it, and perhaps manipulate your flavors, but the rest was up to the vines. They would give you what they would give you, and you would learn what you could.

You had to think like a tree yourself, season after season. You began years ago with analysis. You took soil samples and accumulated weather data and gathered every available morsel of information. You studied the trunks of oak trees to see how big they were, whether the roots were coming to the surface fighting for sustenance, or were deep and content; the oaks didn't like a lot of water, so you could discern something about the drainage from the position of the roots. You determined what variety of grape would flourish in this particular patch of earth. You decided on a rootstock. You chose a clone. You figured out the best way to prune to get the crop you wanted in this soil, under these conditions. What size crop load would strike the perfect balance between productivity and quality? Could these vines on this land hit that mark? What trellising system would suit the conditions and the vines? What kind of irrigation? Was there enough water? Were your men reliable? Then you waited. A year or two later you'd get a teeny crop, and if you were planting for red wine the wait was more like three or four years. It would probably be another year before your crop was sufficient to make a wine from this single vineyard—if that was what you wanted to do. Then you began trying to turn your crop into the wine you wanted to make, an imaginative target. A thousand new decisions confronted you. Did you use oak? Whose barrels? New or old oak? For how long? What kind of yeasts did you employ? Did you stir? How often? Filter? This was just your first time through—when you had no prior experience with the fruits of this land. But you learned as you went. The next year, trying to incorporate what you had learned, perhaps you pruned differently, thinned your buds more, or less. You kept adjusting the second, third, and fourth years. And just as you got as close to hitting your target as was humanly possible, when your knowledge gave you command and the weather cooperated, and neither blight nor bug afflicted you, the market could move.

The crop in Keegan was looking wonderful. The joy of the vineyard made Steve ebullient, and Ava and his boys filled him with a paternal pride so intense he sometimes felt he could not contain it. One night he was with his oldest son in the kitchen laughing and gabbing away, when it hit him that as much as he was like his dad in his stubbornness and his pride, he was breaking the generational chain, he was in some way doing a better job than his father had. He admired his dad so much, and loved him too, but his dad was hard-core—he had knocked him down so much when he was a kid.

Once he had said to his father, "All I want to hear is a compliment." And his dad replied, "You don't need to hear one from me."

Don and Rhonda would be returning from Reno soon to take up residence in Geyserville for the harvest. Don liked his pillow there, Steve knew. Steve called Don the coolest guy in the world—he wished he had 1 percent of Don's smarts. *And* 25 percent of his money. He thought his dad was jealous of Don. And of him, too. His mom had told Steve that his dad was scared of him. That made him uncomfortable as hell, but if he were honest with himself, it also thrilled him in a place so deep he couldn't talk about it. He was glad Don would be here soon. It was a comfort to know he was around.

In bed, Steve began to ask himself if he should throw some crop on the ground. Conditions were almost too good, the developing crop too abundant. He wanted seven, eight tons an acre, but somewhere there was an invisible line he could not cross. All over Napa and Sonoma counties, men and women were asking themselves the same questions, thinking about the glut of international wine already on the market, pondering how much they could sell this year, doing mental calculations that led only to more anxious questions.

At the end of next week—that's when he'd decide whether to drop crop.

IT SEEMED like bud break came earlier every year, that the whole idea of a "normal" season now had to be put in quotes. In the cities and suburbs, global warming was a powerful and alarming idea, but in the vineyard growers lived with its consequences: The entire weather calendar had been pushed to the left, and 2002 looked to be no exception. This was also supposed to be an El Niño winter. Nothing to do but take what precautions you could, and wait.

There were things that were measurable, knowable. Take, for instance, the Sauvignon Blanc grape itself, a classic white grape of Bordeaux, that had first been planted in California in the 1870s. It was a gypsy that grew well worldwide in many different conditions, and produced wine with a variety of different characteristics in different locales. The French bottled it as Pouilly-Fumé, or Sancerre. Seventy-five percent of its weight was pulp, 20 percent skin, and the balance was its two, three, or four seeds. The skin imparted most of the flavor, aroma, and color, and now, at what was called veraison, was the time in the growing year when its true color emerged. The pea-green berries softened as sugars in the pulp, which eventually would be converted to alcohol, began to develop.

The softening seemed to occur because the decreasing water content resulted in a loss of pressure within the cellular structure of the emerging grape. But nobody was really sure—so much of grape growing depended on tradition rather than science, and precious little research money was available compared to such sustenance crops as white rice, or corn. What was certain was that each grape became a little sugar-making factory; as chlorophyll was lost, the skins shaded toward golden. The increase in sugar meant that there was proportionally less malic and tartaric acids; the acids contained tannins, which contributed bitterness as a balance to the glucose. The bitter tannins may have served another purpose as well, making the grapes—at this stage, when they had not finished making their seeds—less appealing to creatures that might eat them, including humans.

At the same time, the grapes were producing a high concentration of methoxypyrazine—the chemical compound that imparted a certain vegetative flavor—the very flavor Steve was trying to rein in.

As Steve stood in Keegan in mid-July, he thought this was the biggest crop he had ever seen there. There had been more rainfall than in 2001, nearly thirty inches in Keegan (where there was a weather station, something Don had suggested), and the weather so far, despite the negligible shatter caused by the May rain, had been close to ideal. He pulled a few of the tiny, mellowing grapes off a cluster, tasted them, spat them out, and declared that the sugar level was between four and six Brix. Brix was a scale used to express the percent of sugar concentration—during fermentation, sugar content would translate into alcohol content. He would harvest when the Brix were at about twenty-two or twenty-three and the flavors had matured to where you wanted them. These were two moving targets that, if you did everything right, and were lucky, would cross like shooting stars precisely at the moment you decided to harvest. If Steve had to guess, calculating one hundred days forward from the completion of bloom, he would predict harvest between September 6 and 10. *If* things went normally.

Meanwhile, he was also thinking about next year's crop. He had men in the vineyard carefully pruning bull vines and retaining sun vines on which the microscopic clusters had already developed that would become next year's shoots. He lived in a three-year continuum, reaping the fruits of last year's practices, making the vineyard ready for next year's crop. That was why any serious imbalance could take years to correct, why the edge was so thin.

He stood in the midst of Block 8, at the epicenter of Keegan Ranch, his sunglasses pushed back onto his broad forehead, his hands resting on the hips of his baggy jeans, and breathed deeply through his nose. "It's amazing," he said, "when you pick up the smell of green leaves, the fruit"—now his hands were making excited shapes in the air—"and the skin. I think Sauvignon Blanc probably smells better than any other varietal." I could hear tractors chuffing as they redisked the rows where the rain had caused weeds to grow and at our feet the emitters went *plop, plop, plop.*

The fecundity and simple beauty of the vineyard was something I was beginning to love. Every time I drove north across the Golden Gate, passing a huge American flag billboard with the words "God Bless America" at the south end of Petaluma (which called itself California's chicken capital), I left behind the greater forces I was seeking in the vineyard. The failed restaurants and bankrupt wineries. The water battles in the West. The influx of immigrants and its attendant tensions. The tourists whose emissions polluted the wine-growing valleys and whose credit cards kept them in business. The closer I came to Keegan Ranch, the farther away they seemed.

What I cared about *now* was how much crop Steve had chosen to drop.

Between 5 and 20 percent in different blocks, he answered, the clusters that were still green. He had left seventy to eighty grape clusters on each of the vines, tied to three fruiting wires that ran between the trellises, which were spaced seven feet apart. The seven-by-eleven spacing and the T-trellises were traditional for Sauvignon Blanc, though Ferrari-Carano was also experimenting with a vertical trellis system.

The same clones grafted on the same rootstock, exposed to the same weather and irrigated identically, could produce vines only a few feet apart that developed differently, bearing grapes with different tastes. At the Estate, or northern end of Blocks 8 and 9, the blocks nearest Dry Creek, the tastes, everyone assured me, were more like honeysuckle. Whatever honeysuckle tasted like. But just a few dozen feet south, they likened the tastes to asparagus and green pepper. The explanation was simple enough: This was where Tim Keegan's apple orchard had stood. The soil was especially rich in nitrogen, encouraging a dense canopy, which in turn reduced the amount of sunshine that penetrated to the grapes. The grapes would only begin to develop their distinctive flavors when they reached fifteen Brix. Then maybe I could taste asparagus and honeysuckle for myself.

Steve swore that each vine had its individual personality, something I could comprehend but never could "see" the way this fourth-generation grape farmer could. Steve experienced the world through his senses, his inherited savvy, and his instincts. I lived mainly through my mind. It was precisely his way of apprehending the vineyard that I was most drawn to each time I descended the steep, short slope from Kinley Drive, past the one-family help-house where the foreman, Robby Bodalla, lived with his wife, Marina, and son José (at school, "Joe"), past the shed and shop, across the tiny concrete bridge over the dry stream bed, through the blocks of Malbec and Merlot that were turning from green to purple, until finally I pulled up beside Block 7. I was taking possession, not of the vineyard but of its Story. It was becoming the stuff of my daily conversation, my reveries, my dreams. I didn't share Steve's knowledge, his dedication, or his anxieties. But my feelings were glommed onto his. One day I drove my wife Carole up to see Keegan. "This is it," I said, as we rolled to a stop with the gravel of the vineyard avenue crunching beneath the tires. "This is my vineyard." I felt no need to revise that.

NEAR THE end of July a spell of cooler, overcast weather slowed things down in the vineyard, pushing the weather calendar to the right, so that Steve was now predicting harvest to begin no earlier than September 10, twelve days later than in 2001. For the moment, though, things were on cruise control. Sulfur spraying had ceased several weeks earlier, and crews of men from El Charco and elsewhere were continuing to thin out leaves. Everybody believed as a matter of experience that vegetative flavors would be reduced by exposure to light and warmth, although the few studies that existed had provided no scientific evidence to support this faith.

Most important, the clusters were nice and even, in balance to produce a uniform crop. "This should make some really, really quality stuff," Steve said. It was nearly eleven o'clock, and the sun had finally burned away the fog and broken through the clouds. I felt its warmth against the back of my neck. Sugars and flavors were accumulating according to design, Ferrari-Carano's stylish design, which began on the restaurant table and spiraled back here to the land.

Within every grape, photosynthesis was increasing the sugar content day by day as sunlight struck the leaves and the fruit. The leaves had pores on their undersides that "breathed"—opened and closed—in the presence of light. Not so the grapes, whose internal temperatures rose with the air temperature. Until veraison—now two weeks in the past—the sugars being delivered to the green berries within a water solution had taken the form of sucrose. Since then, and for reasons nobody fully understood, the sugars had been split into glucose and fructose, effectively doubling the sugar content in the fruit. Grapes have a higher sugar concentration than any other fruit—up to 50 percent in some varieties. This desirable sweetness was the evolutionary way the plants had devised of encouraging animals—and especially humans—to distribute their seeds.

Steve had to get going. Don was due into Santa Rosa Airport. Steve was going to meet the plane and drive Don straight up to Michalek, to the hillside. They had already killed more than fifty rattlesnakes up there this year, a lot more than last year. He knew Don would be interested in that.

BUMPKINS

RHONDA AND DON had returned from touring some of the great châteaux of Italy and the south of France in the fall of 1983 with an idea of what they wanted Villa Fiore to look like.

By then they were wholly committed to Ferrari-Carano. They had begun by making wine for themselves and for the Eldorado, calling themselves Ferrari Cellars. Then Don asked himself, why am I selling my grapes to these other guys when I can make my own wine and profit from it? And away he went. Rhonda started to think about the wine business as an alligator; it kept gobbling up parcels of land the way casinos accumulated slot machines. She thought she and Don had gone goofy, driving over the Donner Pass in the snow to take classes at U.C. Davis so they could become better farmers. But the truth was, she loved every minute of it.

Don had accomplished a father's dream by persuading all five of his children to join the family business. When Rhonda married their father, it took some time before Gregg, Glenn, Gary, Gene, and

Cindy accepted her, but because of her age she had become almost like one of them when acceptance came.

"Years ago," Don's son Gregg told me, "I was interested in joining Ferrari-Carano. But you know what? It's really a place for Don and Rhonda, Dad and Rhonda."

Gregg's sister Cindy made a similar observation. "Rhonda is so talented and has so much energy and is so full of life—to be able to create something for herself, with my dad, is important. So she can call it her own. Here she has to share it."

When Rhonda began to plan Villa Fiore, there was never any doubt about who was in charge. She had an architect, Mitchell Cohan, and an adviser, the Pasadena Rose Parade's Raul Rodriguez, who had done the exterior of the Flamingo Hotel in Las Vegas. But they took direction from her, not the other way around. Cohan's first rendering was of a mission-style building, and Rhonda knew that wasn't what she wanted. Of the places they had visited in Europe, the one that inspired Rhonda most was Michel Guérard's Les Prés d'Eugénie, a resort in the Aquitaine region in the south of France.

"ORIGINALLY, IT was built for one of Napoleon's wives," Rhonda said.

"Or girlfriends," Don interjected.

We were admiring Villa Fiore, with its grand fountain and circular driveway between it and us. John King, the *San Francisco Chronicle*'s architecture critic, was there, too.

"I always laugh when I hear people say it's Tuscan," Rhonda said, ignoring Don's joke. "If anything, it's more Veneto style. But we knew it was going to have to be in California, too."

Rhonda's own style is what it is. She was eyeballing her creation through rimless glasses shaped like cat's eyes; she wore a tooled belt with a heavy silver buckle on her short white linen skirt. There were auburn highlights in her dark hair. She was delighted and intensely serious—King was one of California's most distinguished architecture critics, and he had come specifically to see the Villa.

"I'm an artist, too," she said. "I worked with Raul. Don was always saying, 'Rhonda—budget, budget, budget.'" She laughed happily at how silly her husband had been. Budget! "Raul did a sketch of an Airstream trailer and gave it to Don. It said, 'Don's Villa Within Budget.'"

Don smiled and nodded. You could see how proud he was of her.

"It's grand," said King. "But it's stripped-down grand. Why aren't there nymphs running up the side of the building?"

"That'd be a little too much," she said earnestly. "A little too Las Vegas. I think it's very stately."

What King was thinking, and what he later wrote in a note he sent to me, was that, "Villa Fiore has a lot more to do with theatricality than authenticity. More to do with branding than bedding down." Indeed, the Villa *is* the brand.

"The whole idea is to convey an image of opulence from the dramatic exterior to the limestone detailing to the rooms that don't really match the exterior except in terms of Robin Leachian splendour," King wrote. "What struck me was the way that this loops back toward the casino world—the aura of semi-upscale tourism isn't so far apart from Vegas. Both pick and choose their moods and ambiance, both aim to pull you in with the promise of easy access to the good life, and both are cobbled together by dreamers. It's culture by collage, meant to suggest another time: which we can make fun of, but at the same time, is that any different from Mondavi's fake Spanish mission?"

"So how much did this budget-buster cost you?" I asked Don.

Don laughed, a there-you-go-again laugh. "We haven't disclosed that," he said, chuckling. Another secret.

The facade was done with Roman tile slates, limestone columns, and a stucco finish. In each of three arches at the entrance hung a custom-made chandelier. Flanking the wide, shallow staircase were twin statues—"Summer" and "Harvest"—that Rhonda had found in an English garden statuary catalogue.

"How it was going to fit in with the surrounding landscape was our biggest concern," Rhonda said. The Villa seemed comfortable where it was, but dwarfed anything else in the Dry Creek Valley, except for the dam at Lake Sonoma. Nearby, three Mexican gardeners silently tended a hedge and a bed of red salvia. Rhonda had more than two thousand plants and trees on the grounds, and visitors were encouraged to wander the gardens while visiting the tasting room at the Villa's east side. But a heavy metal gate prohibited the casual tourist from approaching the front entrance of the Villa. Rhonda had had enough of cattle calls in Reno, so she and Don decided that Villa Fiore would be for the trade alone.

You could almost hear Rhonda thinking about how John King might be reacting, and anticipating his criticism. "Yes, it is a grand villa," she said, leading us into the soaring entrance hall. "Yes, it's a little ostentatious on the exterior, but when you walked in I wanted it to be like a home, one of the grand estates you visit in Europe. Very comfortable."

Thirty feet above the jade-colored Chinese marble floor, within a dome, was a frieze of cherubs bearing bouquets as a vineyard goddess blessed them. But what caught my fancy was not the Bordeaux-like tapestry, the coat of arms, or the tiles that had been individually cut by an old German-Austrian. It was the soaring columns, too wide to encircle with your arms. I tapped one—the columns were hollow. They were cast in concrete in Reno, shipped here, then faux-finished in fourteen-karat gold leaf and bronze by three Australian brothers.

"We're big on faux," said Rhonda. "We went by the seat of our pants. I didn't have a plan. I'd sit down with every artisan and come up with a design and put it together. It took a little time. But I wanted every part to be meaningful to us."

You could spend pages cataloging the opulence. The Steinway baby grand; the deep pile carpeting with grape motif, picked up from the faux gold clusters on the columns; the ornate golden picture frames, more than many a museum has; the washroom suites; the table lamps made from antique chandelier glass, each representing a place the Caranos loved—Florence, New Orleans, China; the display cabinets exhibiting Rhonda's personal collections of porcelain and antique glasses and decanters. In the formal dining room a maid was polishing the gleaming, custom-made table that seated sixteen when Rhonda said something it would be easy to ridicule: "We never thought the winery was going to be as substantial as it was, to be honest with you. We were country bumpkins. Still are."

Which is why my favorite part of the Villa Fiore was an ordinary oil painting of a peasant girl on tiptoe drinking from a public fountain. Rhonda had acquired it through a friend from the estate of Dorothy Lamour, the actress who was a pinup favorite among GIs in World War II. It hung above the grand staircase that curved and swept up twenty-nine steps from the hall to the second floor, and as we passed it, Rhonda said she got it soon after she graduated, probably the first objet d'art she'd bought. She always liked Dorothy Lamour, Rhonda said. And that was all she said about the former Mary Slaton of New Orleans, the daughter of a divorced waitress, who turned a sarong into her trademark, and made $450,000 a film when she starred with Bob Hope and Bing Crosby in the road movies. Once you knew all that, you appreciated why the painting might be hanging in Villa Fiore. Little Rhonda Bevilacqua, a home ec major at University of Nevada, Reno, daughter of a furniture mover. She was, in a sense, the peasant girl in the painting—and Dorothy Lamour, too.

"It fits in perfect," she said.

Sweet-Talking

STEVE WAS PUSHING the men hard as August wound down. There were a million projects that needed to be completed—some of them huge, like the new reservoir up at Michalek—and with harvest bearing down on them, it was tense as hell.

Back in the winery, George had concerns of his own. The Sauvignon Blanc, normally the first variety to be picked, was behind in its ripening. So it looked like he'd be getting some Chardonnay into the crush pad first. He was meticulous in his planning because he had to be—he had neither enough men, nor machinery, to handle the cascade of grapes that needed to be crushed unless they arrived in predictable fashion. If the winery backed up, you could have delays in picking and miss an optimum moment in the vineyard. Once harvest was in motion, the winery and the vineyard were like two lungs needing to work in rhythm and balance; their lives depended on it.

George had seen every possible permutation often enough to have a good feel for what would work. He felt he had developed a calm over the years. The key was always to allow himself an escape route, so if the weather turned, he had a contingency plan. "That's why," he said to me, "I'm extremely . . . cautious. It's all about playing the odds. There's a tropical storm down in Cabo. There's weather coming in from Alaska. All the forecasters are saying it's an El Niño year, thinking we might run into early rains. The Sauvignon Blanc is extremely susceptible to rot—that's why Steve leaves a lot of room for air in there. And if we do run into early rains there's a huge benefit to having higher sugar in the bank."

Not only that, but rain absorption could dilute sugars, and mud could slow down the mechanical harvesters. He had asked Steve to harvest the grapes in some of the younger vineyards at twenty-four or twenty-five Brix. "You've always got to be expecting the worst," George said. It was his credo.

From Steve's perspective in the field, George's caution about letting sugars develop was another headache he could do without. Steve did not think it would show off his grapes to their best possible effect. There were times when George's excess of caution could be a royal pain. When George himself, in fact, could be a pain—or so it seemed to others, who observed them both closely.

The enologist Amy Kelsey, who worked side by side with George, believed that she had never met a more insecure person in her life than the winemaker.

"I think George is really threatened by Steve," she observed. "Steve has such a close relationship to Don—great rapport that George never had. And at any winery, there's always some antagonism between the people who grow the grapes, and the people who make the wine. Both sides feel they are the ones making the wine as good as it is. Also, there's this feeling from the vineyard people that the winemakers screw up their grapes, and the winemakers say they would have made a great wine if only the grapes had been better. With George and

Steve's personalities, it's magnified. They put on a good show but those two have a fairly antagonistic relationship. Steve was really frustrated because George was overmanipulating *his* grapes. He nurtured them, brought them to George—and then George screwed them up."

It was a situation tailor-made for Jeffrey Gould's ministration. A tall, rail-thin man with the body of a marathon runner, Jeffrey was by nature easygoing and agreeable. In his thirties, he had about him the air of the perpetual student, the man who at eighty would still be saying "wow" when he learned something new. Year-round his primary duty was research. But his job title was vineyard liaison. The way he saw that part of his job was that he *took* the winemaking into the vineyard—he went out there *to* Steve.

As harvest approached, it became his chief responsibility to bring the fruit in at the moment of optimum maturity. Steve and George talked directly to each other, but nowhere near as often as Jeffrey talked to both of them.

At this time of year, he said while standing in Keegan along with Steve on August 14, "I'm a little more of a liaison, not necessarily between two battling countries." Amy Kelsey had noticed how Jeffrey's personality would alter subtly, depending on whether he was dealing with the mistrustful George, or the outgoing Steve. He would adapt, becoming whoever he needed to be.

Jeffrey loped through the rows tasting fruit as he went, gathering grapes in a large, transparent Ziploc baggie.

"Look at him," Steve said fondly, "Jeffrey's a fuckin' raccoon."

Indeed, there was something utterly natural and unself-conscious about Jeffrey in the vineyard. His long, angular body was seemingly at one with his task, plucking grapes from a variety of different places on the vines to get a fair sampling, popping fruit into his mouth, spitting seeds. The clear juice ran between his fingers and made his hands glisten.

In the beginning, Steve had been wary of Jeffrey. He did not need a watchdog from the winery, and feared it was a blow against his autonomy, and perhaps the trust in which he was held. The relationship began at arm's length, cautious and respectful on Jeffrey's part, proud and defensive on Steve's. Gradually, Steve began to see that Jeffrey truly wanted to help the winery understand the viticulture better, and to bring the winemaking closer to him. If there was a decisive moment, it came when Jeffrey told Steve: "You know what? Your soul's in these vineyards." Steve didn't say anything, just gave Jeffrey a long look. Jeffrey thought that maybe Steve had never heard that said before, and perhaps he had never thought it in just those words, but he knew it. That was four years ago. Now you could see the *simpático* that existed between the two men.

Back at his truck, Jeffrey pulled out a refractometer, an instrument that was shaped like a large kazoo. After mashing a baggie full of grapes between his hands, he poured some juice into an opening with a hinged window in the wider end of the refractometer. He had been careful to gather grapes not only from different places in the vineyard and different parts of the vine, but from different positions on the clusters because the farther from the stem, the riper the grape. He held the refractometer toward the sun and pressed the narrower end to his eye, as if it was a telescope. Within the refractometer, light rays bent by the sugar content cast a shadow across a scale no harder to read than a thermometer. He got a reading of 17.2, which was behind last year on this date. Not surprising. Because the total heat accumulation, measured in degree-days, was also slightly behind 2001. But Jeffrey wasn't concerned. The weather was superb, warm days and nights cooled by coastal fog. The flavors were not yet consistent, but the fruit seemed happy.

———

HAPPIER THAN Steve, who was chafing against George's insistence on the highest possible sugars in the younger vineyards. Don visited Steve in Keegan late on the afternoon of August 29. That morning they had harvested their first grapes of 2002 before dawn, some Chardonnay off young vines around Don and Rhonda's house, and from one other vineyard. George had opened the winery at 5:30 a.m., and declared himself happy with the fruit.

Steve mentioned to Don that he noticed that flavors in the Sauvignon Blanc grapes were coming on at lower sugars than ever before, though why was a mystery.

"I think it's going to be an exceptional year if we can get the fruit off without any rain," Steve said.

"Could be a banner crop," Don agreed.

At the up-valley end of Keegan, the two men paused to taste some grapes.

"Nice Sauvignon Blanc fruit character," Steve said. "Sweet grapefruit. Apricots. Sometimes you can't get that. Still a ways to go, though. I get pineapple, too."

Don looked over his vineyard. There was a lazy feel to it as the sun hovered west of the apple orchard and the creek, casting its rich, buttery glow over the dark-green vines, with their abundance of soft, warm yellow-green clusters. The wispy fog creeping over the mountains from the Pacific would have been invisible if not for the way it filtered the sunlight, creating that hazy late afternoon light that was Northern California's glory in late summer. Keegan Ranch looked like perfection itself.

"It's amazing," Don said, "the way you can train your people to do this."

"It's because they've been with us so long," Steve said. "They do it over and over again." Steve took hold of a cane. "My ranch guy, he'll know this is a good one, save it for next year."

"What are the sugars?" Don asked.

"Twenty, twenty-one. We'll take it up."

"George wants it a little more," Don said casually. "I think George's thinking is more flavors with higher sugars."

The longer the grapes were on the vine, and the warmer the weather, the more sugar would accumulate. Eventually, in the barrel, yeast fermentation would transform the sugar from the grapes into alcohol and carbon dioxide. So the higher the Brix, the greater the amount of alcohol in the finished wine. But if the Brix got too high they might have to de-alcoholize it after fermentation—a process that was a dirty little secret shared by many California wineries, especially the larger ones. But what George had in mind was a second effect of higher sugars—intense fruit characteristics. And, in addition, more sugar meant less acid—pH increased as Brix increased—and thus made for a softer wine.

Steve said, "I think our Fumé Blanc is improved taking it to a little lower sugar. It has a better mouth feel." But he knew he couldn't win an argument with George about mouth feel—viscosity. That had been the subject of George's thesis at U.C. Davis, and his professor had been the one who proved that every wine had an optimal alcohol level for maximum body, and that beyond that, alcohol acted as a solvent and decreased viscosity. Anyway, it was George's call when to pick, not Steve's, though obviously his opinion mattered.

Don didn't say anything, and the subject was dropped. But it was clear that Jeffrey's attempt to persuade Steve of the rightness of George's desire for the highest possible sugars had not done the trick. Don himself needed to step in. The gentle, praise-coated way he conveyed the unwelcome message was masterful. Talk about sweet-talking.

DON LIKED to sit and talk at the conference table in his spacious of-fice, overlooking the pool with its faux ruins, and a corner of the Es-tate Vineyard. The table had a special significance for him. Rhonda had wanted Don to have a desk that was unique. A cabinetmaker at the Eldorado Hotel named Giovanni Collichioni was going to visit his family in Rome, and she had asked him to look around. Giovanni vis-ited his old master, ninety-two years old, and saw a dilapidated desk high up in a remote corner. It turned out to once have belonged to a general in the Croatian wars. Giovanni refinished it, stretched new leather onto the desktop, and commissioned his master to make a matching trestle for his glass-top conference table.

I wanted to know how Don inspired the loyalty and devotion he clearly commanded among his staff and workers. His answer was a portrait of some of the qualities that have made him successful: his modesty, his genuine interest in and appreciation of people and what they know, and his willingness when it was necessary to be forceful. Don could be tough, but never hard.

"I guess a lot of people like to call the shots themselves," he said, and laughed self-consciously. "I've never been so secure in my own abilities to call the shots myself. Two minds are better than one—it's a lot more fun that way, too. I have people working in Reno more knowledgeable in gaming or food than I will ever be.

"I think people grow if it's their area of expertise and they're re-sponsible for the final product. I try to include people who really have ideas and can make them work. If they're not part of the idea, the implementation's not going to be as successful. It's always my philos-ophy not to micromanage. If I have a manager who can't handle a de-partment, who I can't rely on, I better find another manager."

His thoughts turned to Steve Domenichelli. Gary Carano, the old-est of Don's children and the one his siblings regard as their leader, told me that, "Dad's proud of Steve like he's proud of a son."

"When Steve took over the vineyards, under Barney Fernandez," Don said, "he had guys throughout the vineyards he wanted to give responsibility, and Barney was reluctant to move on it. Steve brought that to me and I totally concurred. Now Steve has them in charge of specific vineyards—a lot of personal responsibility and satisfaction because each of them can look at *their* product.

"When Steve came in charge," Don continued, "George felt our reds had a vegetative character as opposed to fruit flavor." A sufficient problem for Ferrari-Carano to cease producing a Cabernet entirely for years. "So Steve—he grew up in this business—he found that the soils were depleted, needed soil amendments, on [a vineyard called] Anderson, especially. And he did that; that was significant. As well as the different trellis systems. Before he put in the two-wire system, everything was bunched—the inner grapes were not getting the sun. So he developed that open U, getting sun. And down in Jimtown there was too much exposure and the fruit was burning. So he trained it up and gave it some cover.

"What you find with Steve is he's very meticulous, very thorough. I don't know how many miles a day he travels. He wants to taste the wines before they're blended, see if what he's doing in the fields has an effect on the wines. He's got a very good relationship with George," Don said.

"I don't want to take anything away from Barney," Don continued. "Barney wanted to do more in governmental affairs; he likes to go to meetings. I said to him, 'Maybe this is the time to do it. Because I want to implement this other organization.' Maybe it was just a younger generation."

There was more to the story than that. A few weeks earlier, Steve had poured out his heart about the conflicts that had existed, and I had gone to Don to ask what his point of view had been. Soon afterward, Don had faxed me a letter, asking me to hold off on scheduling other interviews until we had a chance to discuss his concern about "the personal aspect the interviewing process is taking." When I called him, Don had said he was thinking about backing out altogether from giving me access to finish the project. But he soon got over that, and the conversation we were having at Giovanni's table was the upshot of that short-lived drama. Don's foremost concern, as it turned out, was that Barney's feelings would be hurt.

Throughout the organization, how exactly Steve came to replace Barney Fernandez was a sensitive subject. It was the only change among top management in the history of the winery. The three other princes of the realm—George; the director of sales and marketing, Steve Meisner; and the controller, Dave James—had all been in their jobs since the beginning.

Steve and George were unstinting in their praise for each other, but there was a fulsome quality to their talk about their relationship, and how they had overcome the traditional antagonism between the vineyard and the winery. Back in March, Steve had told me he had instituted weekly conversations with George. "Barney didn't want anybody from the winery on a ranch without twenty-four hours' notice," Steve said. "I had nothing to hide—the more eyes the better. When I was a kid, farmers always hated winemakers. If you want to make a world-class wine, you can't do that. George and I have to be joined at the hip."

But not necessarily at the heart. "George acknowledges," Steve finally told me, "he is not a trusting or a friendly guy. I've tried to be his friend. But George is just a loner."

Don had come up with a way of easing the tension surrounding that most crucial of relationships to the success of Ferrari-Carano—by having Jeffrey Gould as the vineyard liaison. Initially, George had hired Jeffrey to do grape sampling. Jeffrey had quickly won George's trust, and assumed expanded responsibilities in vineyard research. But it was obvious that though his mind was in the lab, his heart was in the vineyard. Don also sensed the bond that was growing between Steve and Jeffrey, who displayed some of the same frenetic enthusiasm. So in 1998, Jeffrey was given his new title. As Keegan produced its first crop, he became the grease between the big wheels, George and Steve.

Seeing the best way to get the most out of his people is classic Don Carano. And Don has the rare and valuable ability to make people feel appreciated, even loved.

It was nearly time for lunch. Don was in good shape for a man of his age, reasonably trim, but by no means a fitness freak. He was under orders to watch his carbohydrate intake. Such strictures should not befall an Italian with appetites. "I have rigatoni once a week," he said. Then he laughed at his little lie. "Maybe twice."

A few times he has had dizzy spells, and his doctor was unsure what caused them. He has insomnia, and takes Ambien.

Once I was standing with a few of the vineyard hands, shooting the breeze and drinking a beer, and they began to joke about how Don is up deep into the night. Somebody said that Don always seemed to begin a conversation with the words *I've been thinking,* followed by a question. That got a knowing laugh.

"I get Oakland Raider and cave questions from him," one man said.

Their tone was affectionate for the peculiarities of a well-liked boss.

"You see his light on at one a.m., two a.m.," another man said. "He's up all night. Reading and on the phone. Storing up questions to ask."

Proudest Moment

ALL ACROSS NAPA and Sonoma counties this August, as always when harvest was approaching, dirt-poor Mexicans—many of them illegal entrants fleeing a land where farmworkers had no work—were decamped anywhere the legions of tourists could not spy them, and therefore the local cops would not roust them. In cars, under bridges, deep in the undergrowth off secondary roads, and in Napa County at two crowded farmworker centers with 120 beds paid for by growers. The county had even erected some circular tents called yurts for workers to live in.

"I'm watching these poor people like serfs, so humble, so hard-working," says Lauren Coodley, who teaches history at Napa Valley College. "And these castles, these people living like lords and kings. And it just struck me, this is feudalism." The notion that there might be a feudal microeconomy nestled within the global economy of twenty-first-century California was as enchanting as it was disturbing. It offered a picture of history as being as layered as the alluvial flood plain beneath Keegan Ranch.

In all, according to research by the Pew Hispanic Center, there were 2.5 million farmworkers in the United States, about half of whom had entered illegally, largely from Mexico. Stories abounded of growers and contractors who took advantage of their laborers' fear of the law by not paying them. In Northern California the U.S. Immigration and Naturalization Service did not seem inclined to bust up the cozy arrangement that allowed growers to produce some of the world's best wines on the cheap. "Very seldom does Immigration come to this area," says Aurelio Hurtado, a program manager for the California Human Development Corporation. "I haven't seen it for years and years. They are inclined to look the other way. It's just politics," says the old United Farm Workers organizer. "Cesar used to say, 'If we had a miracle we'd be able to pull every worker out of the field for a week—the whole Mondavi empire would go down the drain.' I'm not advocating for that because that would be hardship for the worker, too."

In late August, the UFW had begun a 165-mile march to the state capital in Sacramento, retracing the route from Delano Cesar Chavez had followed in 1966 when he first drew national attention to the farmworkers' struggle. The decades-long battle between growers and *campesinos* showed little sign of abating. A few hundred people were approaching Thornton, about twenty-five miles south of their destination at the state capital, accompanied by support vans and police on a two-lane road that ran between vast, industrial-sized grape fields, when I arrived on a Thursday. It was sunny but breezy. I parked in Thornton and walked back toward the marchers, and heard them chanting and singing before I saw them. Then, above a hedgerow, I saw their flags—black Aztec eagles against red fields—flapping in the breeze.

I fell in beside Arturo Rodriguez, the union president, who explained that this was called The March for the Governor's Signature, specifically on Senate Bill 1736. The bill would force growers whose workers had elected union representation to reach agreement in a reasonable amount of time, or else be subject to binding arbitration. It was Rodriguez's contention that growers practiced delaying tactics. For instance, Dolores Huerta, the seventy-two-year-old cofounder of the UFW, who was also marching, told me she had been at the negotiating table with Gallo of Sonoma for six years, and it was seven years before a contract was signed. Huerta was a tiny woman, who spoke softly but firmly. In September 1988, at an anti–George H. W. Bush rally, she had been beaten with clubs by San Francisco cops—suffering two broken ribs and a ruptured spine. So she was tough and could not be deterred. She had an aura that made me think of Jimmy Carter after he was out of office—an airy soulfulness.

The bill had been sitting unsigned on Governor Gray Davis' desk for weeks, and Rodriguez said he was hearing that Davis—a Democrat whose unpopularity was usually attributed to his ceaseless fundraising—was planning to veto it, but that its sponsor, State Senate President John Burton, of San Francisco, a liberal, was working behind the scenes to salvage a compromise. "We're extremely hopeful," Rodriguez said. "The governor's going to see the tremendous support we have with the people of California and his heart's going to be touched."

"And what makes you think he has a heart?" I asked Rodriguez.

"Let's put it this way," Rodriguez said, laughing. "It's my faith in humanity."

Governor Davis had received one hundred and fifty thousand dollars in campaign contributions from winegrowers in just the few weeks since the bill had passed. "I have no idea why they would do that," Rodriguez said. "Other than the fact that for some reason they don't want to see the farmworkers have a better quality of life."

He had statistics at the ready: "Seventy-five percent [of field workers] make ten thousand dollars or less [annually]. Only nine percent have health insurance. Overwhelmingly, they are the poorest of the poor."

When they reached Thornton, the marchers rested and ate lunch on a school lawn; many needed to be treated for blisters, aches and pains, and heat exhaustion.

The next day Senator Burton would say: "To see seventy-year-old *campesinos* marching one hundred miles to get a Democratic governor to sign a labor bill is not the proudest moment in my life." Two weeks later, agreement was reached on a weaker bill that the governor did sign, requiring mediation—not binding arbitration—when contract talks were stalled.

IN THE picturesque hamlet of Graton, in the Russian River Valley, I talked with Ignacio, who did not want me to know his last name. He had come to the Golden State at great risk. Ignacio was twenty-eight years old and living in a makeshift tent—a blue tarp lashed between some boughs in dense undergrowth near an overpass just outside of town. Other encampments were haphazardly scattered throughout the tall, dense weeds. Perhaps twenty men with stories not unlike Igancio's were hidden here, out of view but with the tacit permission of local authorities. Starting at 5:30 a.m., the men would shape up on Graton's block-long main street, and growers who needed cheap, casual labor, and did not care whether the men they hired were in this country legally or not, drove by and selected the workers they wanted.

Ignacio and a friend had arrived from Oaxaca about a month earlier, each of them borrowing thirteen hundred dollars to pay a coyote. Ignacio had left behind his wife and four children, seeking to make some money, but he had yet to earn what the coyote had charged. He was paid eight dollars an hour on the days when he was lucky enough to be hired. So far, he said, everybody had paid cash, and nobody had cheated him. He had saved five hundred dollars, spending money only for food. Sometimes he ate in the town's only Mexican restaurant because he had no stove or refrigerator.

People from his village who preceded him had told him how beautiful the living was in the United States, but so far all he knew was this place, with his laundry hung on a line, and a portable toilet some kindly person had left nearby. Ignacio bathed in a thick brown puddle of a creek, the water dense as oil. In order to wash, he strained the water through a towel into a bucket.

He missed his wife and kids something awful, Ignacio said, and was living in fear of the police and his economic circumstances. He wanted to hear his wife's voice but there was no telephone in their village, Mano de Señor, Hand of the Lord. He had to fight the impulse to get up and walk away, go home. The loneliness was always there, threatening to overwhelm him, but he needed the money so badly. He hoped some day to find work for a *padrón* who would treat him right.

THE MEN who worked at Ferrari-Carano may have worked for an owner who was adamantly opposed to unionization, but Don Carano also considered it a point of pride, as well as good business, to take care of his people. All the Ferrari-Carano workers were in the United States legally, Steve Domenichelli told me. I visited one of the Ferrari-Carano help-houses, as they called them, one afternoon soon after the men returned from a day in the vineyards. It was a simple bunkhouse, with the men sleeping two and three to a room. The lodgings were basic, but clean, decent, and free. A radio was playing mariachi music, and a lot of the guys were in the communal kitchen, making sandwiches or cooking. On the stove jalapeños, tomatoes, and dried peppers were boiling, and somebody was frying a rib-eye steak. I had never seen so much Mazola corn oil in my life. The men had planted their own kitchen garden with tomatoes, beans, peppers, corn, and the cactus they called *nopales*. If they had the water and conditions to grow all this in El Charco, they wouldn't be here.

Some men were drinking beer—no Coronanitas in the United States, that would have to await their return home in the winter—and others soft drinks. No wine. Twenty men lived here; there were sixty-two, all told, in company housing. This particular help-house was near Jimtown, on a ranch called Carinalli, after the man who sold it to Don.

Young Jaime Ruiz was here, sporting a clean gray bandanna around his neck. He could hardly wait to tell me: On June 4 he had passed his citizenship exam. It was, he said, a proud moment. The size of his smile confirmed that. Now he believed that Milagros and their first child, due to be born any day, could join him in as little as six months.

Pull the Trigger

IT WAS STILL dark at three thirty in the morning on Tuesday, September 10, and the crew had already been harvesting grapes off the Estate Vineyard, behind Don and Rhonda's home in Geyserville, for two hours. The men were hungry, so Steve set up a portable grill and he and another man were making what they called Mexican hamburgers—plenty of chiles and ketchup—when everybody was surprised to see the *padrón*. Don couldn't sleep, so he'd come out with his hair sticking up, his face bleary, and a question on his mind.

"What are you doing?" he asked Steve, gesturing at the burgers Steve was flattening in his hands as he knelt over the Sputnik grill. "You can't be doing that." Don was paying Steve something like a couple of hundred grand a year to be making hamburgers? But the men had to eat. So Don got himself presentable, then drove to Healdsburg and bought doughnuts for them. On the way, he used his car phone to leave a message for Joey Costanzo, his chef, to cook breakfast for the crew and truck it out to the vineyards until the end of harvest. You could say it was fifteen years overdue, but that would be churlish.

I had been expecting that they would decide to harvest Keegan overnight, on Wednesday, September 11. I drove up early on the tenth in anticipation and walked onto Keegan Ranch by myself. The temperature was at seventy degrees and rising, and the sun had been up for about three hours. In the Dry Creek Valley the sound of distant machinery mixed with the nearby hum and buzz of insects, and the indistinct staccato of a walkie-talkie somewhere nearby but hidden from view by the dense green canopy. Engorged with sweetness, the clusters of golden grapes hung plump and heavy from the vines. Keegan Ranch was a pregnant woman nearing her due date, I thought. Steve Domenichelli's anthropomorphizing was catching.

Jeffrey Gould arrived at 11:20 in shorts, a wine-colored T-shirt, a sweat-stained baseball cap pulled low over his long, narrow face, and a pair of beat-up old hiking boots. "I'm hoping this pair of shoes is going to make it," he said, walking back to me. "If I can get three more weeks out of them."

His wife, Karen, had left for San Diego a few days ago with their girls, a trip she took to her family home every year at this time. She was a harvest widow.

"It's such a special time," Jeffrey said, and loped into Block 7A, the farthest from the creek of the three planted in Sauvignon Blanc.

He was here to make the preliminary call about the harvest; the final decision would rest with George. Jeffrey had a baggie in hand, a refractometer in his pocket, and, as he went up and down the rows, he talked for my benefit, a kind of stream of consciousness.

"It's been interesting this year. This is maybe my sixth time in here. Taking about eighteen berries or so. Beautifully, mindlessly random. A little bit off the front, these are maybe off the top, it's automatic right now. As long as we're looking at ripe flavors and the pH is about three point four or three point five, we're okay. I'll take some of these grapes back to the lab and test there. It's just, this year we have moderate Brix, and low pH, and I haven't figured out yet why it is. I think we built such strong canopies early in the season, and canopies are fine, but maybe because of the canopies it's taking a little bit longer to build flavors.

"Earlier when my crew was coming through here, they were getting a little bit higher sugars than I was getting. What they were missing was the fruit higher up in the canopy, not getting sunlight, that's still really sour. I'm tasting a lot of citric acid, like mangoes. Grapefruit. I want to push it a little more tropical." The back of his long neck was burnt a deep reddish brown.

"See these clusters right here?" he said, coming to a halt. "They're starting to have lost their roundness, getting square. Starting to dehydrate." If you waited long enough, water would no longer be delivered to the fruit, and they would dry up and become raisins. Already the ground was grayish, and as dry as an octogenarian's scalp.

"So," Jeffrey said, "what percent are dehydrating? What percent are a little sour? What percent are really sweet? Trying to balance all that, but we're getting really close.

"The seeds, we're starting to get some mature seeds." He crushed a grape. "Look, deep brown, and if you bit into them they're crunchy. Haven't completely lignified," he said, referring to the same chemical process by which the vines had gone from green to their current gnarled, woody appearance. Jeffrey squinted at the blue, cloudless sky. The temperature was about eighty degrees. "This is ideal ripening weather. Tomorrow's supposed to be a cooling trend. I'm looking at the canopy also, starting to get a lot of yellow. Another indication the vines are really, strongly in the reproductive cycle—want to get that fruit off."

So this was it, then?

Jeffrey shook his head no. "I want to push it a little bit more tropical. I'm not real excited to move on this block. Next time hopefully I won't find *any* of those neutral flavors. Because I haven't found anything that's so sweet it's cloying."

Jeffrey hurried back to his truck and poured some juice from Block 8 into his refractometer. "Huh," he said, surprised. "I wouldn't have thought it but this is at twenty-three point five, too." Just like Block 7, which traditionally ripened first. "This is a block that's really going to have to get riper sugar-wise to show some flavors."

So, I said, disappointed, it's not ready?

"Got to keep that patience," Jeffrey said, perhaps recalling the mistakes he had made his first year in Keegan when he pulled the trigger too fast, "and wait for good things to come."

His cell phone rang. "Hey, Hoss," he said. "I'm at Keegan Ranch. Okay. Okay. Okay. I'll give Steve a call."

He turned to me. "The winery is maxed, we're shutting down." Then Jeffrey wandered away and punched up Steve. Steve was out in a vineyard driving his men to get in crop, while back at the winery a full crew was hurrying to get already-harvested grapes crushed and on their way to becoming wine. But when Hoss Milone, who as the cellar master for George Bursick oversaw the delivery and crushing of the grapes, needed to tell Steve enough for today, he called Jeffrey. It was a time of year—with high stakes and frayed nerves—when tempers flared, and Jeffrey kept George and Steve separated at the ends of his long, thin, sinewy arms. Nobody screamed at Jeffrey, and if they did, it was all right with him.

He must have seen my disappointment at the delay because he said: "Just gotta be, *gotta* be patient."

I GOT to the Smoke House in Geyserville before Steve arrived, and had a chance to catch up with the newspaper. There was the kind of scary story that brought the world crashing back into the vineyard:

> One of Napa Valley's oldest and most prominent family-owned wineries has been sold to the world's biggest wine producer. E&J Gallo bought the Louis M. Martini Winery in St. Helena in a deal made final yesterday. . . . The sale was a result of market pressures that squeezed the Martinis' ability to distribute their wine. . . . "You have to either be really small or really big," said Carolyn Martini, a granddaughter of founder Louis M. Martini. "We were somewhere in between." The winery produces 80,000 cases, while Gallo produces 55 million, primarily from its operations in the Central Valley. . . . The purchase is Gallo's first big move into Napa Valley. They have been producing wine in Sonoma County since the early '90s.

The purchase was a chilling reminder of the changes that were occurring in the industry, changes anticipated by Don and Rhonda when they had drawn up their business plan years earlier. An old-fashioned winery with out-of-date ideas, Louis Martini had relied more on its long history and reputation than on advertising, public relations, and aggressive sales techniques.

Gallo was moving into what had been Mondavi territory.

"Mondavi's not going to be too thrilled," said Steve, after he'd arrived and we both had a glass of wine in front of us. He had cleaned up after a long day in the vineyards, and was glowing with vigor and good health. "I talked my daughter to sleep last night," he told me. "Just kept talking to her until she nodded off.

"I wanted to make a legacy with my family but it didn't work out that way," he said, because he and his father could not work together.

"My mom's really sick, she's got an autoimmune disorder. She was raised in a cotton-picking family, hard-core. I wrote a story about her in ninth grade. They told me to write about a saint. She takes care of my dad, she does everything for him and she's sick and he's healthy. It's crazy. She's incredible.

"I really looked up to him so much. We'd hunt together, fish together. I still look up to him to this day. I've called him three times in the last two weeks and he hasn't returned my calls. He's busy? I'm busy, too. I miss him. I just miss him."

THE NEXT morning the sun had just appeared above the ridge east of Storey Road Ranch—a one-hundred-acre vineyard whose steep, narrow hillside rows beside the Russian River had to be harvested the old-fashioned way, by hand—when Steve showed up, talking on his cell phone.

"He's not going to shoot anybody," he barked into his phone, a cup of steaming coffee in his other hand. "If he threatens again, call the sheriff. That's all we need, somebody to get shot on September eleventh."

The man with the gun was a neighbor of the Estate Vineyard, an old biker who objected to having his sleep disturbed by the noise of the mechanical harvester. With the harvester, they picked before dawn, when the grapes were cool and firm. Gunplay was no stranger here at Ferrari-Carano. One Christmas, Steve was trimming his tree when an El Charco man shot another in a card game at a help-house, then knocked on Steve's door, gun in hand, to confess.

Now Steve slapped his phone shut, squinted at the hazy, molten light above the ridge, and exclaimed: "Morning light! Isn't the sun beautiful!" Without a pause, he hopped aboard a forty-ton lug being hauled by a tractor that was filling up with purple Merlot grapes—*las huvas*. He reached in to help the two men who were already busily clearing vines and twigs by hand. Then he leapt to the ground, hugged an elderly worker with gray stubble and a straw hat, shouted at another man, and whipped out his cell again, hurrying out of range of the clamor to have a shouted conversation.

The Mexican hands were doing the harvesting, working their way gradually up the hillside. Squat, grab, cut, drop, move on; squat, grab, cut, drop, move on. It was relentless, thigh-aching work. The clusters were dropped into a rectangular plastic basket called a *bandeja*. A full *bandeja* held about thirty pounds, and a fast worker could fill six in thirty minutes, earning $1.30 per load. If you took it easy you could make $50 a day during harvest, and if you worked hard about $150. The record was $250. When a *bandeja* was full, you ran toward the lug being pulled up the next row at about two miles per hour; you hoisted your load over the top of the vines to another man whose job was to dump the grapes into the lug, then rush the empty *bandeja* back to you. A young man in a 100% Technology sweatshirt— a boy, really—was waiting impatiently to be noticed, his thirty pounds hoisted aloft.

"Dude!" he shouted.

"Aquí, chico, aquí," came the answer.

His *bandeja* emptied, the youngster rushed to the vines farther up the hillside row, leapfrogging his *compadres,* whipped out his *cuchillo,* and resumed: squat, grab, cut, drop, move on. It was 7:05 in the morning and already the kid was pouring sweat. This would go on for another eight, nine, ten hours. The pace would increase as the chill burned off and as the sun, turning the hillside earth a rich golden brown, warmed a man's bones.

As the men reached the crest, the river came into view, reflecting the dawning light. In the valley were as yet unharvested rows of Sauvignon Blanc, although twenty acres afflicted with phylloxera had been pulled and discarded. A crew from another winery was working in the next vineyard over. It seemed the whole valley was in a focused frenzy to bring in the 2002 crop. Every few minutes, a truck rolled by hauling two full gondolas toward a winery, or empty gondolas being rushed toward a vineyard. An orange school bus navigated the curving road.

Jaime Ruiz had been made a subforeman for the harvest, so he was not picking, but following along, keeping a watchful eye out, looking as serious as his added responsibility required. He had the ultimate symbol of working authority slung on his hip—a walkie-talkie.

So did Boa, who was looking entirely relaxed, this being old hat to him. "I came from Mexico twenty days ago," Boa told me. "I drove my truck for my new daughter. She is named Lacy." So a daughter, and not a son. I offered congratulations.

"En el agosto primero," he said. He'd spent twenty days in El Charco, but wouldn't return again until the beginning of December. "I want to make a party for my little girl. A compadre will be her godfather."

Boa hailed Jaime. "He has a daughter, too," he said, displaying a lot of gold with his contagious, good-spirited smile. For a moment Jaime dropped his subforeman's face, and showed his delight.

Karen Michelle was born August 20, he told me. She and Milagros were well.

It had been a good year, I said, what with becoming a citizen, being promoted, and the birth of his first child.

"Yes," he said in English, another milestone. "A very good year."

AT TEN o'clock George Bursick drove the eight miles southeast along Dry Creek Road from the winery to Keegan Ranch. Once there, he wasted no time, heading quickly along the rows of Block 7. He was wearing khaki shorts, a cranberry T-shirt, and ankle-high white socks. His pale skin had seen some sun, but not much. George was difficult to describe. He was of average height and middling build—thick rather than thin, soft rather than hard—neither handsome nor homely. What struck you most were his eyes, those nervous eyes.

Here and there in Block 7, George grabbed a few grapes in his right hand, shook and squeezed them like a gambler would dice, and poured the juice directly into his refractometer, a five-hundred-dollar Leica that he kept under lock and key. A wine man's refractometer is like a major leaguer's glove—broken in, comfortable, reliable.

"Twenty-five and a half," he said, peering. Right on target. "This time of year there shouldn't be any surprises." He tasted a grape, then spat most of it out. "I'll spit out maybe ten pounds—that stuff goes right through you. The flavors here are nice, light, grassy, herbal."

The grapes were soft—the cell walls had broken down, converting large molecules to small, and making the juice more viscous.

"I'm motivated to have these guys pick the whole thing in one pass," George said, although Keegan was usually picked over two, even three, days because the blocks ripened at different rates. "The real driving force is flavor. A lotta people watch pH and acidity. But I don't put a lot of emphasis on it because I know those can be easily tweaked. You can add acidity, it's legal. What's really the tough one is sugar, because you want flavor but you don't want eighteen percent alcohol wines, either. That's a real balancing act.

"You're just trying to achieve a goal, dealing with all these moving targets, and all these variables. This block"—we were in Block 8 now—"doesn't have as much flavor as those guys there. I'll be honest; sometimes you've got to sacrifice one for the other. It's more if you can be efficient *and* get flavors." Times had changed, and no self-respecting winemaker would now say that he harvests based on numbers alone— or on sugar content exclusively. George also had logistics to consider— especially concerning the mechanical harvesters—questions of where the equipment was, and how quickly it could be moved. "I've got this tidal wave of reds ready to come crashing down, and if I don't get the Sauvignon Blancs crushed, settled, and fermented in barrels, through that pipeline . . ." The thought remained incomplete but clear—disaster.

"I could gamble and wait for a little bit more in the flavors, and the fruit could be a tiny bit overripe and then the fruit's blown out," George said. A year of farming, of constant monitoring, disking, thinning, spraying, dropping crop, and now the moment of decision was at hand.

"A big moment," I said.

As always, George deflected credit. "Every moment's big," he said. "You've got to live by your decisions. It looks good, it's uniform. Steve's such a clean farmer. I'm spoiled."

The winemaker put his refractometer in his pocket. "Ready to go," he said. "I've made my decision right here." He took out his cell phone and called Jeffrey.

HARVEST

FRIDAY THE THIRTEENTH. Talk about bad omens.

The fog off the Pacific lay heavy over Keegan as the first men rolled up at 12:45 a.m., their headlights stabbing the night. They left their cars and trucks near the shed and shop, and stood in knots, talking quietly among themselves. Three mechanical harvesters were being fired up, their motors muttering loudly. They machine harvested at night, in the dark, when the grapes were cool and firm and didn't cling as tightly to the stems as they did in higher temperatures; that way there was less need to rev up the rpms, and risk tearing up vines and machines alike. They had told me to expect something like a battle scene when they hit the vineyard—fast, furious, and confused—as they and their machines struggled to bend time and nature to their wills.

The clock had run out on the growing season. The answers to all the year's questions were about to be picked clean. Had they succeeded in reining in the vegetative characteristics that could threaten the market share of their Fumé Blanc? Had they been patient enough? Had they, on the other hand, in their patience, allowed the more melonlike flavors on the Estate end of the vineyard to develop one day too long? Had they caught the moment of perfect balance between sugars and flavors?

The plan this morning was to take about 106 tons of fruit out of Blocks 7 and 8, then speed away to Storey Ranch, giving Block 9—with its thick, soil-nourished canopy—another day to develop flavors. They expected they would get seven tons an acre off Block 7, and seven and a half tons off Block 8. Right here, right now was the biggest piece of what was going to become the Ferrari-Carano 2002 Fumé Blanc, the third-best-selling Sauvignon Blanc in American restaurants, a huge bite of their reputation and their future.

The bulky harvester machines muttered and rumbled and waited, along with the gathering men. Just across the bridgeway, the taut clusters of midnight grapes, nature's perfect packages of sweetness and flavor, the fruit of drunken love and elusive glory, waited for their purpose to be fulfilled.

"Almost ready, Frank?" asked Dave Bacci, the vineyard manager, of Frank Machado, a mechanic who went everywhere the finicky but efficient harvesters went. "We want to get going at one o'clock. So . . ." said Bacci.

Frank, who was a Portuguese from Bodega Bay, nodded. Right now he had his head inside one of his machines, just listening: He knew exactly how they were supposed to sound. He could hear a problem before anybody else would notice it. The harvester produced a deeper, steadier roar than the throaty grumble of the John Deere tractor that would haul the two-ton gondolas. The harvester's cab was perched high above the front of the machine, open to the night. In the absence of sun, there was no need for the awning. It had a metal mesh floor that allowed the operator to look down into the works. Operating this buster was one of the easiest and most lucrative jobs. Not surprisingly, the man in the cab, Ruben Ruiz Lopez, was the brother-in-law of the paymaster, René Ruiz.

Bacci turned to Frank. "I think we're missing Tony," he said. Tony was another driver.

"Okay," Frank said. "Put Peanut on the tractor. Peanut knows how to drive tractor."

Dave went off to find the man they called Peanut, as another guy came up. "I fucked up my back last night, Frank," he said, his inflection rising, as if he were asking a question.

"You're hurting?"

"Yeah, real bad."

"Hang around," Frank said. "We'll talk." He turned to me. "First thing in the morning you get the usual problems," he said. "But once it gets going, it's a sight to see."

The operators kept the motors idling. Many wineries refused to use mechanical harvesters because early on they had a reputation for damaging vines. Don had become interested in them when he read they were becoming more efficient. George had been skeptical, and so had Steve. The harvesters seemed like a foreign presence in the vineyard, in violation of tradition, inimical to the romance of wine. But expensive as they were—each one cost $126,000—if they could do the job, they would save Don a small fortune. It took five men about eight hours to pick ten tons of grapes. To harvest the one hundred tons or so of Sauvignon Blanc this morning by hand would have required ninety men if they wanted to be done before sunup. The arithmetic was simple: It cost Don $120 a ton to harvest by hand, and $30 a ton by machine. Ferrari-Carano expected to harvest about one thousand tons of Sauvignon Blanc, and about four thousand tons of grapes total, and the harvesters would be used for a fair portion of their work. Still, if the machines damaged the vines, they would not be a wise investment. But they had been using them for three years and were more than happy with the results.

Don had bought the first harvester in 1999, and another in 2000, and now was renting a third one that he was considering purchasing as well. Back in winter he had taken me to Ferrari-Carano's shop near Jimtown to have a look at them. Not only were they economical, he told me, but they saved money and headaches in the winery. White grapes needed to be pressed quickly, and using the harvesters allowed the winery to open at three a.m., and get to maximum efficiency almost at once. Don said the harvesters posed no threat to the men's jobs because there was still plenty of work to be done. But several of the men had expressed trepidation because, wherever possible, Ferrari-Carano was having them install new trellis systems that were compatible with machine picking.

Don seemed almost as proud of the harvesters as he was of his children. But, says Deep Cork, when the winery's public relations person, Nancy Gilbert, wanted to publicize them as an innovation that made Ferrari-Carano a leader in the trade, Don and Rhonda decided against it. The harvesters were seen as industrial rather than artisanal. They did not fit with The Story.

Frank showed me how the harvester worked, his flashlight picking out the moving parts within the green chassis behind and below Ruben's cab. The harvester mechanism sat above the vines, high enough to pass over the tops of the vines. Its hard but flexible plastic bow rods moved around the trellises without snapping or breaking loose pieces of metal, though if metal flew into the machinery there was a strong magnet nearby to attract and hold it. The bow rods looked like the cooling coils at the back of a refrigerator. They fit snugly around the vines and shook at 460 rotations per minute. The loosened grapes dropped onto revolving catcher plates that were adjusted to a level beneath three fruiting wires between trellises. The plates moved up conveyer belts, and at the apogee of their circuit tipped the fruit into a long troughlike arm. Just before the flip, a strong fan blew loose leaves clear of the fruit and out a dangling hose. At the bottom of the trough, the grapes tumbled through a thick tube and into a gondola being drawn along the adjacent row by a tractor. This tube was an adaptation of Frank's that had been incorporated by the manufacturer, Tuff Boy. Frank liked that the machines were American-made—it meant he could get parts without having customs hassles. They were lubricated with biodiesel, derived from vegetable oil.

The bow rods *hugged* the fruit, said Frank, who let the beam of his flashlight linger over them. "Most people thinks it pounds 'em," he said. "But it actually caresses 'em."

What the machine could not do that human hands could do, however, was sort the good fruit from the undesirable. Everything went into the gondolas. So meticulous farming practices were essential.

It was a few minutes after one a.m. when the three harvesters rolled across the bridgeway, along the avenue, and lined up facing three rows in Block 7.

"Hundreds and hundreds and hundreds of hours of work," said Dave Bacci. "And now, bam! One hour of picking and you're done."

He told me to climb the ladder to the cab and stand beside Ruben, where I would get the best view over the vineyard, and down into the harvester mechanism as well.

"Okay, Frank?" he shouted over the noisy motors.

Frank waved.

"The game is on," he said, as the harvester lurched forward in concert with the other machines.

Machine or no machine, this was farming, and the need for backbreaking work could never entirely be escaped. I had asked Dave earlier how many men were attached to each harvester and he had replied, "Five." The operator, a mechanic, a tractor driver, and two foremen, one walking ahead and the other behind. "Not counting the Hispanic guys."

As the harvester started up the row, whipping up a fierce wind that made the vines sway as if they'd been caught by a tornado, I watched from above the two guys in the gondola. I could not tell who was who under the yellow jumpsuits, goggles, gauze masks, and white hard hats. A waterfall of grapes and juice rained down on them, twenty-two pounds of grapes per vine; they stooped and plunged both hands into the glop to remove the leaves not blown clear, tossing them overboard.

Delicate as the harvester was—it had originally been designed to pick raspberries, which required the gentlest handling imaginable—it still knocked loose a lot of leaf and some cane. The *campesinos* were slip-sliding all over the place, but they had to maintain their footing and not allow the slipperiness to slow them down. They worked frantically to keep up. Juice was sloshing around in the gondola almost immediately, and as we proceeded along a row the tide of grape and juice rose up their bodies until, finally, they had to climb out onto a running board and reach back in. It was hard, dirty, deafening, relentless work. And worse—they were serving a machine that, despite reassurances from their bosses, might be the engine of their obsolescence.

In action the harvester looked like an enormous insect, with its conveyer and extractor dangling like twin proboscises. Its headlight illuminated the vines ahead. The true miracle was the precision with which the machine removed the grapes. It did not snatch off whole clusters as it progressed at two roaring miles per hour down rows of vines. It took the grapes but left the stems attached to the canes. After the machine passed it looked as if deer had supped on the grapes; the harvester was that precise. Leaving behind the stems benefited the wine because stems imparted bitterness. I saw what

Frank had meant about the rods caressing the fruit. Though the ground was tangled with discarded leaves and canes, the vines were substantially intact. I would return Saturday morning to find that the plants had lost their vibrancy, their leaves yellowing. But there were hardly any grapes on the ground. Nearly the entire crop had gone to the winery.

Down one row and back along another we went, in the darkness before dawn, and then down a third, when the machine had to be halted for a repair. Frank was jogging along the entire time—he said he ran ten to twelve miles a day during harvest—and now he dove into its innards because there was a bent or broken bow rod making a screeching noise. Or it was possible a piece of trellis had broken loose; the trellises had to be in perfect alignment for the harvester to work at all. Frank had a wrench in hand, and he and Dave Bacci were struggling over the machine when Steve Domenichelli suddenly appeared in the fog, giving his arrival a mysterious quality. He didn't look like a spirit, though; he looked like a man with a cardboard coffee container in his hand and a broad smile.

"The other ones are picking clean as shit," he said cheerfully. "This one a little dirty?"

Dave wiped his hand on a rag and straightened up. "It's picking heavy," he said, talking about the vineyard. "We really got some nice weight to them." Indeed, before the morning was over they would harvest seven tons more than they'd anticipated from Block 7 and extra tonnage from Block 8 as well. It was a bumper crop, the largest ever off Keegan.

In a few minutes the bent bow rod was fixed, and the harvester was on its way again. Every five hundred yards or so a tractor pulling an empty gondola hurried up, and the full gondola peeled away, accelerating toward the eighteen-wheeler waiting at the avenue that would haul the first twenty tons to the winery.

It had been nine months since Steve had snapped the canes to wake them up, long enough for Ava Sophia Domenichelli and Lacy Gonzales and Karen Michelle Ruiz to be born, and Marlene Ing to go through chemotherapy. The vines bloomed. The earth was disked. Water was dripped and dripped and dripped. The canopy was thinned and tended, the vines were sprayed, and sprayed again, to fend off dangers; veraison came and went, the flavors and the sugars matured, the acids were absorbed. All mysteries were solved, and all problems held at bay, as Steve and his men struggled to keep nature in balance and their crop consistent with their aims.

Now they would learn if they had succeeded.

3

BARREL

September 2002–October 2002

RIDE THE PONY

AT 2:35 A.M. THE first big rig loaded with Sauvignon Blanc grapes harvested off Keegan Ranch eased onto the scales at the winery. The winery was already lights-on. The crush pad—its long dock open to the cool night air, and a huge American flag draped from its roof—was ratcheting up for the day shift. Sleepy-headed workers bundled up in sweaters and knit caps were moving about. At the center of activity was Hoss Milone—two hundred and fifty solid pounds in shorts and a sweatshirt, moving through his domain with a grace that was strikingly light-footed for a man of his size. His given name was Frank, but there were too many Franks in the Milone family, he explained, so when his grandpa gave him a ten-gallon hat as a toddler he became Hoss, and then grew into the name. Hoss' title was director of cellar operations. He was George's foreman.

Hoss greeted me. "It's early. It's Friday the thirteenth. It sucks. My must pump is still not working—ahh, there it goes," he said.

Meanwhile, pulleys above an enormous container, called an auger, were hoisting Doug Skinner's load of ten gondolas. Two by two the gondolas were tipped, spilling a waterfall of grapes and juice into the auger, which had a rotary at one end that fed the grapes into a de-stemmer/crusher, a horizontal machine that broke open the fruit and separated out stems. The rate was metered and controlled to prevent the grapes from spinning out of the auger. The juice, skins, and seeds, in a pulpy mix called *must,* were pumped from the crusher through stainless-steel pipes toward a dejuicing tank, stationed high on a mesh catwalk where it sat atop a press that contained a bladder and a screen.

Just as the crew began to fill the first dejuicer, another eighteen-wheeler from Keegan rolled in at 3:19; they were expecting four additional truckloads from Keegan 7 and 8 on this shift, plus more from Storey Creek.

The must pouring into the dejuicer was a greenish liquid, its foaming churn still holding fibrous grape skins and some stems and leaves. The air was perfumed with its vegetative odors. Within the vertical dejuicer was a screen, which would allow the juice to run freely into a surge tank, and from there into a press. The press would extract the remaining juice from the mush of skins, seeds, and some pulp. Finally, the clarified juice would be pumped into a stainless-steel storage tank inside the winery.

This was the end of the line for Steve Domenichelli and his crew, many of whom had already departed Keegan for Storey Creek, about a half hour away, to continue harvesting Sauvignon Blanc before the heat of the day called a halt. The story of the 2002 Ferrari-Carano Sonoma County Fumé Blanc was now in a new stage: the transformation of fruit to wine. After the crush was completed, the wine would be settled for two days. After that, it would be racked—when some of the heavy solids called lees were removed, and bentonite, a clarifier, added. It would be settled for another day, then racked again. At that point, yeast would be added to set off fermentation, and, finally, it would be pumped into either barrels or tanks to ferment.

The Ferrari-Carano ads in *Wine Spectator* and other trade publications invited customers to savor—their verb—their *handcrafted* wine. But the four-day process of getting the juice and yeast into the barrel was industrial, and it took place in a factory. "Everyone thinks winemaking is the great romance of the agricultural industry," Hoss said. "You pick grapes once a year, nothing else to it. Yeah—your mutha.

"In the field, lots of hands-on," he continued. "And then in processing, it's industrial. That's the way agriculture's always been. But it's still a handcrafted wine; there's still lots of manual labor in the cellar. Guys always smelling, tasting, making sure it's okay. It's not like Budweiser."

The facade of the winery, the part seen by tourists as they strolled through Rhonda's gardens on their way to the tasting room with its multiple spending opportunities, was right on Story; it had weathered wood siding, heavy French doors, a tiled roof. It was a long building, set attractively low in the landscape. But behind its facade was this factory, where generators hummed amid banks of control and monitoring gauges. One cellar worker would say to me that pumping so many thousands of gallons of premium wine—wine that would ultimately retail for fifteen, twenty, thirty dollars a bottle—through the wide hoses into barrels was "just like working in a refinery." Oddly enough, the inspector from the Environmental Protection Agency who had done the 2002 compliance check at Ferrari-Carano had also inspected the Chevron facility at Point Richmond, on San Francisco Bay.

The twenty-ton dejuicers, shaped like surface-to-air missiles, hung with their cones noses-down. Each dejuicer wore a dimpled refrigeration jacket so that the juice from the cool, night-harvested grapes could be kept at fifty degrees to prevent oxidation, and more important, to forestall the growth of unwanted microbes. The evolving juice would be held in a dejuicer for several hours, during which time an enzyme would be added to help begin breaking the skins, encouraging juice flow that maximized product and eventually profit. The amount of sugar in the juice would determine how much heat was generated once fermentation was underway. For the Block 7 crop that had arrived so far, the Brix were uniformly between twenty-three and twenty-four. That was slightly higher than Steve thought optimum to showcase his fruit, but right where George had wanted it to be.

Every dejuicer—"DJ," in the lingo of the crush pad—was labeled with a code detailing what kind of grapes, what vintage, what vineyard, and what block it held. Each block would be separately stored and tracked right up until blending began in late winter. Hoss had a standing board that could be changed by hand, like an old-fashioned baseball scoreboard, that he used to chart the progress of each block from machine to machine. He called it his air traffic control board. He had a lot of grapes, a lot of machinery, and a lot of men and women to keep tabs on. At harvest, both day and night crews were on twelve-hour shifts.

Beyond the dock, the crush pad looked like a particularly vexing jungle gym, a bewildering array of levels and interconnections, most of them constructed with heavy steel mesh that was now getting slippery because there was so much juice and water around. The whole setup was messy, complex, and infinitely detailed. But large as it was, the winery was close to getting maxed out, thanks to Don's appetite for land, and for creating a ninety-nine-rated Sonoma red wine. That was another reason for building the new gravity-flow winery on-site to handle the hillside reds. Ferrari-Carano simply couldn't accommodate any more grapes here.

"I'm starting to run short of barrels," Hoss said. "So it's a juggling act. I had to save barrels for Keegan and Storey Creek—they're two of our best Sauvignon Blancs. Our luxury is that ninety-nine percent of what we crush is what we grow, so we get our flavors off the vineyards and we pick 'em for those flavors, so we know exactly what we got coming in."

For Hoss it had been a busy twenty-four hours. He was a volunteer fireman—so was George—and they kept an antique fire engine on display which today, September 13, 2002, was draped in American flags and the legend: "We Remember." Just when Hoss had been knocking off after a twelve-hour shift yesterday, he'd gotten a call that a baby was choking in Hopland, so he and his brigade had rushed there. As they arrived, the eighteen-month-old coughed up what had been choking her, a LifeSaver. Hoss went straight home to bed before returning to work at two a.m.

Now it was time to ride the pony. The must was going to fall from the DJs into a press, where a bladder would squeeze the remaining juice out of it. But first they poured eight cubic feet of rice hulls into the press to create channels that would filter out the remaining skins and seeds, called the pomace. Eventually the pomace would be disposed of by spreading it in the vineyards. You wanted to process the juice quickly, to minimize flavors from bitter and astringent tannins in the pomace. At a few minutes past five a.m., the must began to course through the stainless-steel chute with a winery worker straddling it, riding that pony, making sure not a drop spilled or was wasted. In his cowboy hat, he looked like Slim Pickens riding a missile into Moscow at the end of Stanley Kubrick's *Dr. Strangelove.*

Hoss turned to the photographer shooting the scene. "Send this picture directly to Cal OSHA," he said.

IT WAS just about then that George Bursick was driving from his home in the town of Healdsburg. Along Dry Creek Road, he was struck by how few other wineries were bringing in their crop. Faced with the wine glut, reduced demand, and intensified competition, many wineries had dropped a significant amount of their 2002 crop on the ground, and were letting flavors and sugars mature for as long as possible, taking a gamble on producing less wine of higher quality. George saw almost no activity on properties belonging to Gallo of Sonoma and Dry Creek Valley Vineyards. It was his devout belief that Ferrari-Carano's superb land, combined with Steve's meticulous farming, allowed them to reach that optimal moment a step or two quicker than others, and with a minimum of dropped crop.

Once at the winery, he stopped briefly in his office, which had a window overlooking a barrel room but no view of the gorgeous land outside. The office was plainly furnished, and might just as easily belonged to a mid-level government bureaucrat—no Roman general's desk here. What was uniquely George's were the cymbals. Mounted and framed, the cymbals had pride of place behind his desk. Ringo Starr had given them to George. A friend of George's was a roadie who traveled with Ringo and with Paul McCartney. George was disappointed to learn that Ringo didn't drink. But Sir Paul had sent back word that he'd loved George's Chardonnay.

"It's kind of fun," George told me once. "I live vicariously because that's what I wanted to do, go on tour and play rock 'n' roll. I was a music major in college, I came from a musical family, and my aunt played with the Dorseys. I actually thought I was going to be a musician, but you realize the commitment it takes. So I said, 'I don't think I want to do this, it's a tough life.' " The most excited I ever saw George was when his band, Private Reserve, was paid to play at a local fair. And this was a man who earned a substantial six-figure salary—some say as much as half a million dollars a year.

"I have drum sets that would fill this office," George had said. "You just have to come to this life's realization: You like something but don't have the passion to practice ten hours a day. My wife, that's what she did, she was a pianist. But she was in an auto accident when she was in college and broke her back. That ended her piano career."

Later, George would complain to Don about the personal nature of the interview—I was supposed to be writing about a bottle of wine, not him. After that, I understood that George was as guarded as Steve was open. I began to think about Ferrari-Carano as a pseudo-chivalric court—that coat of arms in the Villa Fiore—with Steve as Lancelot, and George as Merlin the magician, guardian of the alchemy.

But on September 13, George strolled onto the crush pad at six a.m. with a steaming mug of coffee held with his thick, wide fingers.

"Smell that grassiness?" he said, inhaling deeply. "Sauvignon Blanc. Nothing like it."

LATE ON the afternoon of Friday, September 13, Hoss Milone and Jeffrey Gould were relaxing for a moment over a beer in Jeffrey's lab in the winery. It had been a long day after many long days, and there were more to come. Jeffrey had been anxious to taste the grapes from Keegan in the gondola, but had overslept, not arriving until after Blocks 7 and 8 were harvested, and the gondolas had already departed for the winery.

"Keegan Seven went into a ten thousand and a two thousand," said Hoss. The ten-thousand-gallon tank held the equivalent of 160 barrels. "Keegan Eight just went into a ten. Those extra tons, man."

Jeffrey looked at the figures on his screen. "It seems like all the Sauvignon Blanc is about ten percent higher than projected," he said.

In the end they would harvest 1,288 tons of Sauvignon Blanc, by far their largest crop ever—enough to increase production over 2001 by something like 25 percent.

"I need barrels," said Hoss.

"I know," said Jeffrey. "'I need wood. I need wood.'" He had heard this from Hoss before.

The need for more barrels was no laughing matter to Dick Andersen, the longtime night barrel supervisor, who preferred to have all the wine barreled by October. "But that's not happening anymore," he said, on Monday, September 16, as he prepared to move the first batch of Keegan Sauvignon Blanc to barrel. "We're getting too big."

By then the juice had been racked and the solids, or lees, left behind—although a portion did go into the barrel, and was stirred every month or so as it gradually broke down.

The barreling operation, like the crush pad, was now running on twelve-hour shifts, seven days a week. This time of year, Dick said, was all about overtime. He had a man quit on him last night, he continued, and that threatened to mess things up, but he had managed to assemble a full ten-man crew. They were gathered in a barrel room, a warehouselike area with rows of fifty barrels stacked from floor to ceiling. Prior to arriving here, the Sauvignon Blanc had been warmed up in the tanks, and yeast had been added, at a concentration of between 1 percent and 3 percent. But now that it was warmed up, and fermentation beginning, the juice—it wouldn't officially be wine and subject to alcohol taxes until October 1—needed to be rushed to barrel before the foaming fermentation made a godawful mess. The 673 barrels Dick's crew would be filling on this shift were still being set up on the shelves with the oldest, neutralized barrels on the bottom rows, intended only to hold the fermenting juice until they could get the barrels they wanted in place and ready. For the most part, the barrels they were using for the Sauvignon Blanc were from 2000, had been used new for the 2001 Chardonnay, and would be sold after this second usage, when they no longer met George's exacting standards.

One of Dick Andersen's men, Tony Muzzin, who was twenty-nine years old and from a wine industry family, was busy lining up barrels on their sides, making sure they all extended precisely the same distance over the shelf edge. Like everybody on the crew, he wore high rubber boots because of the water sloshing around, some of the ten gallons of water it takes to produce a single bottle of wine, much to the chagrin of conservationists. The water emerged badly polluted and in need of careful disposal.

Other members of the barreling crew were setting up the thick hoses. The men ran the two-inchers from the tanks in the winery, across an industrial courtyard, to the pumps here, then split them into one-inchers between the air pumps and the barrels. When the juice was coursing through the heavy hoses, they writhed and bucked, and could be dangerous; one of the crew was recuperating from a hernia he had sustained when he was knocked off his feet. But that was only one danger in barreling. There was a noticeable shortage of oxygen in the air, and noisy extractor fans were removing carbon dioxide fumes coming off already fermenting wines. Sensors kicked in the fans automatically when the level of fumes rose, but pockets of gas built up regardless. "You gotta be really careful," Dick said. "You can get yourself in trouble." Workers at other wineries had died from carbon dioxide asphyxiation while shoveling out the last of the skins and seeds from a red wine fermentation.

The crew was blowing water sanitized with ozone through the pumps to clean them, and earlier they had used trisodium phosphate to sanitize the equipment, and citric acid to neutralize the TSP. Flu-like symptoms were common, caused by the ozone-loaded water and lack of oxygen. Sometimes the men had to work on legs made heavy by the fumes they were breathing, Dick said.

"Actually," he added cheerfully, "I'd say this is as dangerous as when I used to work in the woods in the timber industry. There's hidden danger here—you always knew what was happening in the woods. People get hurt here, they slip and fall and strain their backs, not catastrophic like in the woods. But there are things that can affect you twenty years down the line, exposure to these chemicals. I'm careful. We have a pretty good safety program; everybody's well versed. We do have our toxic chemical signs up everywhere so an unsuspecting secretary doesn't walk in on it. Now there's a lot of things chlorine doesn't want to be around, and we use a lot of chlorine—chlorine and ammonia mixed are deadly—and ammonia is part of fermentation. And some acids, and caustics," continued Dick, who was fifty and the father of two. "I'd say they take pretty good care of us here. We have a health plan that's one of the benefits of being full time. We're like a family."

Tony Muzzin and Kevin Rogers, another member of the crew, had joined the conversation, and Tony said he had trouble living on what he made, but it was good experience. Kevin said they needed a union: "Then we wouldn't have to kiss so much ass to get a raise. Ninety percent of wine industry workers can't afford to live in Sonoma and Napa counties."

There was a lot of preparation involved. Once you began pumping, you didn't want to have to stop, because then the wine already fermenting in the tanks would blow the pumps off. But now everything was ready to begin pumping. Kevin hoisted a one-incher and started down the first row, inserting the hose in the bunghole on the top of a barrel. They used a stopwatch to determine when each barrel had forty-five gallons in it—it took one minute and forty-five seconds. They left an empty space at the top large enough to accommodate another fifteen gallons. In a couple of weeks, when fermentation slowed down, they would consolidate the barrels.

When the first barrel was as full as he wanted it, Kevin moved to the next barrel. Another member of the crew, working behind him, inserted a device in the first bunghole to double-check the level, then inserted a fermentation lock, a "bubbler," that let carbon dioxide out but prevented air from getting in.

They kept moving down the line from barrel to barrel, slapping a label on each completed barrel that said: *2002 Sauvignon Blanc Keegan Block 7*. Although the barrels were not temperature controlled, their relatively small volume allowed the heat thrown off during fermentation to dissipate. The temperature in the room itself was kept at fifty-five degrees. The air pump pushing the yeasty juices through the hoses made a loud but gentle sound. It operated on a diaphragm like living lungs, and with each "breath" it sucked wine in and pushed it out. It sounded like a heartbeat: *thwump, thwump, thwump.*

Dick's walkie-talkie squawked. It was George, wanting to make sure everything was copacetic.

"Piece of cake, George," Dick told him. After he turned the walkie-talkie off, he turned to me. "They were awfully worried about how they came in hard and fast." With the crop larger than ever before, it was going to take three days to get the Sauvignon Blanc into barrels. Dick said they were using two different levels of toast—the caramelized carbohydrates in the wood—as well as new and older barrels.

"That's George's magic," Dick said. "He knows which grapes do well with which forest, and which do well with different toasts. We'll come back every month and stir it all up. At some point he'll say, 'Okay, hold off on stirring the Sauvignon Blanc.' He's got the flavor he wants. He quits."

It didn't take long before the juice in the barrels began to burble. Dick motioned me to put my ear to a barrel.

"*That* is a happy camper," he said. And so was he.

In the Barrel

THE FIRST THING you want to know about barrels is what forest provided the oak. Trees in Vosges, for instance, west of Alsace near the German border, grow faster than the same species in Burgundy. The growth rings accumulate more quickly and are spaced a bit more widely. Not that it is ever a rapid process—it will be a century or two before any oak is mature enough to be harvested. The species of oak most commonly found in Vosges, one of four hundred kinds of oak in the world, is *Quercus robur*. It grows on the hillsides, above the fir and pine, and is much sought after for its straight, wide grain with no knots.

The rule is, the slower the growth of the tree the tighter the grain of the wood. The tighter the ring, the less the penetration of the wood by the wine, and therefore the less the extraction of flavors. No small consideration, because the barrel is second only to the grapes in imparting flavor to wine. It is a well-worn joke in the industry that Chardonnay is just a delivery system for oak.

The trees in the oak forests, which have been owned and managed by the French government ever since Napoléon wanted to be certain his navy had a steady supply of wood, are harvested as a crop. They are closely spaced, which encourages them to grow up, not out; only the trunk will be used in barrels. Typically a tree will provide enough wood for between two and four barrels. Usually they are felled in autumn or winter, when the sap is low.

The oak wood is auctioned off throughout the forested regions of France in September and October. The buyer has the right to go to the forest, measure the trees, even bore into them to examine the grain. The auctioneer sets a high price, then comes down until he finds a buyer. On average a cubic meter, which makes about ten barrels, costs in the neighborhood of three thousand dollars.

Wine has been stored in oak barrels since before the birth of Christ because the species is rich in tyloses, a natural plug that makes the wood liquid-tight. In all that time, the method for making barrels has hardly changed. You begin at the stave mill by measuring off useable lengths, and then—nowadays, employing mechanical axes—you split the logs lengthwise into four staves. Sawing would produce more staves, but also raise the level of astringency. You remove the bark and the sap wood. This process is the first of three each stave will undergo, and combined they are what make good French barrels so expensive. To master the technique, a French cooper today undergoes a seven-year apprenticeship.

Next, you dry the staves in the open air for one to three years, until the level of humidity in the oak is no more than 15 percent. (Only winemakers who want to make a hundred-dollar bottle of Chardonnay will insist on trees that have been dried for as long as three years.) During the drying, certain molds and enzymes form, neutralizing the natural bitterness of the wood. Some researchers believe that in the process, polysaccharides are released, sweetening the wood; others disagree. There is no doubt, though, that the flavors in the oak evolve as the drying proceeds. But a buyer must beware—the men who produce staves, called *morrondier,* are not uniformly scrupulous in their attention to make-or-break details. How deeply has your *morrondier* stacked your staves? One pallet? Two? Three? Are the staves at the bottom seasoning properly? Have they been turned to assure equal exposure to the air? Or is one side well seasoned, and the other raw and green?

When the wood is sufficiently dry, you cut the staves more precisely and taper the ends. The staves are cut from transversal sections, so that the end of each one will show the growth rings. You fit them into a temporary metal frame by toasting them until they are soft enough to be shaped. But by what method do you heat them? You can use electric ambient heat, natural gas, steam, boiling water, or wood-chip fires. Most French coopers use wood fires because of the demands of the wineries, and offer different toast levels. The toasting process caramelizes carbohydrates in the wood, imparting micro-amounts of extractable sweetness to the inside of a barrel. It is the interplay of the kind of wood you have chosen, the length of drying, and the method of toasting that combined will determine the characteristics and quality of the finished barrel. As with the wine it will hold, there is disagreement about which barrel is best for a winemaker's particular purpose and goals.

You custom-make the flat ends to fit them into grooves you have cut at the top and bottom of the stave and remove the temporary metal hoops, replacing them with permanent ones that bind the joints of the barrel into a double arch. Once you scrape and smooth the exterior, *voilà,* you have a barrel. A finished barrel will weigh between 110 and 127 pounds, and cost an average of about six hundred dollars.

So a winemaker in California begins by knowing the style of the wine he is trying to create and choosing a compatible barrel. Heavy toast or light? New or previously used barrels? Style, quality, and the ultimate price of the wine all figure into this decision. A winery the size of Ferrari-Carano uses thousands of barrels a year—and buys new ones continuously. Don Carano has never skimped on quality.

"Many times Dave James, our controller, will say, 'What if we didn't buy these barrels?' " George told me. "Dave's the bean counter. And every time, Don overruled him. *Every* time." There are wineries that use a heavy wallop of oak to cover up the inadequacies of their fruit, the way a mediocre cook will use hot spices to cover up the poor flavor of a dish. But in the hands of a master winemaker with first-rate fruit, for whom cost is not the first consideration—in other words, in George Bursick's hands—the barrel is chosen primarily to contribute to the style of his wine.

For his Fumé Blanc, George sought a template against which the blend of herbaceous and melonlike flavors that characterize Ferrari-Carano's best seller would show to best effect. He did not want the oak to disrupt that balance, but only to add a subtle complement, so he used barrels from a cooper called Gillet Père et Fils. Ferrari-Carano replaced about 70 percent of its barrels with new ones every year, but George did not use new barrels for Fumé Blanc, which went into second-year barrels. Most of the caramelized sugars had been extracted in their first year of use with Chardonnay. Once a white wine barrel, always a white wine barrel. When all went well, the barrel would add a subliminal sweetness and a buttery quality in the mouth. "I want to showcase our grapes," George said, "not our cooper. I mean, I like the guy. But *I* denote our style, and our style is fruit-forward."

Decisions such as what barrel to use are one juncture where creativity enters into winemaking. There are dozens of barrels to choose from, as well as stainless-steel tanks. George likens it to a painter choosing colors, and in *The Wine Bible*, Karen MacNeil says that advances in the technology of tank fermentation—not all wines, and not all Ferrari-Carano wines, are fermented in barrel—have given winemakers the ability to *sculpt* their wines.

Characteristically, George worried about the prying eyes of competitors who wanted to steal the knowledge he had acquired through time-consuming, expensive experimentation. "Our barrel-mix is something we don't like to talk about; it's proprietary," George said. He told me that there are French winemakers who turned their barrels bottom-end out, so the stamp of the cooperage will not show. To which some coopers responded by stamping their name on both ends of the barrel—leading certain winemakers to take up their sanders. "A barrel," George said, "is the one variable that anyone could buy— that flavor is readily available."

But George's hypercaution may have more to do with who he is than anything he truly needs to protect from competitors. Amy Kelsey, the young enologist who had worked closely with George for four years, said that, "The culture of Ferrari-Carano tends to be very private, very tight-lipped. George sets that tone—'We have our secrets; we don't share them with anyone.' That's always made me laugh. Everybody knew what we did—it's a small industry, everybody talks. George really does maintain this illusion that there are secrets."

Indeed, Mel Knox, a barrel broker who wrote the entry on oak barrels for *The Oxford Companion to Wine,* knew all about George's cooper. Gillet Père et Fils is located in Saint Romain, in Burgundy, and the barrels Ferrari-Carano buys from them are made not from *Quercus robur* but from the equally desirable *Quercus sessiliflora*. Trees in Burgundian forests such as Bertranges grow slower than those from Vosges, and have growth rings about three millimeters wide, tighter than the trees in Vosges.

Claude Gillet is a small cooper who supplies a very few California wineries. "It's a brilliant move by Don Carano," said Knox. "He's able

to say, 'We have this unique little cooper who makes barrels for us.'
He was probably able to cut a deal, save some money. Claude Gillet is
not wealthy, so it's a good deal for him, too. He gets his money on the
front end."

After using them for a year or two, Ferrari-Carano sells its barrels,
but George preferred not to say to whom. Some buyers pop the head
off a barrel, shave off perhaps three-eighths of an inch of oak, put the
barrel over a toaster, and begin to use it again. The problem is that not
all the caramelized sugars deposited by the original toasting have been
extracted, and the retoasted sugars add a burnt flavor to the resulting
wine. If you are mass-producing really inexpensive wines, even retoast-
ing is too costly. What you can do instead—and it *is* being done: can
you say Two Buck Chuck?—is to buy three tons of oak chips for about
the same six hundred dollars just one good barrel would cost, and toss
the chips into the stainless-steel tanks with the fermenting wine.

Caramelized flavors from a good barrel are imparted gradually,
and the longer the exposure, the more flavor is extracted. George
didn't want his Fumé Blanc to spend a lot of time in barrel; in general, Sauvignon Blanc didn't need that. That short fermentation, plus
the use of second-year barrels, are two reasons Ferrari-Carano is able
to sell it for about half the price of their Chardonnay.

Not everyone likes George's approach. Lisa Minucci, the sommelier at Martini House restaurant in St. Helena, which is renowned for
its wine list, says she is not a fan of oak on Sauvignon Blanc. That is *all*
she says, but in a world where an eighty-five from *Wine Spectator*
amounts to a failing grade, even that is heavy criticism. But what the
heck, you can't please all the oenophiles all the time. That minimal
exposure to *Quercus sessile* barrels from Gillet Père et Fils works for
sommeliers at plenty of fine restaurants. And in the marketplace, it
transforms a workaday Sauvignon Blanc into a smoky, seductive
Fumé.

LIKE A DANCE

GEORGE WAS IN a darn good mood. For weeks, the accumulated pressures and demands of harvest had caused the Private Reserve musicians to miss a couple of their regular get-togethers, but last night they had been jamming at winemaker Mike Martini's studio in Calistoga. They worked on an old Statler Brothers a cappella tune, ate pizza, and drank some older reds.

George had enjoyed the music, the company of his wine business musician buddies, and the wine, but the latter not the way you or I might. His palate was not inborn, but perhaps the ability to acquire such a palate was. He had learned at U.C. Davis to focus on an individual element in a wine, a flavor or aroma or texture within the complexity of the whole, and to the momentary exclusion of all the other components. When he tasted a wine, he picked it apart element by element, and rated each against what he perceived to be the winemaker's intent. That was the pleasure he took in wine, the pleasure of deconstructing it based on his knowledge and understanding. This was true no matter how exquisite the wine. At his fiftieth birthday party, for instance, they had poured a flight—a group of wines with something in common—of French first-growths, some of the world's most precious and sought-after wines. George had wished, albeit fleetingly, to be able to sit back and enjoy them just for what they were. He couldn't, of course, but hadn't felt sorry for himself. Rather, he experienced a deeper pleasure in his ability to taste and smell wine granted to very few: to truly know what he was drinking, and how it had come to be, a knowledge available only to professionals, and even among these, only to the gifted.

But when Private Reserve—a guy from Beringer who played guitar, a wine lawyer, a grape grower, and a marketer—practiced and drank some wine, there was no picking apart. The fellowship and the music were paramount—it was no time for wine criticism.

George tried to keep his assessments specific and understandable. Everyone could understand what "flavors of asparagus" meant, or bell pepper, or melon, whether or not they had the capacity to taste or smell them in the glass. "But Algerian honeysuckle grown on a north slope?" George asked rhetorically, as we headed to check out the progress of the 2002 Fumé Blanc. "That only means something to some wine geek, not to me. There's no need to make it so complicated. Hell, I don't even remember the last time I tasted a kumquat."

When George arrived in Barrel Room Number Nine, a crew was consolidating the wine from 45 gallons per 60-gallon barrel to 59½ gallons per barrel. The wine was becoming drier—less sweet—as the sugars burned off during fermentation. One of the decisions that George had yet to make was whether to induce malolactic fermentation, which chanced detracting from the varietal character of the wine, the pure taste of the grape, but would add body. How a wine felt in the mouth was, after all, George's specialty. He was still making up his mind about that particular trade-off, one of an incalculable number of decisions he juggled as he

shepherded fifteen different varietals and blends, sitting in barrels
and tanks for anywhere from a few months to four years, toward
their release.

There was still some Merlot to be harvested off Keegan, then that
would be it for 2002, except for a bit of late harvest sweet wine: For
that, the vines would be wet down to encourage the "noble" rot that
translated into Brix of thirty-five or higher. Sauvignon Blanc was perhaps the easiest of the grapes to deal with—it was malleable both in
the vineyard and as juice. But whatever path he took with malolactic,
and he had perhaps another week to make up his mind, the flavors he
had now in the barrel and the tank were pretty much it.

George paused in his explanation. That sensitive nose of his—its
cherry tip no surprise in a man in his occupation—picked up an odor
he did not like. It was like watching a setter take a scent. For George,
a summer cold would be a professional disaster.

"We've got a little bit of funk," he said. "Could be sulfites, might
just be in one barrel or two," among six thousand. The dread TCA is a
mold compound that smells of wet dog and onion. He raised his assistant winemaker, Andrew Levi, on his walkie-talkie, and asked him to
hurry over. It was the kind of thing you wanted to nip in the bud, before it had a chance to spread.

That having been taken care of, we entered row C1, where wines
from Keegan 8 were being held. George removed the fermentation
lock from a barrel and peered inside, then told me to take a look. The
wine was still topped with a debris-strewn foam, but wasn't on the
boil, the way it had been a couple of weeks before. "Almost dry,"
George said, picking up a wine thief, a long plastic tube with a vacuum device that he used to suck up an ounce or two of grapefruit-
colored liquid. George emptied it into a glass he held the way
oenophiles do, with the foot between his thumb and the knuckle of
his index finger—whenever I tried this, the wine spilled—holding it

up toward the light, then swirling it. The wine was cloudy because yeasts were still suspended throughout the barrel.

"If the sample was clear, I'd know I have a problem," George said.

"Actually, he'd have a problem with me," said Andrew Levi, who had hurried to join us before searching for the source of the funky odor.

Andrew was thirty-one. Four years earlier he had come to Ferrari-Carano hoping to learn from a master, from George. Andrew came from an illustrious midwestern family—his great-uncle had been the attorney general of the United States—and he had attended Amherst College, majoring in philosophy, but was nagged by a feeling that he was not where he belonged. He disappointed his parents when he dropped out of Amherst and, seeking his future, came—where else?—to California, where he moved in with an aunt who was something of a black sheep, a hippie sort who lived in Calistoga, in Napa County. Andrew's epiphany came gradually but irresistibly when he realized that, as he puts it, "I could smell all that stuff on the wine label—melon, fig, honeysuckle. I knew it was my life. There's nothing else I want to do until the day I die."

One of Andrew's jobs was to monitor fermentation, the process by which yeast converts the glucose and fructose in the grapes to alcohol. Enzymes in the yeast also act as catalysts to convert the chemicals present in the grapes into flavors. The chemical precursors are bound together with the sugars; when the sugars are burned off, the flavors remain.

To produce the flavors you wanted, you needed to keep track of the complex interrelationships among sugar concentration, the heat generated by its conversion to ethanol, and the volume of alcohol in the baby wine.

This was the kind of thing Andrew had studied at U.C. Davis Department of Viticulture and Enology. Once he had his degree, and his parents saw the depth of his commitment—hard to miss in somebody who proclaims, "I'm willing to live and die for wine"—they came around, and the family was reconciled.

The yeast reproduces by budding. Daughter cells separate from the mother cell, which dies after producing about a dozen buds. At first, when the yeast is added to the grape juice, there is a period of adjustment to the new environment. Within days, the culture zooms ahead, growing exponentially, then begins to wane as it was doing now, until all the sugar that provided its nutrition has been metabolized. Exhausted of their vitality, the yeast cells begin to die off.

Saccharomyces cerevisiae—the yeast used for winemaking (and to bake bread)—means sugar-loving. It's regarded as humankind's first domesticated organism. A fungus, its cells are organized in the same way as those in our bodies, and are heavily studied. Some eight thousand researchers worldwide are devoted to yeast, and they have their own journals (*Yeast, Yeast Research*). It was almost to be expected that its genome would be the first to be sequenced, and become the model for the Human Genome Project. We're talking staff of life, after all.

The initial environment of *Saccharomyces* was not bread, though, but grapes. It is highly adapted to grapes, and if you throw some *Saccharomyces* into a vat of grape juice where it is outnumbered a million to one by other strains of yeast, it is going to be victorious in the end.

You can use wild yeasts in wine fermentation, but they have considerable disadvantages, not least that they are relatively alcohol intolerant and unpredictable. So winemakers turn to commercial strains developed specifically for their craft. In a general sort of way, what a winemaker is seeking is a predictable and reproducible fermentation, one that will tick along until all the sugar in the grape juice has been converted to alcohol. A good yeast must also be tough: tolerant of alcohol in concentrations as high as 18 percent, as well as high temperatures, and the sodium dioxide used in winemaking.

The commercial yeasts available to George and all winemakers (produced by a handful of manufacturers worldwide, none in the United States since Red Star was sold to a French company) meet these criteria, so he made his selections on more esoteric grounds. There were certain characteristics in the grapes he wanted to bring forward, others he hoped to deemphasize. The rate of vigor was also tremendously important, but temperature was more crucial than the yeast strain in controlling the rate of fermentation.

I asked George about the kinds of yeasts he was using. He looked as if I had asked him what sexual position he preferred. His yeasts were a proprietary secret, he said, the product of his own innovations, one of his greatest sources of satisfaction. Weeks later, he mentioned in passing that one yeast he used was called VL3. (Eventually I asked Dr. Linda Bisson, a yeast specialist at U.C. Davis, about VL3, thinking I was impressing her as something of an aficionado, and that I was about to penetrate closer to the heart of George's magic. "Oh," she said, "VL3 is one of the standard yeasts. Run-of-the-mill. Its enzymes are supposed to bring out grassy flavors.")

But George had apparently neglected to tell his closest winemaking associates, Andrew Levi and Amy Kelsey, that their yeasts were to be kept secret.

Andrew talked readily about their yeast mix. He seemed happy to describe the process because, while on the one hand George was continually cautioning him to be careful what he said around me, on the other hand his own inclination was to cooperate, as he had also been told to do by Don and George.

For the Fumé Blanc, they used three yeasts—VL3, VL1, and one from E. Begerow, a German company. "SIHA—it stands for something, I can't remember what," Andrew said, "It's a moderate fermenter." The SIHA yeast is used for delicate white wines with lots of aromatics and acidity. "It provides very fruity characteristics," Andrew said. "VL3 is vegetative. VL1 is the fruitiest. You add the yeasts at the get-go—one lot, one vineyard, one yeast. By using all three, you're trying to get a little bit of everything."

Andrew's colleague Amy Kelsey had worked with the celebrated Paul Draper at Ridge Vineyards, who readily taught her whatever he knew—but that wasn't George's style. And that was one reason why, in an industry characterized by collegiality—wine had been made more or less the same way for thousands of years, and though every winemaker's gestures were unique, there were no real trade secrets as there were in California's other hot industry of the nineties, high-tech—Ferrari-Carano was sometimes mocked for its Mafia-like silences.

"The yeasts really aren't proprietary at all," Amy said. "George really has a fear all out of proportion that some other winery will get hold of his recipe, and be able to copy it."

LIKE ALL good winemakers, George liked a long, slow fermentation, one bubble at a time. The more rapid the fermentation, the more carbon dioxide bubbles it produced—bubbles that could trap aroma compounds; in other words, the faster the fermentation, the fewer the flavors. Especially with Chardonnay, George favored nail-biters that depended on his knowledge of yeasts. The danger with a slow fermentation was that it could become stuck, the way a low flame can blow out. But George was depending on Andrew to watch closely—really closely—so that if the rate of fermentation reached a critical level, you could jump in and add nutrients or yeast vitamins. "If you let a fermentation stop," George said, for Andrew's instruction as much as my edification, "then you weren't paying enough attention." Nonetheless, it sometimes happened. "I'm riding the line with stuck fermentations," he said. "I'm taking it right down to the edge."

In some ways, George felt the most anxious time in the winery was the final stage of fermentation, but not because he was afraid it might stick. It would be another three months before the true color and nature of the Sauvignon Blanc would be revealed, but even now, in early October, it was nearly too late to affect what would be going into the bottle. For example, there had been two blocks from the Storey Creek harvest that were too aggressively herbaceous, threatening the overall design for 2002, and George was hoping that exposure to the barrel would temper those tendencies. He was close to being certain of what he did and did not have, where the flavors were heading. He could by now "taste" the outcome, the way a golfer can "see" the line of the putt into the cup before he makes the stroke. But George could not afford to miss.

"We have our style," he said, "and if we're not going down that path, it would be really serious. You don't know quite yet if you blew it or nailed it." Soon, when the wine was in its last stages of fermentation, when it was too late to manipulate the wine in the barrels and tanks, he would know.

Consistency in the bottle was, after all, a major part of what Ferrari-Carano was selling, and in the perilous new marketplace a slip could be economically fatal. The chill off the marketplace had blown through George's musician friends. Mike Martini's family had owned their winery and vineyards for three generations before they had been forced to sell to Gallo. The industry was consolidating, and smaller operations, some of them quite venerable, were being swallowed. In fact, Don himself had been approached several times by large operations interested in buying Ferrari-Carano. He has never responded, except once, when he felt that the potential buyer deserved that respect; one can only assume that it was Robert Mondavi, but Don wouldn't say.

We moved on to another row, where fermenting grape juice from Keegan 9 filled the barrels. George dipped the thief again, bringing up a few ounces.

"I'm stealing the wine," he said, smiling. He looked, swirled, looked again, tasted. "[Keegan] Eight, to me, had a neutral citrusy thing, but this—something's going on." It sounded like something good. "Down by the creek, it gets a little more . . ." He didn't complete the thought. "It's pretty dry, maybe one-half percent sugar. Everything's cool. Right where it should be.

"Our susceptibility to oxidation is increasing as fermentation decreases," George said. "It will stay like this for a week, then we have to add sulfur dioxide as oxidation protection. So we're slowly putting up the stop sign."

The sulfur compounds used as antioxidants by most American wineries are controversial because they cause severe allergic reactions in a few people. That is why wine labels warn that the wine "Contains Sulfites." The warning was vehemently opposed by the wine industry. But its addition doesn't seem to have hurt sales.

When precisely the right moment arrived, "We get a bunch of guys and nail it like that," George said, snapping his fingers. If they left it even a moment too long, the oxidation might impart the odor of a burning match to the wine, in which case a quality house like Ferrari-Carano might as well feed its wine to the fishes in the deep blue sea. That was why they reserved a half-gallon's worth of empty space in every barrel, so that when they added the sulfur dioxide the barrels weren't full, or foaming over, and they could speed through as many as five hundred barrels in a night, topping up each barrel as they went.

"It's going to be in shock when you take this nice little baby wine, essentially nesting with its friend the yeast, and throw sulfur dioxide on it. We do it in one shot, just nuke it. Sauvignon Blanc's pretty forgiving.

"It's like a dance," George said. "Walking that line." A line he had the gift to be able to sense. "It's all personal interpretation. There's no right or wrong. It seems like you're constantly reacting to what's happening because it's so unpredictable. It's fun; I enjoy that. You've got to be on your toes—like that smell. We've got to do some detective work and see what's going on. It's kind of amazing to me," he marveled, "how many people in this industry think they've got it all figured out."

His comparing his work to a dance was thought-provoking. There are those who consider winemaking an art, and others who scoff at the notion. Could something so ephemeral, something made to be consumed, ever be art?

"There is nothing so irascibly difficult [as] making a truly fine wine, given a thousand unpredictable variables," the novelist and oenophile Jim Harrison has written. "Is winemaking an art? Maybe for a few, and their identities are somewhat concealed except to a few. The apprenticeship requires the entire life. You often have to wait twenty years or more . . . to have any idea if art has been 'committed' . . . Ultimately you are working in a medium that is rarely understood beyond the immediate sensation of pleasure. Like a fine chef, your work only reaches fruition when it disappears into someone's mouth."

I wondered what George's view was.

"It's got to be a balance," he said. "There's a lot of hard-core science involved. If you're going to be making decisions about fermentation, all this stuff, you must know a lot about chemistry. But it should be used as a tool, not as the focus of your direction. Where art comes in, you've got to be able to go with your gut instincts. If you make wine just by the numbers, you can taste it. I can taste it in other people's wines—whether there's a passion. You can't be a technoid winemaker because you come off sterile, nor can you come off as a flaky artist because the wine won't be sound. I think you have to approach it somewhere in the middle. It's more fun for me to approach it in a more artsy way; I'm more left of center. But I need balance."

Naturally there were artistic yearnings among people as creative and complex in their sensory appreciation as George was. But in the end, you made wine *primarily* to sell it. It was a business. Every composer, painter, and poet wanted to sell his work, too, to reach the widest possible audience, to be fully appreciated, to earn a living. But that wasn't *why* they played music, and painted canvases, and wrote poems—they made them because they had no choice. Although Andrew Levi had said, "I'm willing to live and die for wine," he had added: "But I'm not going to cut my ear off." Artists did what they did because it was who they were. The process of making this wine—I could not speak for all wines—was so safe, the variations held within such strictures, the possibility of genuine surprise or inspiration so thoroughly guarded against, that at its very best it was craft, high craft perhaps, but never art—pottery, not poetry.

AUTUMN LIGHT

IT WAS A perfect autumn morning, clear and crisp and sharply etched, and on my way to the Ferrari-Carano harvest party I stopped at Keegan Ranch. There were deep ruts left behind by the tractors in the rows between the yellowing vines in Block 9, nearest to the creek; in Block 7, the drooping leaves were a dull and lifeless brown. Nearby a lone bird twittered and called. The life cycle of the vineyard was complete, but a new cycle was already underway—spurs on the gnarled wood that would become shoots, then bear clusters. Steve's continuum.

Driving from Keegan Ranch toward Geyserville I passed by a new Indian casino in the shape of a teepee, with a lake-sized parking lot, that was rising east of Highway 101. I had driven this way with Don a number of times, and he always made some comment. California's Indian casinos were competitors of his casinos—upstarts, from his perspective—and indirectly because of them he was embroiled in a politicized land use controversy in Reno. Many of the gamblers whose losses had enriched Don were from Northern California, and now they could gamble closer to home. Don believed that Reno needed to offer new reasons to come to Nevada; he was part of a group that was going to build a downtown center to host conventions, exhibits, concerts, and boxing. The site was partially on land he owned, and when the package was assessed, his parcel, which was on the street, was more highly valued than the others. There was organized opposition to the scheme from some city council members and slow-growth advocates, who claimed the downtown center was more about enriching Don Carano and his partners from Harrah's and Mandalay Bay than enriching the civic life of the city.

Don was backing a slate of council candidates in the November 2002 election who saw things his way. The mayor, Bob Cashell, was already his guy, and Don was spending many hours brokering deals that would allow the first shovel to be put into the ground. He was also deeply concerned at accusations that he had undue influence in local politics. His reputation was his pride and the source of his effectiveness; it offended and weakened him to be accused. On the day before Keegan was harvested, he had flown to Reno on his jet, then back again that same evening because he and Rhonda had invited me to dinner at John Ash & Co., a wine country restaurant in a luxury inn they had bought on the outskirts of Santa Rosa. The first thing he said when we met was, "I'm getting too old to do this." But he continued to do what he had to do.

The harvest party for the vineyard crews was at Steve Domenichelli's headquarters on the Carinalli vineyard in Jimtown, where there was an office in a trailer, maintenance shops, and sheds. This was where the heavy equipment was kept, and where René Ruiz ran the payroll operation. Officially, it was also Steve's office—but Steve's real office was inside his head, as he raced around in his truck. He seldom used his desk; he had no need for notes on paper, not when it came to his vineyards.

There were picnic tables set up under a long canopy, and four men in chefs' whites were preparing food. Quite a few of the Mexican guys were there when I arrived, gathered by themselves at the opposite end of the tables from where the Anglo bosses were hanging out closer to the outdoor kitchen.

Boa had a new haircut that looked like something a ten-year-old would have sported in the 1950s. A bowl-on-the-head look, nearly bald over the ears and standing straight up on top. That wasn't all, though. He had colored it with henna. I couldn't begin to imagine what he thought he looked like. Had he wanted to obscure the scar on his scalp? His baby daughter, he said, was going to be christened on December 14.

Many of the Mexican guys were gathered around a second, smaller grill where there were bushel bags of fresh oysters from Tomales Bay. Boa told me the oysters they could get at home in El Charco were "not fresh. These are very fresh." Over the next several hours, oysters were continuously shucked, grilled on the half shell, slathered with Tabasco, and gulped. Nearby was an ice chest filled with beer, soda, water, and bottles of Ferrari-Carano 2001 Fumé Blanc. There were tequila bottles on some tables at the Mexican end. Beer and tequila were being drunk, and soda and water, but nary a single bottle of the wine these men had cultivated and harvested.

A volleyball game got going, supervisors versus hands. The Mexicans won the first match, and then Dave Bacci rounded up better players for a rematch. I wandered away to where the meal was being prepared. Javier Rocha, a chef at the Eldorado, had flown down, and Don's chief pilot, Fred Barrie, was here, too. Javier told me that he and his staff were preparing 100 pounds of pork, 280 tamales (half of them pineapple), 40 pounds of rice, 50 pounds of ranchero beans, and 130 pounds of beef tri-tip. He sliced me off a piece of the grilled tri-tip to taste. He had marinated it in butter, diced onion, garlic, honey, and four kinds of chiles: poblano, ancho, pasilla, and chipotle.

Javier's crew included Rhonda's father, Dario Bevilacqua, who was seventy-eight. "I want to stop working," Dario joked, "but Don and Rhonda won't let me. I moved houses all my life"—his old truck was still in use at Ferrari-Carano—"but when I hurt my back, Don said, 'Why don't you come up to the hotel?' I run the pasta shop; we make all our own pasta." Dario had two girls, Rhonda and her older sister Charlene. Rhonda, he said, "always had a mind of her own. I'll tell you, she was a good student. Always A's."

The new volleyball game was going strong—the reinforced bosses were now dominating play—when I sat down to talk with George. The sugar in the Sauvignon Blanc, he told me, "was down to dryness," meaning that virtually all of the sugar had been eaten up. The barrels had been consolidated, freeing up some barrels for other varietals, and the sulfur dioxide had been added. The decomposing yeast was releasing lipids and fatty acids, and the wine had been stirred to keep those fatty elements in suspension, which would add mouth feel to the wine. "We don't want them clear, we want to keep them dirty," George said. This lees aging—*sur lie,* the French called it—was an expensive, labor-intensive process—unusual in white wines other than Chardonnay—that enhanced flavors. Another aim was homogeneity.

Thirty percent of the Sauvignon Blanc had never seen a barrel, but was fermenting instead in stainless-steel tanks, and George had also added an *oenococcus* bacterium in the tanks, setting off a malolactic fermentation. The additional fermentation—sometimes called spring fermentation—turned tart malic acid from the grapes into lactic acid, such as is found in milk, thus softening the wine, which he thought was a smidge too thin. It was a classic example of how the introduction of steel tanks in the 1960s had added to the ability of winemakers worldwide to "sculpt" wines. By the time George had been sure he was willing to sacrifice some varietal flavors for more body, he thought it was too late to risk inoculating the barrel-held wine. But the tank-held wine, fermenting more slowly and under greater control, and intended to produce a crisper wine to complement the fuller wine in barrels, could still be played with. The stainless-steel tanks were the most significant advance in the science and craft of winemaking since Pasteur had learned in the 1850s that living yeasts converted the sugars in the grapes to alcohol. It had been a breakthrough in the understanding of an ancient process that expanded the tools available to winemakers for their wizardry—the craft that could not be taught, although it had to be learned.

"Really, no problems," George said. "We put the Sauvignon Blanc to bed and it's resting comfortably. I know where it is; I've got my hand on it. I don't have to keep after it."

George had an ego. But he lacked the confidence to be combative. He had all but stopped doing wine judgings because he felt the most dominant person always got his way. "A lot of times people don't feel that confident, and let people bully them," he said. Despite Don's obvious appreciation of his talents, George could not help but hold his employer at arm's length. It struck his young associates, Andrew Levi and Amy Kelsey, that George was afraid of Don. "Andrew and I talked about it a lot—was that his basic personality?" Amy said. "Was he always fearful? Or did he become that way at Ferrari-Carano? I was amazed how he was afraid of Don. Don would have loved a close relationship. Don gave him carte blanche to run the winery, a huge paycheck, lifetime security, loyalty. But George couldn't be close—he would sort of shake in his boots whenever Don was around."

As part of the company's marketing efforts, George did interviews, especially with the trade press, and appeared at wine events, often with Don and Rhonda, but sometimes alone. "There's a side of me the public sees," George said. "Then there's the side I don't talk about. What my beliefs are, and everything else, is sacred to myself, and my family and friends. Everything I do I wear on my sleeve—even music. Everything I do, someone is critiquing."

I left George alone as quickly as possible because of the sense I got that it was painful for him to be answering my questions, and soon was talking to Steve about the 2002 harvest.

"We brought in close to four thousand tons," he said. "And every bit of fruit, besides the machine-harvested, was thrown on a table and hand-sorted before hitting the winery. That's huge—that never happened before at Ferrari-Carano. I've been here sixteen years and I've never tasted fruit like the fruit this year. Some of those blocks were over the top—big, soft flavors. It's got to show up in the wines."

I asked him why the 2002 crop was so good.

"Climate—dynamite year. And quality control. Modern viticulture at its best." Listening to Steve, I imagined a mental exclamation point after every phrase: "We're hip! We're with it! Most people are ten years behind us! We threw five hundred, six hundred tons on the ground! That's a huge commitment! Walls of fruit on the ground! I showed Don—and he was like, 'Jesus Christ, am I going to make any money?' "

IT WAS time to eat. The harvest feast went on for hours, and still the men could not finish all the food. But as the day began to wind down, I took away two images. The first was of René Ruiz. The men were getting bonuses, anywhere from a few hundred dollars to two thousand dollars depending on their jobs and their tenure, and René, immaculate as always, strutted about all day with a wad of checks sticking out of his back pocket. Better even than big *cojones* was a wad of bucks.

The second image was bittersweet. Photographer Eric Luse

rounded up all hands for a group portrait. The afternoon light on this last day of October was the most beautiful California possessed, buttery soft. The men stood in front of a yellowing vineyard. The mellow light and the death of the reproductive cycle in the vineyard created nostalgia for the moment before it had receded into the past. Eric clicked off shot after shot. There were perhaps one hundred men there in all, and no women, not even Rhonda. The vineyard was a male domain, and the womenfolk stayed up at the Villa. Every one of these *campesinos* was being paid for coming to this feast as if he had worked a regular eight-hour day. That was thanks to the man who stood almost shyly near the periphery, not in the suit and tie he wore in Reno, but wearing his down-on-the-ranch jeans and a shirt open two buttons over his white T-shirt. Their employer, their *padrón*—the man who said he had no undue influence.

Right then, I understood something about Don that had eluded me. He was ambitious, certainly, and confident, as well as capable. But Sonoma County played second fiddle to Napa, and Reno was Nevada's second city. For all that Don thought big, as Pat Kuleto had said, he liked to roll the dice where the limelight was not at its brightest. Was that modesty, caution, or fear?

4
A THING OF DESIRE

November 2002–January 2003

Box Warrior

HERE IS THE first thing Steve Meisner, Ferrari-Carano's director of sales and marketing, ever said to me, when I called him to set up an interview: "I designed this program, in terms of specificity, from day one."

So it hardly came as a surprise, when a few weeks later he also told me: "Like a lotta guys in this business, I'm pretty intense. Very competitive." He had the eyes of a linebacker just before the snap, and had been a load master for the air force in Vietnam.

The first time Don introduced me to Meisner he had called him his "Box Warrior." Don said it with the indulgent affection of a monarch talking about a soldier who was willing to die in battle for the greater glory of his majesty. That is precisely what Meisner does—he wages war in the marketplace. There are a lot of good wines in the world, a lot of attractive wines. Some wineries will make it onto the list at Four Seasons and Boulevard, and some won't. Their fortunes will rise or fall accordingly. It is Meisner's job to make sure Don and Rhonda's fortunes are never swept away by an ebb tide.

We were standing near the busy tourist entrance to the Villa Fiore. I had followed Meisner from his office when he needed a cigarette. Meisner positioned himself in the shade under a small balcony and behind a massive clay pot full of geraniums and azaleas. His posture could only be described as skulking. He wore a white shirt and a tie amid the visitors, many of whose sunburned knees were visible below their Bermuda shorts. He never even saw them, and seemed to hope they wouldn't see him either. There were so many other things they were supposed to look at. Five acres of gardens. A gigantic bronze water sculpture of a wild boar that Rhonda had named Boardeaux. Beyond a stone balustrade, vineyards. A summer sun in a cloudless sky. Rhonda's design for heaven on earth.

"People, they look at the beauty of this place," Meisner said, waving his cigarette, "and they forget. It's a business."

He was the son of a father he described as "the man in the gray flannel suit," a Connecticut businessman. After four years in the service Meisner had traveled, roaming through Europe, where he found that wine and food interested him. In 1978 he came to Mecca, that is to say, California. He went to work for a distributor and acquired outside sales experience. He never handled anything but fine wine.

In 1984, before there was anything to sell, Don recruited Meisner. Don was a supremely successful marketer himself, so he knew what he wanted and how to go about getting it. "I came from two wineries where I had to turn things around," Meisner said with characteristic modesty. "Chateau Souverain and Chateau St. Jean—which I did over the time of my tenure. One of the great things about Ferrari-Carano, we started with a clean slate and I could take everything I learned, and going in, didn't make any mistakes."

He seized that empty slate that Don handed him, and although he had the luxury of time, and the meticulous attention to detail of both Rhonda and Don, he was hardly one to go with the flow.

"The first three or four years are the most important," he said. His voice was raspy. "That's when you establish your brand as a thing of desire. Let's face it, is a twenty-six-dollar bottle of Chardonnay really something a man needs? What the whole job amounts to is creating demand and creating the image that your wine is a thing of desire. It's what Lexus wants to do. What Gucci wants to do. What every luxury marketer wants to do. I would say that we have an image that is one of elegance and consistent quality. I think that sums it all up."

All it took for Meisner to succeed in those crucially important first years was to have no life. "The first six years I did all fifty states myself," said the man who now ran a national sales staff based in Los Angeles, New York, Chicago, and Miami. "I opened every state personally—I was on the road seven months a year." It began in 1985, when Ferrari-Carano produced five thousand cases. Nothing was coming out of the vineyards as yet but Chardonnay and Fumé Blanc. A new bottle on the street. Out there selling like there was no tomorrow, because if he didn't succeed, there wouldn't be. Calling on distributors, hoteliers, and restaurateurs who had never heard of Ferrari-Carano, chain-smoking his way across the USA to build a brand.

How did he sell something new and unknown?

"Steve Meisner is not new to you," he said, demonstrating his pitch. "Steve Meisner has been calling on you every month for ten years," for Chateau Souverain and Chateau St. Jean. "Steve Meisner has a reputation for keeping his word. Basically, I knew every fine-wine distributor in the country. Some," he conceded, "were doubtful."

Of Steve Meisner? Just a minute here.

"I said to them, 'Do yourself a favor. Take this. If you don't sell it, I'll personally buy it back. You have my word.'

"Instead," he said, "they were begging for more. When I came back from my first trip the entire production of the winery was committed to, before it even left the winery. It's not just 'Put good wine in the bottle. Know who your competition is'—you have to survey, and come in a little under them. When you're an unknown brand, you have to marshal all your resources, and everybody has to know who your competing wineries are. You survey thirty wineries per varietal, both up and down in the price point. You want to go to places that do sell your competing wines."

Today, for Ferrari-Carano Fumé Blanc, those competitors include a couple of New Zealand labels, Cloudy Bay and Babich, as well as California brands such as Conundrum, Mondavi, Caymus, Frog's Leap, Dry Creek, Murphy Goode. In terms of price, Ferrari-Carano is in the middle, higher than Frog's Leap, Murphy Goode, and Dry Creek, lower than some of the others.

"You have to have incentives for the sales people," he said. Incentives were a key. What distinguishes one nice Sauvignon Blanc from another? For the aficionado, the style and quality. For the casual consumer, the price, or perhaps the rating. But for the distributor and the restaurant, the best deal: What are you offering *me?*

"The smartest thing Don did was start buying his own vineyards early," Meisner said, because it allowed Don to control quality and quantity, price and growth. "Don's a very, very bright guy. I'll tell you how I see it. Without his long-term vision, buying vineyards you don't need for another ten years, giving George state-of-the-art equipment, giving me the leeway to hire the best people, of which I have nine, and building the Villa for purposes of image and entertaining—and he did everything in the exact right order."

How could Don, a novice in wine, know so much about how to go about it?

"Beats me," Meisner said. "The guy had vision. Had *vision.*"

He led me back to his office, the least adorned place in the Villa. He sat down behind a lacquered desk that was all but bare. Outside his window was a trellised golden hillside, the very image of symmetrical abundance. Why did I get the feeling that Meisner never took the time to enjoy the view? Meisner picked up one of the few objects on the desk, a heavy, gold Mark Cross pen. Another thing of desire. His hands trembled almost imperceptibly.

"The bottom line for a guy in my job is to keep the demand curve ahead of the supply curve, and ours always has. To accomplish that image of desirability. And how do you do that? Served in the finest restaurants." *Tap* went the gold pen on the lacquered desktop. "Served in the four-star hotels." *Tap* again. "Served in the best resorts." *Tap*. "Common sense, not rocket science." His right leg was pulsating faster than a hummingbird's wings. "It's execution that counts.

"For your distributors, you say: 'Here's your allocation.'" In California, you are forbidden by law to tell your distributor where to place your wines, but wineries and distributors work hand-in-glove. "You say: 'To meet our criteria I need fifty good wine shops and maybe one hundred white-tablecloth hotels and restaurants.' So this is how it really started," Meisner said. "Had it in the bottle. Had great packaging. Had a detailed program for distributors. Established our image by giving a large percentage of each vintage to restaurants that were individually targeted." Then the second vintage of Chardonnay made it onto the cover of *Wine Spectator*. Overnight, George Bursick became a star, and Ferrari-Carano was on the fine-wine map. It became a little easier for Meisner. Next thing you knew, Ronald Reagan was serving their Chardonnay in the White House. Steve Meisner had the framed menus to prove it.

The Fumé Blanc was the winery's "friendship wine," Meisner said. If you liked it, maybe you'd move up to the Chardonnay next. "No matter how much we make of Fumé Blanc, we never have enough." And the more they made, the easier it was to hold that fourteen-dollar price, which was essential. It was, for instance, the least expensive white wine good enough to make it onto the list at Four Seasons in

New York, and when the Four Seasons talks to Meisner it never asks how much it will cost—only if he can guarantee the goods. "We could be getting a lot more for that Fumé Blanc. But we're not going to. My goal is to get the customer to buy ours at fourteen dollars and say, this is better than the other guy's at eighteen dollars. That's called price/value relationship—very important in a competitive industry. Price/value is everything in the consciousness of what is now a great deal of awareness on the part of the average consumer. When I started thirty years ago, it wasn't. Now it's there in spades.

"Line that sums this all up? It's not the *quantity* of distribution that counts when establishing a high-image label; the *quality* of distribution is everything. That's a good quote," Meisner said, pointing his Mark Cross at my notebook to make sure I got it down.

"It's about time for my next cigarette," he said. But first, a point. Steve Meisner was not resting on his laurels. "I go out on the street all the time." He touched his chest: I, me, Steve Meisner himself. "If you lose touch with the street you lose touch with what your competition is doing. Can I give you my whole philosophy? Two phases with every brand. Getting there. Staying there. As difficult as getting there can be, under today's conditions staying there is even more difficult." He frowned. Today's conditions were a cloud on his horizon. "It's more of a battle than it used to be, not what it was before nine eleven."

Los Angeles and Chicago were running ahead, but San Francisco had lost convention business and was slumping. "Especially back East. Restaurants and stores that you knew are gone forever. Everybody's fighting for what remains. So." Deep drag. Don Carano's Box Warrior. "You have to work a little harder. And I'm going to make another statement that's important about this place.

"Decide who you are. And be it."

Grown Men Crying

MARTINI HOUSE IN St. Helena, at the heart of the Napa Valley, is a beautifully designed, place-specific restaurant, both rustic and sophisticated. Because of its location and its pedigree—it was designed by Pat Kuleto, the chef is Todd Humphries—local wineries feel they absolutely must appear on the thirty-six-page wine list.

Only one Ferrari-Carano wine had made it in mid-2002—a Reserve Chardonnay. The Fumé Blanc had not. Michael Ouellette, the wine director and manager, made a Sauvignon Blanc himself—it was, of course, on the list—and he said a white wine faced a tougher marketplace. "There's not enough fear with white wine," he said at nine-thirty on a Wednesday morning as he prepared for the weekly onslaught of desperate producers and distributors. "It's never, 'I didn't get to taste that Sauvignon Blanc and now I missed the boat.' With red wine, your friends say, 'You haven't had the '98 Screaming Eagle? You're kidding me.'

"If you're a winery with a national sales force out there, you're insisting they place their wines in high-profile restaurants in this market. It's your own backyard. People come in, the first thing they look at is the list—to see if they're on it. People stop you on the street—it's a small valley. Every week, there's a new winery. Ten years ago it was every year."

Ouellette is a thin, casually elegant man with a floppy haircut, designer jeans, brown suede shoes, and, at fifty-three, an aching back. As he talked, he was sipping an Odwalla tangerine juice, and casting a snake eye at the blinking red message light on his phone. His tasting room/office—in the part of the restaurant never seen by customers—is six feet by eight feet, with cases and loose wine piled higgledy-piggledy on the linoleum floor.

"This is actually a luxury space," he said. "Look, here's our community spit bucket." The bucket had a Moët and Chandon champagne logo. Taped to the inside of the door was a list of wines that were being eliminated from Martini House. The wine list was updated every week, some wineries dying a little death, others being granted new life.

"Look, here's a wine." Ouellette grabbed a bottle from his cluttered desk. "It was dropped off yesterday, by two women. This is classic—'Hi, we love your restaurant.'" He squinted at the label. "A Tuscan blend—'An intriguing, succulent blend,'" he read. He sighed loudly. "And, look, it's fifty dollars a bottle wholesale—they don't have a rock star winemaker, they don't grow their own grapes. *How* do you come out of the gate like that?"

There were six wines lined up to be tasted this morning, arranged from least to most intense—the earlier in the morning a wine is tried, before Ouellette is tired, or fed up, the better its chances. He held a list of sales reps who had succeeded in getting appointments with him and the Martini House sommelier, Lisa Minucci. "It's very, very difficult to get an appointment," Ouellette said.

"There's only so much wine you can buy. The plethora of producers is bringing you wines made with great skill, but when you look at your list, they're just redundant. How many Carneros Chardonnays do you need?"

Six was the answer, according to the whimsical wine list, which had categories such as Women Winemakers We Love, and Restaurateurs Who Make Wine, which included Ouellette's own Zinfandel and a Kuleto Sangiovese. The list also specified markups—2.5 times the wholesale price for wines under fifty dollars, 2.0 times for more expensive wines. Serving wine requires very little labor compared to preparing food. It doesn't slow down table turnover, as an extra course will. Nor does it add to overhead. Its considerable net is at the core of a fine restaurant's profitability.

The first distributor's rep showed up just before ten, a guy named Jeff. Jeff's appointment was later in the morning, but he'd arrived early—ahead, in fact, of the first scheduled appointment by one of his competitors. A go-getter. Just before he appeared, Ouelette had been saying: "These guys are under so much pressure—they want you to at least taste—then they can say to their wineries, 'I tasted Michael and Lisa.' They're off the hook. They all put their wines in front of your face—sometimes I feel like a French goose. You see them walk through the door with a great big bag, and they know damn well chances are ninety-nine percent they're not going to make your list."

Now, Jeff said, putting down his large case: "I've got a lot—you can just pick through them." He put six bottles on a low stool. Ouellette picked up the first, shook his head no. Tried the second, a Sauvignon Blanc. He sped through the routine: pour, swirl, examine, sniff, spit into the bucket. After his fourth tasting, he said to Jeff, "Can we eliminate some of these?"

"Dude," said Jeff, plaintively, "I waited three months to see you."

"And you have to go back and tell these people," Ouellette said, waving at the open bottles now surrounding Jeff's chair, "that you tried these things on us."

"You know me so well," Jeff said, his attempt at humor tinged with bitterness.

After Jeff, others came and went. Ouellette recorded every wine, left-handed, in a log.

"Of all the wines we tasted," he said, when we were alone again, "the reality is we probably won't buy any. You know, I've seen men come in crying, because if they don't get their wine on our list, they're out of a job."

CHRISTMAS BLUES

ON SUNDAY, DECEMBER 8, the *San Francisco Chronicle* carried a full-page, full-color ad for Cost Plus World Markets, a home-furnishings chain that carried wines in its outlets in twenty-five states. Right there, between a bottle of Bonny Doon Big House Red, and a Renwood Old Vine Zinfandel, was a bottle of Ferrari-Carano Fumé Blanc with its familiar invitationlike label. The price was $11.99. Two dollars under retail.

Meisner had said the whole trick was to decide who you were, and be it. So what was going on?

"I know, I know," Meisner said when I called him. "People see us the first time in Cost Plus and it's, 'Oh Christ, what's going on with Ferrari-Carano?' Cost Plus were taking advantage of something, and we were taking advantage of it, too. And that's something we didn't have to do before."

At Cost Plus headquarters, Mark Albrecht, their national wine buyer, said, "That item is doing really, really well. I wouldn't call it a discount; it's a promotional price." Albrecht said there was funding available from Ferrari-Carano's distributor, Southern Wine and Spirits, to help Cost Plus advertise the promotional price. When he bought one hundred or more cases, he maximized his savings. "We're not a discounter, like Costco," Albrecht continued. But, "going from fourteen dollars retail to that twelve-dollar promotional price has gotten it into a lot of people's hands."

Was that a good thing? Meisner had said that the only thing better than scarcity itself was the image of scarcity, that in a perfect world his winery would make five bottles and sell them for a million bucks apiece. Now here they were in the holidays ad, flying out the door at a place where people shopped for inexpensive Christmas trinkets.

For years, Albrecht said, Cost Plus had sold some Ferrari-Carano wines, however much they could get their hands on, which was not much. "Fumé was always an issue," he said, "but now we're seeing a much better amount. This year it's basically wide open for us. We're scheduled to do fifteen hundred [cases of] Fumé alone, and we'll probably do two thousand. We're definitely seeing that occur with many brands."

Nor was Cost Plus the only shop that was taking advantage of the promotional price. The following week at Trader Joe's, which *is* a discounter, I saw it on the shelf again for $11.99.

Albrecht was happy because never before had there been that much Ferrari-Carano available. "Their total product is not that much," he said.

I asked him to guess at their production.

"The Fumé? I'd probably say thirty thousand. I know their total number of cases is one hundred and fifty thousand." He took a moment to consult his Gomberg-Fredrikson review. "Hunh," he grunted. "Lot of cases." One hundred eighty-five thousand in 2001, according to Gomberg-Fredrikson. "They're getting up there. The consumer still sees them as boutiquey. To their benefit."

But how long could that image be propped up when they were being advertised at a reduced price? Their competitors looked at this, and smelled blood in the water. Bryan Garbutt, who sold Sonoma-Cutrer—the top-selling Chardonnay in restaurants—understood exactly what it meant. "Their on-premises sales are suffering, and they're resorting to Trader Joe's and other places of that ilk to move some inventory. So Trader Joe's is a sign that you've lost your luster. Cost Plus—I've dealt with their buyer—you've got to drop your pants. Sonoma-Cutrer, the day we sell to Trader Joe's we're looking into the grave."

DON AND Rhonda were home in Reno with their families for the holidays, but I asked Don about it early in 2003.

"It's definitely a concern," he said. He seemed tired, but as cordial as ever. We were at the glass-top trestle table in his office. "But you find that, the answer, I think, is that so many knowledgeable wine-drinking people are buying their wines from these establishments. In Cost Plus you can find Lafite, from first growths. And some of the finest California wines. So we're not the Lone Ranger." But in marketing, where perception is reality, Cost Plus was not perceived as a high-end retailer, as Garbutt had made clear, and Don had assured me earlier that insofar as Ferrari-Carano was tilting more toward retail, it was high-end retail. Now he put the best spin he could on the change of strategy forced on Ferrari-Carano by slumping sales.

"Actually, Cost Plus is one of the finest, most aggressive retail outlets in the United States. But that's not our decision to make, that's the distributor. If you say, 'I don't want my wines there,' you'd probably end up with a lawsuit."

What he told me a few minutes later, though, put that concern into perspective. Rhonda had been diagnosed with breast cancer.

Don walked me to my car that afternoon seeming older than I had ever seen him. Those legs that had made him a high school football star—Fast Don Carano—were thinner now. His shoulders appeared to have narrowed. He walked with his hands in his pants pockets, his shoulders hunched. His wife was twenty-two years younger than he was, and he adored her. Words could not directly express such sadness and fear. Don talked instead about his father, who had died when Don was seventeen.

"You know, I saw Seabiscuit race once," he said. "I was just this high. My father loved the ponies. Too much, he gambled too much. He took me to Santa Anita, I saw Seabiscuit in a three-horse race. I like the ponies, too." He laughed at his own folly. "I don't gamble," said the man with a gazillion slot machines, but only one Rhonda. "But I bet on the ponies. I like them, too."

THE GOMBERG, Fredrikson & Associates annual wine industry review is to the business of wine what the census report is to population—the final word. And likely a good deal more accurate. It seemed every time I asked somebody in the trade a question about sales or size, they referred to their copy.

Eileen Fredrikson, who runs the consulting firm with her husband, is a handsome, gracious woman of middle years whose office is in her home on a hillside in Woodside, south of San Francisco. I visited her there in July, and we sat sipping coffee on her large deck, with the Pacific visible in the distance.

Ferrari-Carano, she said, had shipped 185,000 cases of wine in 2001, a number her firm gathered by collecting and analyzing data available from state and federal sources, such as tax records. The number, she explained, was not necessarily identical to production, but very close. As we spoke she held a copy of the review, referring to it.

"Bonny Doon. Simi. Villa Mt. Eden. Same approximate size. There aren't too many as big as they are. Franciscan. Beringer. Murphy Goode." She glanced up from the page. "Just above them you get people like Raymond, generally positioned in much lower price points. It is extremely hard to reach the volume of Ferrari-Carano with the price points of Ferrari-Carano. Robert Mondavi undoubtedly has a number of the same price points, but we call their strategy the halo effect—they build tiers of quality at every price point," while producing millions of cases.

"But at Ferrari-Carano's price point," she said, "there's nobody really exactly like them. Simi is pretty close, but owned by Canandaigua," a subsidiary of the giant Constellation Brands. "Franciscan is very close, but is also a division of Constellation Brands. Raymond is close, but owned by the Japanese. They really have done something unique," she said, the surprise of a discovery in her voice.

So it is not hard to imagine the grim atmosphere at Ferrari-Carano's national sales meeting at the Villa Fiore on December 3, 2002, where the focus, Don later explained to me, was on moving as much product as possible away from slumping restaurants and into retail outlets.

I wanted to attend the sales meeting, but Don refused. Much of what was discussed was proprietary, he said, when the sales staff from around the country came together to plot strategy with their boss, Steve Meisner, the Caranos, George and Steve, and Dave James, the controller. From the mid-1990s up until September 11, 2001, these meetings had been giddy affairs. It was as if they had been harvesting money. They could have charged almost anything they wanted for their wines but had chosen not to price gouge—as they easily could have, and as some wineries did. Like other things of desire, wine was not priced based on the costs of production but on whatever the market would bear. Ferrari-Carano's strategy had always been dependent on offering a high-quality product at a price that allowed restaurants to reap handsome profits. Year after year their Fumé Blanc was among the most frequently poured Sauvignon Blancs nationwide by the glass, which is where restaurants rake in money.

Don told me afterward that at the sales meeting they acknowledged that, after the terrorist attacks, especially in New York, the second-largest market for premium wines, "Everything that Steve [Meisner] and his crew had, in effect, crumbled." Nonetheless, they elected to keep their by-the-case price exactly where it had been. Don refused to divulge the price of a case of Fumé Blanc to the distributor, known as the F.O.B. (freight on board), nor would he tell me what his margin was. "That information potentially has serious implications for us, for our distributors, for our retailers, for our restaurants. And quite frankly, I'm not going to give it to you. It's asking for a lot of consequences we don't need," he said.

I told him I understood, and would try to get that information from other sources.

"Be reasonable," Don said. "Be reasonable."

Other people in the trade had access to the F.O.B. for the 2002 Fumé Blanc, and said it was ninety dollars, as it had been for three years. It was right in the middle of what premium Sauvignon Blancs cost. If Ferrari-Carano succeeded in maintaining a margin of 30 percent, the industry standard, that meant it should have been netting about twenty-seven dollars a case before taxes and operating expenses. A net total close to $2 million.

Ferrari-Carano's overall production, meanwhile, was leaping to its highest point ever in 2002—201,000 cases, up 16,000 from 2001. Much of that growth was because of its abundance of Fumé Blanc. In 2001, it had shipped between 45,000 and 50,000 cases of Fumé; in 2002, that number would be more like 70,000. In part this was simply, as Steve Domenichelli had said, because it had been a great grow-ing year. But it was also the fruit of a strategic marketing decision. Given their escalating operating expenses as they expanded into the hillsides in pursuit of Don's dream of a ninety-nine-rated wine, to hold the fourteen-dollar retail price that was so important to them for the Fumé they had to increase production.

Virtually every bottle of the 2001 vintage had been allocated, that is, bought by a distributor. That was because, Meisner explained to me, he and the salespeople gathered in December for their annual meeting had been "nimble" in shifting their strategy into greater retail sales. He had provided incentives for his salespeople, such as restaurant meals and trips to the Villa Fiore, if they met their goals. The sales force had been authorized to offer their distributors the kind of inducements they needed to implement this change in direction. But promotional and marketing costs—incentives, again—rose, he said, by one dollar a case.

"In the past we did not encourage this kind of thing," Meisner said. "It's simple—where it's legal, we offer a discount. You get a ten per-cent discount if you buy three cases. The distributor benefits from part of that, we benefit from part of that." The more a restaurant buys, the bigger the discount. And if a restaurant buys a lot, it is likely to feature the wine by offering it by the glass. In California, by-the-glass sales remained strong.

Every state had different laws, but the big markets mattered most. In New York, getting the quality of distribution they wanted was al-ways something of a problem; they had already changed distributor-ships once, and would soon change again. Southern Wines & Spirits was a national powerhouse that distributed Ferrari-Carano in Florida as well as California. In an industry in flux after the breakup of Sea-gram's, Southern had real clout, very important to any winery. Many restaurants relied on the advice of their wholesaler in building their wine lists.

"They've got a beautiful thing going," says Jack Brennan, the Northern California vice president and general manager for Southern. "Times are tough but not too tough for Ferrari-Carano. They're almost exempt from it, because they're so much in demand. We're very close partners. We meet with them monthly, take it right down to accounts. They understand their role, and understand the wholesaler's role properly. They are the best; they go to market as good as anybody."

Don was monitoring the operation of his Box Warrior closer than ever before. Allocated wines flowed from the winery to the distributorship, and from there to retail shops and restaurants, month after month—a steady, uninterrupted stream. With Fumé Blanc in particular, a wine that is meant to be drunk when it is young and vibrant, it is crucially important to make sure one year's allocation is sold out before the next year's arrives in May or June. They were staying in profit, Don said, but their net had sunk. Nonetheless, he preferred offering discounts to lowering their F.O.B.

What Don had told his salespeople at the Villa Fiore in early December 2002, while the baby 2002 Fumé Blanc was still in barrels and tanks, was to focus on "quality. Quality, quality, quality. The good price/value relationship perceived by the consumer, the retailer, and the restaurant."

In January 2003, Meisner sent his guys back out to do battle in the marketplace armed with everything he and Don could give them. "You can't tell the distributor what profit to take, that's illegal," Meisner explained. "And you don't tell the retailer how to promote, that is legally prohibited. We never say to distributors—this is what you *have* to do. We say—this is what we think [would work], what do you think? My guys did that after I provided them guidelines in December. My guys only deal with distributors. But key players, like Julian Niccolini at the Four Seasons, Bob McGinn," the Northeast regional manager, "he knows those people."

Indeed McGinn visits key clients regularly. As do Don and Rhonda and George, who go on the road several times a year to keep up those personal connections. Distributors and restaurateurs love that personal attention. And they in turn are wined and dined at the Villa, and suitably impressed with Ferrari-Carano as well as their own importance. The marketing is seamless and relentless.

Bob McGinn would fly back to New York and visit the Four Seasons, or the Palm Court at the Plaza Hotel, and let them know that, "our distributor has a special deal on Fumé," Meisner says, but the distributor's rep is the one who would take the order. "All my regional managers are totally professional. Crux of why we were successful? Understanding what distributors and the trade needed. Doing it quickly."

McGinn himself would put it slightly differently a few months later over a seventy-five-dollar brunch at the Palm Court, where the 2002 Fumé was receiving its vintage debut. Distributors, he said, respond to two things. "First, make the product profitable for them. Second, do I have a lot of inventory? That's why it's so important to make sure they have enough product. Those are the two main factors. Distributors respond to greed and fear."

5

WINE

February 2003–March 2003

ROMANCE

ANDREW LEVI HAD a cold; his eyes were red and matched his hair. The assistant winemaker had just returned from his parents' home in Kansas City and was experiencing a transformation known to many California emigrants: When he left Kansas City now, after a visit, it felt as if he was headed home.

We were walking along a catwalk high in the barrel room, watching as the Fumé Blanc was racked for the last time—consolidated into stainless-steel tanks prior to the blending and final tasting. The tile floor of the warehouse, packed with barrels stacked six levels high, was damp, and the room smelled yeasty. Steam rose toward the rafters. In the distance but out of sight were voices, a lot of voices, suggesting just how labor-intensive it was to make a bottle of wine.

"I call this place the Death Star, from *Star Wars*; you can see above and below," Andrew said. "It's really called Location 9. Very romantic."

He dipped a stainless-steel straw with a tiny window through the bunghole of a barrel to be sure that the lees, the heavy solids saturated with carbon dioxide—mostly exhausted yeast cells—had sunk to the bottom. It took four minutes for each barrel to be emptied, the air pump making its familiar *thwump thwump thwump*. As the barrel emptied, the carbon dioxide expanded, keeping out air that could cause oxidation, ensuring that the wine was fresh.

They had begun to rack the wine into the tanks on February 3, nearly five months after it went into barrels, still keeping each block intact. It was going to take nine days to complete the transfer. Then the lees left behind in the bottoms of the barrels would be filtered to extract the last remaining drops of wine.

The finished wine had yet to be blended, and was still no more than a sensory imagining in George's mind. But in 2002, as in every year, Ferrari-Carano's reputation, and thus its success, was on the line. Soon *Wine & Spirits* would release its annual restaurant poll—"50 Most Popular Wines in America's Favorite Restaurants" read the cover copy—and among Sauvignon Blancs, the 2001 Ferrari-Carano Fumé would rank second in sales only to Cakebread Cellars. On menus it sold for an average per-bottle price of $34.50, $11.43 less than the Cakebread—but somewhat higher than in 2000, according to the magazine. In total restaurant sales, Ferrari-Carano would rank seventh among all American wineries, trailing Kendall-Jackson, Cakebread, Sonoma-Cutrer, Jordan, Robert Mondavi, and Sterling. Its ranking had slipped two notches in a year.

Meisner's perpetual frown was even deeper than usual. His people, he said, were hitting their numbers—he did not say how much of the product was showing up at Trader Joe's and its like—but it was harder than ever, and the net would be down again. Even though there was more product to be moved than ever before, the Box Warrior claimed he was close to being fully allocated. As if there wasn't enough pressure on him, he had slipped onboard Don and Rhonda's company yacht, the *Eldorado*, while entertaining customers in Newport Beach, and was wearing a splint on his broken thumb. "He's a bundle of nerves," said Deep Cork. "There's astronomical pressure on him. He doesn't get a great deal of liking, or appreciation, but the brand exists because of him and his salespeople. He's the one who has to listen to the price point Don sets, and then go and sell the volume. That's bottom-line stuff, the scariest stuff in the whole business."

Setting prices was done in concert. Like perfume, another thing of desire, the wine industry supported a range of prices not always related to the quality of what was in the bottle. Deep Cork described how it was done at Ferrari-Carano: Meisner said what he could sell a bottle for, then Dave James, the controller, would say how the bottom line looked at that price point. But in the end it was always Don and Rhonda who made the final decisions behind closed doors, and nobody else knew exactly what their dynamic was. Their closeness and loyalty made others marvel. People referred to them, not without affection, as "Donda."

A more visible dynamic involved the four princes of the realm— Steve Domenichelli, George Bursick, Steve Meisner, and Dave James—and their monarch. Meisner felt he had built the brand single-handedly. Steve thought the quality of his farming practices and the fruit they produced were paramount. George was the highest paid, and the most visible star. Quiet Dave James, meanwhile, held the keys to Don's treasure—he was the man who knew the monarch's most closely guarded secrets. Don's gift was to keep them all in harness and in relative harmony, to make each of them feel valued and appreciated, just as he had managed that even more difficult feat at the casinos in Reno with his five grown children.

Nothing amid all these tensions ever came close to threatening the central relationship of Don and Rhonda. Don was grave and chivalric about his wife, always. He never failed to emphasize that what Rhonda brought to the table was the essence of their success.

"What we're selling," he once said to me, "is a lifestyle."

"Wine country lifestyle," Rhonda said, taking her cue from her husband. For example, she continued: "Gardens are very natural in this area; why not incorporate it in a gracious way of living?" Their ads were precisely targeted, not scattershot, Don explained. In a gourmet magazine like *Saveur,* they emphasized wine and food, how Rhonda's recipes and pairing tips were available on their Web site, where customers were also invited to join their Circle of Friends. In *Wine Spectator,* the wines were paramount, specifically the Chardonnay and Fumé Blanc. In *House & Garden* the beauty of the property was front and center.

You were not welcome at the Villa Fiore, however, if you arrived on a tourist bus. Buses were barred from the Ferrari-Carano property on Dry Creek Road, as they were from any number of upscale wineries. People on tour buses weren't likely to buy an expensive bottle of wine, and selling wine at full retail through the tasting room was much more profitable than selling to a distributor. In addition, the presence of bargain tour buses would clash with the ambiance, The Story.

"People have this mystique about wine country, we just sit out in the gardens eating wonderful food, drinking wonderful wine," Rhonda said. "To me, when people come here, if they can experience that lifestyle even for a minute . . ."

"Seventy-five thousand people taste wine here every year," Don interjected.

"Oh, no," Rhonda said. "More than that. A hundred and fifty thousand plus."

More tourists came every year to see the stunning hills and valleys of Napa and Sonoma counties than visited Disneyland—which might help to explain why Prohibition was a short-lived failure. But the tourism brought with it overcrowding, the consumption of fossil fuels, and the degradation of air quality in the bucolic valleys. I wondered how the wineries got away with boozing people up at free tastings, then sending them out onto the roads of Napa and Sonoma counties to wreak what carnage they might. Clearly, the local sheriffs could not afford Breathalyzers.

Rhonda was a hardworking businesswoman, who was sincere about what she was selling: It was, when all was said and done, the realized dream of her own experience. That sincerity, both about the product and The Story, was the hallmark of Don and Rhonda's marriage of talents. "Our Story, the time was right. I really believe that. I really do," Rhonda said. "Wine to me is not commercial; wine is romantic. Wine is experience."

Experience was exacting its losses and sorrows, as it always does. Although the cancer had been detected in only one breast, and early, she elected to undergo a double mastectomy. The surgery was performed in early March, and the initial prognosis was excellent. The malignancy had not been invasive and she looked to be in the clear. The relief in Don's voice when he told me—he was nearly whispering—was palpable.

FAT MID-PALATE

FOR GEORGE, BLENDING was pure enjoyment. It was where his exquisite palate came to the forefront, where his powers served him best, where he was most fully an artist. His talent for blending—white wines especially—was also why he had his job.

Don and Rhonda returned from Europe in 1983 having decided that unlike the French, who made wines from single, designated vineyards, they wanted to grow grapes under myriad conditions, then blend them to take advantage of the variety at their disposal. They would need a winemaker who approached things that same way. Don once again turned to the late Justin Meyer of Silver Oak to help him. Meyer produced three candidates, all of them qualified. "Really," he told Don, "it's a question of who you have the best chemistry with."

Don met first with George, who was making wine at McDowell, a small Mendocino County winery of no particular fame. Meyer and Don rode up to Hopland to meet George, taste his wines, and talk. Then George came down to the Alexander Valley several times. Don and Rhonda and George talked shop; the Caranos were assessing what kind of impression George would make on customers. Your wine-maker is your most visible employee; he or she must market as well as make. Don thought George had a wonderful way with words, express-ing himself in great detail but in a way that was easy to understand. The Caranos never bothered to interview the other two candidates.

George had been with them ever since, although he was not lack-ing for other opportunities. Now and again another winery would make a run at him. A wine business headhunter who tried to pry George loose says, "We didn't ever get to serious dating. George is a risk-averse personality, and his ego's under control. A lot of wine-makers are totally whacko. And their egos!"

The headhunter estimated that George is paid five hundred thou-sand dollars plus perks annually. But pay, said the headhunter, is the fifth and last thing winemakers usually care about. The first four are: ownership with plenty of money, the equipment and personnel he needs, the freedom to do the best work he can, and owners who are dedicated to the quality of the finished product. George had all that.

On a mid-January morning, George sat down in his tasting room to continue the process of making the 2002 Fumé Blanc. Don had asked him to think about making a 2002 Fumé Blanc Reserve, a limited-production wine that some years they bottled and some years they did not. His primary purpose this morning was to see which lots might lend themselves to the Reserve, a different style of wine that they would re-barrel in new oak. But this was also an opportunity to assess the progress of all the different lots that were eventually going to be blended into the regular Fumé. "Everything's settled down," George said, "started shedding their baby fat, started showing their true character."

There had been one minor disappointment: They weren't getting as much malolactic fermentation as they had hoped for; they just couldn't get it to take off in the tanks. But that was okay, George said, you worked with what you were given. The Fumé was not supposed to be cushy like a Chardonnay, anyway, but racy. So the loss of the additional softening the malolactic might have provided was not irreparable.

Joining George were his assistant, Andrew Levi, and Amy Kelsey, the enologist. It was the artistry of the process that attracted Amy, although she had been hired as a technician because she had a biology degree from Princeton. At twenty-eight, she had done hummingbird research in the Andes and performed on the London stage. She resembled the actress Emma Thompson, with a long, pale, empathetic face, and straight brown hair.

Amy had been just passing through, and that allowed her to be candid in a way that her friend Andrew could not afford to be. "Andrew didn't have very much respect for George," Amy said when we talked a year later, after she had departed from Ferrari-Carano to attend medical school. "He was frustrated because George wasn't teaching him anything, and Andrew really wanted a mentor."

The three of them had developed a shorthand working together, a common vocabulary. George always listened to Andrew and Amy's views, but in the end he made the decisions.

They sat at a mid-sized conference table, Amy and Andrew facing George. There were windows on two walls that, like the window in George's office along the corridor, overlooked a barrel storage area. The room was decorated with testaments to success: White House menus from state dinners where Ferrari-Carano Chardonnay was poured, and a framed copy of that 1987 *Wine Spectator* cover that had made George a star and validated Don's choice.

For the Reserve, George explained, they wanted a wine with a strong floral, or honeysuckle, quality. In front of each of them, and me as well, were eight glasses, each with a quarter-inch or so of the cloudy, grapefruit-colored Sauvignon Blanc. The wine was between fifty-five and sixty degrees, not so cold as to suppress its full aromas. They began to taste them one at a time, remaining quiet, concentrating as they took notes. George wrote on a legal pad with a Ticonderoga #2 pencil. He picked up a glass, held it up to look at the wine; swirled it to lift aromas and flavors toward the surface; stuck his nose into the glass and sniffed; sipped, letting the wine linger in his mouth; and spat into a white plastic cup. They repeated this ritual eight times apiece, George very nearly chewing the wine in his mouth. Then they did it all over again.

They were using Riedel stemware, of the same quality a white-tablecloth restaurant would eventually use to serve the Fumé. And also, all three of them assured me, because wine tasted better in high-quality glass—that's what most oenophiles believed. There was no proof that the quality or shape of the glass changed the chemistry of the wine, but it did change the setting and the context in which the wine was held, and thus perhaps the perception.

Amy spoke first.

"I think it's showing well," she said.

"I do, too," George agreed.

Amy began: "Really starting to—"

George completed her thought: "—settle in. They're all in the herbal camp."

"That first one is total pineapple," Amy observed.

"Really something fun going on with that," George said. "The next-to-last one really smells like dill weed. Although I smothered my green beans in dill last night."

Ferrari-Carano raised about 95 percent of its own grapes, and was moving toward 100 percent, but they still had some unexpired contracts with growers, including one hundred tons of Sauvignon Blanc grapes from McDowell, George's old employer. That was glass number five.

Glass number two was from Keegan, Block 9.

"That's racy," said George.

Andrew consulted his notes. "I actually had that, too. Something wild."

"I really liked it," Amy agreed.

"That's good," said George. "Because we've got a lot of it."

"Number three is Keegan Eight," said Andrew.

"Citrusy," said Amy.

George said, "Real tight. Focused. Nose subdued. Just kind of hunkered down."

A while later, Amy commented that they had "such a good arc this year. A few grassy, a few tropical, a few varietal." The varietals were from their coldest vineyard. A lot of vegetable tastes and aromas, they said, and very little fruit.

"This is for the purists," said Andrew. "There are people who would only like number four and number eight; they're the only two that are very varietal," he explained to me. "If you don't have that, you don't have any hint of Sauvignon Blanc."

Yet those were my least favorite in the flight we had tasted. My friends John Storey and Eric Luse are partners in a small winery, Eric Ross, in Sebastopol. John had told me that the best and most truly varietal Sonoma Sauvignon Blanc was made by Rochioli. He liked its acidity and crispness, and thought it went well with food. It was almost impossible to find in shops. But one day I drove many miles up a winding country road to the winery, where I was able to talk the lady in Rochioli's tasting room into selling me two bottles— one per customer was the limit (that all-important image of scarcity). It cost about twice as much as Ferrari-Carano Fumé Blanc. When I drank it, I thought it was almost sour. But the differences were apparent; the Fumé was so sweet and round and tricked out it seemed far more commercial. Of course, what commercial means is appealing to popular taste, to an untrained palate like mine, a Babbitt's palate.

But that was precisely what bothered Amy about George's winemaking. "George is a fun guy in many ways, and a good boss to work for," she would say. But her opinion was, "He's limited as a winemaker—because he's really consumed with the newest technology, consumed with the word 'trick.' He would put his absolute faith in something not tested at all, because it was the newest thing. Like lees freeze—basically, while you're stirring the barrels, part of the idea is to agitate dead yeast cells into the wine to increase mouth feel. We had been throwing around all sorts of ways to accelerate that process, all the ways you could get the cells to burst without stirring. Freezing will cause the fluid inside to expand and break up the cell. So we froze the lees with dry ice, and returned it to the wine. It was biologically plausible. But most wineries with an idea like that will do a small experiment, then evaluate it a year later—be cautious and conservative. George jumped on it because it was a new technique, decided it worked, and applied it to every lot of Chardonnay in the winery."

A year down the road, Amy says, "So far, there's been no ill effects. This kind of thing happened all the time because George was so consumed with getting a jump on everybody else, to the detriment of basic, sound, traditional winemaking. You know, people have been doing this for thousands of years. Sometimes the simple, hands-off approach is best. Not always. But that's George's style—he really wanted to *make* the wine. It broke my heart—he'd keep manipulating it until it lost its soul—I know 'soul' is malarkey, but sometimes he bludgeoned wines to death. That's George's fatal flaw. He couldn't keep his hands off the wine."

At the tasting, though, George was considerate and thoughtful—trying to help me understand not only his technique, but also his purpose.

"We want the final blend," George said, "to be recognizable, as knowledgeable people understand it. We want this wine to be delicious, and for us, it's primarily going to be sold by the glass in restaurants, so it's an introduction to Ferrari-Carano wines. The craving for a second glass is very important to us." His goal was not to please purists.

He explained that some of their grapes had an aggressive vegetative taste he called "bell pepper." George said that the bell pepper quality was imparted by a specific chemical compound, methoxypyrazine. "It's amazing what a chameleon grapes can be. It's not that it tastes *like* bell pepper, or asparagus, or melon, or whatever. It's that the grapes have *formed* that chemical compound. The grape is the only fruit that mimics other flavors."

There was a brief interruption before the second flight of eight glasses, while George made some arrangements for Joey Costanzo to prepare a box lunch he was going to bring over to Marlene Ing's house after the tasting. Marlene had just completed her last round of chemotherapy, and was not faring well.

"There are," Andrew said, "a lot of heavy hearts."

It must have been especially difficult for Rhonda, who worked so closely with Marlene. Marlene's cancer had begun in her breast, as Rhonda's had, but had metastasized. But I also wondered what effect those heavy hearts had on what George, Andrew, and Amy were tasting. We all know that food and wine tastes best on festive occasions; when we're in the dumps, our appreciation is blunted. Were these three people able to disregard such emotional considerations because they were skilled professionals doing their jobs?

While Amy was setting up the second flight of wines to be tasted, George left to talk to an auto dealer because he was thinking about buying a new BMW to replace his SUV. When he came back, the three of us were trying to decide what word best described the color of a wall that was covered in suede.

"Fuchsia," George said, jumping in.

"It speaks of Rhonda," Andrew said. "A pink suede wallpaper. That's Rhonda Carano, right there."

"It speaks," George said, "of Raul Rodriguez and Rose Bowl floats. Are you writing that down?" he said to me, aghast that I was taking notes.

When they resumed the tasting, they decided that for the 2002 Fumé Blanc Reserve they would blend one lot from the vineyard at Don and Rhonda's home in Geyserville with a second lot from Carinalli.

"Shoot from the hip and do seventy-five percent and twenty-five percent," George instructed. Amy fetched a glass container, called a graduated cylinder, measured out the two wines, poured them into a beaker, and swirled.

"Nice body on that!" Andrew exclaimed after tasting it. "See, that's what blending gives us."

George said, "You might even want to try ninety-ten." They did, and then Amy suggested adding 5 percent from a third vineyard for its aroma.

"That's pretty," George said. "I like where we're going with it. We're trying to keep it crisp and fresh and lively. Descriptions of flavors are fun, but the importance of these tastings is to look for strengths and weaknesses. I care less if it tastes like grapefruit or apricot."

"The flavors are fleeting," Amy explained. "And will change in a year."

"I do care," George said, "if the finish is long or short." In other words, if it lingered in your mouth. "And how it feels in your mouth." It could be buttery or acidic.

"It's got a fat mid-palate," Amy said. There was a pause, then we all laughed.

"No," said Amy, "that's a good thing."

Rough Deal

MARLENE ING DIED in the springtime, just as the 2002 Fumé Blanc was about to go into the last shipment of bottles she had purchased.

A few weeks earlier, Don had driven to Clearlake to say goodbye. Rhonda hadn't come; it was too much—like looking at a nightmare version of what might become of her. At fifty-two, Marlene Ing had been only about four years older than Rhonda. So Don went alone. As Pat Kuleto said, "He's got the right name, Don. All his people are treated like family."

He sat at Marlene's bedside, and did his best to comfort her. "Goddamn, Marlene, I need those figures by four o'clock," Don said, his mock anger a way to lift the spirits of the dying woman.

The night before Marlene's funeral, Don had an attack of vertigo, not for the first time. The cause baffled his doctor, although he suspected it might have something to do with the Ambien Don took for his insomnia, and how it combined with vitamins and wine. Don would stop taking the Ambien—he didn't sleep well even with its help. Nor did Rhonda, who also suffered from insomnia. But Don's attack on the eve of Marlene's funeral was scary enough so that at three in the morning Rhonda brought him to the hospital. He spent the entire day there, Rhonda sitting with him.

THE CHRISTENING of Boa's daughter, his fourth child, had come off without a hitch. In El Charco it was a happy time of year. The men were home for winter, their pockets stuffed full of money, and they set to making more babies. In his house in the upper part of the village, painted a jolly red and green, it was now Boa and his second wife Flor and their two daughters, and Flor's fourteen-year-old daughter from her first marriage, Lillia.

There were only two problems. First, it was the anniversary of when Boa had run his truck into a boulder, killing his young wife and their son, Arturo—an anniversary better forgotten than remembered. But Flor didn't want her husband to forget. That was what the men would say later, in the months to follow. Now more than ever, with a new baby in the house, she told him that he drank too much for his own good, that he could accidentally kill her and their children, too.

The second problem was that he had fallen for Flor's daughter, Lillia.

At Christmas, Lillia broke it off with her stepfather—that was what everybody heard. Boa went out with some buddies on the night of December 27 and got a huge heat on; they had to carry him into his house. He and Flor got into it. Boa went for his gun. He staggered back out to his truck. Flor heard two gunshots and began to scream, but was too scared to go outside.

It was one of René Ruiz's brothers who came and saw what Boa had done, then called the police. He didn't stick around to talk to them: A *campesino* in Guanajuato State did not want to be involved with the police.

Not many men attended Boa's funeral in El Charco. René thought it was a bad thing that his friend had done, leaving Flor widowed for the second time, with children to feed and no means of support. On the day of Boa's funeral, René found he had something else to do.

Back in Healdsburg, Steve was distressed to hear the news. "He was a jokester, a prankster, and honest good guy," Steve said. "Oh, shit, you know I worked side by side with that guy for so long, he was seventeen, eighteen when I first met him and I was fifteen, sixteen."

As the *campesinos* returned from their homes and families in El Charco, they brought with them an evolving version of what had driven Boa to take his own life. More emphasis was now being placed on his ineluctable sadness on the anniversary of the deaths of his first wife and their son. He had been drinking when he crashed and killed them, and blamed himself for their deaths, so he drank more to forget—a cycle no less heartbreaking for being familiar. René had taken up a collection, and everybody had chipped in to help out Boa's widow and remaining children, workers and bosses alike. Steve gave one hundred dollars. "A rough deal," he said.

Rafael Paniagua Gonzales, dead by his own hand at thirty-six. Cause of death—loving all the wrong things.

MOMENT OF TRUTH

"MOMENT OF TRUTH," said Andrew Levi.

Amy Kelsey left the tasting room and went along the corridor. "George," she said. "We're ready."

The morning had begun with Amy pulling wine from twenty-three different tanks, the fruit of six vineyards where Sauvignon Blanc grapes were grown: Estate, Stang, Beverly Hills, Carinalli, Storey Creek, and Keegan. Altogether they had harvested 1,288 tons of Sauvignon Blanc grapes, which had been turned into nearly two hundred thousand gallons of wine, thirty-four thousand gallons of it from Keegan Ranch. Block 9 alone, Tim Keegan's old orchard, had yielded about seventeen thousand gallons. A lot of wine. It took Amy a number of trips back and forth from the lab to the tanks, each time carrying a wandlike thief and a tray with six plastic beakers. She lowered the thief as deeply as she could, snaring a few ounces from each of the thirty-foot-high, ten-thousand-gallon tanks.

When all twenty-three beakers were set up on the conference table, Amy took out her calculator, and Andrew began to blend the

241

separate blocks based on her calculations. They were blending a total of six hundred milliliters, an amount from each block proportionally equivalent to all they had in tanks.

"Eighteen mils of seven-oh-seven," Amy said, consulting her calculator. The tank number was 707. Andrew carefully measured the eighteen milliliters, pouring it into the collection beaker.

"Six mils of nine-oh-two."

Until, at last, the twenty-three lots were blended.

In a perfect world this would become a default procedure. There would be no lot that failed to meet their standards, and thus needed to be sold in bulk to buyers who blended cheap wines like Two Buck Chuck. Trader Joe's, the discount chain, would sell 2 million cases of the $1.99-per-bottle wine in 2002. Two Buck Chuck represented yet another economic assault on premium wines. When I had told Don that I found Two Buck Chuck Chardonnay drinkable, his face registered denial and dismay. At a loss for words, he shook his head in disbelief.

Ferrari-Carano had bulked out lots before. But if all went well today, everything grown by Steve and his men not only would be good enough to market under the Ferrari-Carano name, but would also balance tastes and aromas in proportions that characterized their Fumé Blanc. This was the first moment when they would actually taste what they had—not the discrete components they had sampled up until now, but the blend itself, the end product of Don's acumen, Steve's roots, Boa and Jaime's labor, George's wizardry.

Now George came into the room looking positively ill and sat down without a word.

Andrew said, "I always hate this. It's for all the marbles. The moment of anticipation."

In front of each of them was a single, long-stemmed Riedel Sauvignon Blanc glass about one-third full of the still-cloudy, still-young, still-evolving 2002 Fumé Blanc. George lifted his stemware and observed the wine. He was caught in the grip of one of life's decisive moments, a moment for which he had long prepared. He might have been a midwife, or an executioner—that's how pale he was.

He swirled the liquid in the glass, watching it. He thrust his nose deep into the glass and sniffed. At last he tasted it, mulling it over in his sensitive mouth. Then he raised his other hand to his forehead, as if to cover his face, a gesture of thoughtfulness. Or despair?

He looked up and spoke. "Almost, like, a little apricot coming through," he said. "Peach?"

Andrew said, "Yeah, something like that."

George nodded. "It's a keeper," he said, and the tension in the room burst. Everybody was talking at once.

"It's pretty long," said Amy. "Keeps on coming."

"It's going to benefit from being in the cold," Andrew said. "Open up."

"You get a little alcohol," George said. "Just in the finish. Pretty hot. It causes a little evaporation on your taste buds." When finally bottled, the wine would be 13.7 percent alcohol. One thing George never mentioned to me was de-alcoholization, which was becoming an increasingly common practice, and one, according to someone who worked for the Caranos, that Ferrari-Carano used when necessary. Through a process of reverse osmosis, the alcohol content—at high sugar levels, such as those George had insisted on this year—could be reduced before it damaged the cell walls in the yeast. Of course, de-alcoholization was anti-Story, and so hush-hush.

Even though Sauvignon Blanc was one of Ferrari-Carano's easier wines to blend, far easier than the reds that contained five or six different varieties of grapes, the process would still take weeks. George would be taking a bottle home with him every night, drinking and thinking. He would never be entirely satisfied. It was a matter of coming to grips with his own limitations, as anyone who did creative work could tell you. George and the others tried to control everything they could, from planting to harvesting to fermenting. Along the way they had made an untold number of decisions. But at last George reached a point—this very point—where he had to say to himself, *this is the best I can do.*

"But you always want to take one last shot," George said, laughing loudly and spontaneously at his own expense. "And sometimes I do."

The excitement in the tasting room was rising.

"Yeah. This seems to be correct—where we're going," George said. "Got the varietal snap to it. Then there's that citrusy, melony thing in the background."

"It's in our style," Andrew said.

"Damn good," George said. "You see, Mike," he said, turning to me, "if you treat every lot like your best, there shouldn't be any surprises."

Ah, but there were always surprises. George knew that. Don had just surprised him by letting him know that he was hiring a consultant winemaker for the hillside reds, a Frenchman named Philippe Melka, who was two decades George's junior, and the hottest winemaker going. At the Napa wine auction, a filthy-rich Texan had paid $1 million to have Melka make him three hundred cases of Cabernet Sauvignon.

Don had told George about Melka with the utmost tact. Don said that once you reached a certain size, there was a danger of quality suffering; he did not point out that that was contrary to what George had maintained from the beginning. But the hillside operation was so important—there was not only going to be a gravity-flow winery up there, but also a new name for that winery and a new label. It was asking too much of George to do all of that, Don said; the geographic considerations alone were daunting.

The truth was, Don had banked all his hopes and remaining aspirations on those reds. He would not, *could* not, spare any effort. George, of course, Don said, would remain the ultimate supervisor. But the reds would benefit from Melka's ideas as well. He did not say that George seemed better at white wines than at reds. But some people at Ferrari-Carano believed that to be true.

"George was getting pushed aside, and put on the less important programs," Amy Kelsey said later. "Most people consider reds a higher position, and red winemakers are better looked upon. At this point in his career, it was George who should have been making the hillside Cabernets.

"It was a slap in the face, and very difficult for Don," she said. "And embarrassing for George. I feel sorry for George. In many ways he's really an endearing guy."

Naturally George was upset, as Don knew he would be. George was sensitive, and Don knew George had a tendency to undervalue himself, didn't always appreciate how truly good he was. Don did his best to soften the blow, but in the end also had to tell him there would be yet another new winemaker working with Melka, an even younger man named Aaron Potter. And within a short time, Andrew Levi, seeking to learn more than he felt George could teach him, received Don's permission to work under the new men.

Melka himself was the soul of tact—he was a Frenchman, after all—with a Gallic nose, and a slight, unintimidating presence. In conversation with Melka, Don had come to the conclusion that what Melka would bring to the hillside vineyards, and the red blends, was exactly what he needed.

"My style, how I'm recognized, is to show through the wine the site," Melka would say when I spoke to him at Quintessa, one of several small, prestigious vineyards where he was a consulting winemaker on bottles that cost $110. "To respect as much as I can the grapes. I'm working very much to show the estate," he continued. Then he added something that George would not have enjoyed hearing: "You have to minimize as much as you can the technique, the winemaking, if you like. The science side—so basically, really, with no numbers, making wine with intuition. I didn't do Davis—I did Bordeaux."

But no surprises for George, thank goodness, in the 2002 Fumé. Or none George would talk about with me in the room.

"I could drink that," George said, touching his glass. "Let's do it."

It was a huge weight off his shoulders. They were going to use everything they had harvested. A perfect world, in that respect at least. That was a special accomplishment, and George gave credit where it was due.

"We owe it to Steve and the guys," he said. "They work so hard."

THE WINE now needed to be blended, and heat- and cold-stabilized. A wine sold at this price would not be bought exclusively by oenophiles who treated a bottle as if it were a precious, only child. At $11.99 in Trader Joe's, folks who just wanted something nice to drink were buying it.

"Ideally you wouldn't have to do anything to it," Amy explained. "But the bigger you get, the more you have to prepare for. The fact that someone leaves it in the trunk of their car in summer—so it has to be heat-stable. Or in the fridge for a month—so it's got to be cold-stable." I thought: *You mean I'm not supposed to do that?*

But, by and large, the wine was 95 percent there, and as it sat in the tank, and then in the bottle, only good things would happen to it—it would round into shape. Or so they hoped.

It was due to be bottled beginning around the end of March, and to be on the road to distributors on May 1, its release date. Meisner was champing at the bit. His customers were running out of the 2001, and he wanted to get the 2002 into their hands. His whole philosophy: getting there, staying there.

"This is a wine with a lot of expectations. Just because of the market share we own of this varietal, we're a major player," George said. "This time next year, this will be gone. And you'll lose this fresh, vibrant, exciting flavor pretty soon. It mellows out. It's still good, it's still Fumé Blanc, but you lose the vibrancy. When it ages, the molecules combine and you get a deintensified aroma. The real appeal of this wine is to get it to jump out of the frigging glass."

But what of the Reserve Fumé Blanc that they been blending since January? In the end, George told me, he and Don had decided not to make a Reserve in 2002. It was a curious decision, considering the lake of Sauvignon Blanc they had available. "Our best lots were going there," George said. "We didn't want to put five, six thousand gallons of our really top-end stuff there."

It was something they had done in the past. What was different this year?

"Because the regular Fumé is so popular, we decided we didn't want to sacrifice quality."

Amy put it less tactfully: "We were pleased with the quality of our top lots," she said. "There were only so many of those. If you took that away, you were left with crap."

It was unclear how truly confident they were about the 2002 Fumé having come back from its drift toward an aggressively vegetative style. The lots that might have gone into the Reserve were those that were the fruitiest and sweetest—or honeysuckle, as they called it. Over the next few weeks everybody—Don, Rhonda, George, Andrew—made a point of telling me this vintage was their best in a long time, that they had wholly succeeded. I took that as one part public relations, one part reassuring themselves. But soon they would make another decision that, when combined with deciding they could not spare even five thousand outstanding gallons out of two hundred thousand, seemed to indicate a certain nervousness about how good their wine was.

Big Bertha

BIG BERTHA HELD forty thousand gallons. So if you had something like two hundred thousand gallons—exactly what Hoss Milone did have—you ran sub-blends in and out of Bertha five times, then measured out proportional amounts of every sub-blend. It would take a month from barrel to bottle.

"Final blend in Bertha," Hoss said, a few days after George had green-lighted the Fumé Blanc, as we stood beside a ten-thousand-gallon, ice-encrusted stainless-steel tank. "She comes out, she goes to these smaller tanks." Altogether, he had 165 tanks of various sizes. "Then she goes through heat and cold stabilization, is what it's called. Both done at the same time. Heat is bentonite clay, otherwise known as food-grade dirt," he explained. In addition to protecting the wine against extended exposure to a parking lot in Miami in August, the bentonite removed any remaining haze, leaving the wine clear. "We slurry the bentonite up with the wine itself—pump it over the top of the wine, and mix it in. The bentonite's pretty heavy; it attracts protein, falls to the bottom. That's actually part of the lees.

"We top the tank up, set the thermostat to twenty-four degrees, and walk away," Hoss said. "Can't freeze because of the alcohol in there." When Hoss turned down the temperature, jackets of ice formed on the exterior walls of the tanks. The chill precipitated the remaining tartaric acid from the wine onto the inner wall of the tank, which eventually looked like Carlsbad Caverns. Cold stabilization was a purely aesthetic precaution. Because it had been cold-stabilized, when some unknowing fool like me kept the wine in the fridge for a month, unsightly crystals wouldn't form in the bottle.

George and Hoss consulted many times every day. There were fifteen different varietals and blends at some stage of the winemaking process to talk about. But after twelve years together, Hoss said, "It's to the point where I know what he wants, and what he needs, and, you know, I just get it done."

Amy Kelsey had a different view of their relationship. "George was afraid of Hoss," she said. "I don't think he liked him, but he liked having him around. I think Hoss was a terrible manager; he was a bully. And George looked the other way. George would say, 'He gets the job done.'

"Hoss just does exactly what George says. George was usually surrounded by people trying to climb the ladder, become winemakers," people like Andrew Levi, Amy continued "and Hoss couldn't do that. That made George feel safe with him."

The last stage before the wine went to the bottling area was to filter out any remaining living cells down to bacteria. This sterile filtration assured that errant microscopic bugs wouldn't begin to feast on remaining nutrients in the wine—or in white wines, on trace amounts of sugar—setting off an unwanted secondary fermentation. They hooked a hose from the tank to the filter—a cute little wheeled critter resembling a moon-landing vehicle—and scrubbed the wine by passing it through an ultrafine membrane. It emerged still cold and almost literally polished, then was slowly warmed before it was pumped into a filler bowl that was the first stage of the bottling operation. If the wine arrived too cold it would chill the bottles—then labels wouldn't stick and corks might pop loose.

Ferrari-Carano's bottling apparatus was antiquated, one of a very few areas where they were not state-of-the-art. Even so, it involved at least a million dollars' worth of machinery, machinery that Hoss said was "worse than a hay baler for moving parts," and prone to time-consuming malfunctions. It was going to take longer than it might have to fill those ninety thousand bottles.

But that was okay with Meisner. The Box Warrior was in a fine mood, as close to happy as I had ever heard him. "You're catching me at a good time," he said. "Unlike ninety-nine percent of wineries in this economy, we are totally on schedule. Not that I can give you any numbers. There's various ways to spread your risk and keep from putting too much pressure on U.S. markets. I just opened two new markets, Manila and Seoul, South Korea." A Marriott and a Ritz Carlton. "The other is cruise ships. And their business is increasing because there's a lot of people still don't like to fly and want to go on vacation. So there are ways to deflect pressures from increased production.

"And I said this to Don Carano in year one, as long as you have the quality, and as long as you have the demand curve exceed the supply curve, you're gonna be successful. I shouldn't shoot my mouth off," said Meisner. " 'Pride goeth before a fall,' you know what they say."

IN THE bottling area, an unadorned warehouse at the southern end of the winery where forklifts were stacking pallets loaded with sealed white cardboard cases of wine, the flint-colored bottles were spinning on an orbiter that took them into the clean room, a glass-enclosed sterile environment. The machinery was a twentieth-century invention, but putting the wine into glass went back to the twelfth century. Those early bottles were carafes, open-neck containers, and in addition to their beauty were an improvement over clay pots used by ancient Greek and Roman winemakers. Glass was nearly inert—it did not interact with what you put in it.

The bottles on the orbiter were the last Marlene Ing had selected, Burgundy-style, with high shoulders, and inside the bottoms were high punts, or dimples, that had been traditional in Sauvignon Blanc bottles since the nineteenth century. The orbiter ran the upright bottles under a metal udderlike device with twenty-four nipples, called a filler. As the bottles went around and around they looked like little toy soldiers, and they made a sound like *theta clunk theta clunk theta clunk*. The bottling area was loud with the rattling of bottles and the roar of machinery, loud enough to drown out the mariachi music turned up full blast on a radio brought along by the Mexican ladies who did the manual labor here, just as the men did in the vineyards. Some of the women were clerks or housekeeping staff drafted for the bottling, and others were temporaries. Many wore earplugs.

From the filler, the bottles passed beneath stainless-steel corker heads operated by vacuum pumps. The remaining air was forced out of the full bottles, and corks were plunged into the neck, a marriage of elements that began in the seventeenth century when the technology was developed to produce relatively uniform bottles. Next, the foil capsules were attached by hand—eighty capsules a minute were dropped over the necks of the corked bottles clanking by the ladies' workstations, on their way to a spinner where Teflon wheels flattened and anchored the foil. Last was an old-fashioned glue labeler that slapped on and flattened front and back labels, turning every bottle 180 degrees as it did so. A series of brushes smoothed out the back label with its text written by Rhonda, with help from Marlene Ing and Nancy Gilbert, the public relations person, and approved by the Bureau of Alcohol, Tobacco and Firearms:

> *Well-balanced and crisp, this Fumé Blanc is produced from selected Sauvignon Blanc grapes harvested in several vineyard locations. These varied grape sources give the wine lush melon and fig flavors complemented by light herbal aromas with hints of wildflowers. Partial barrel fermentation, extended lees contact, and French oak aging add a rich, lingering finish. Wonderful as an aperitif, this Fumé Blanc is also an exceptional match with pasta, shellfish and chicken dishes.*

That was it. Ready to ship, distribute, buy, pour, and drink. Except, of course, it wasn't. There was a hitch.

6

MARKET

April 2003–May 2003

This Is Ferrari-Carano

DON AND RHONDA and Steve and George all lifted their stemware to their lips, and tasted, chewing over the wine. It was a cold, damp Easter Monday, 2003, and they were gathered to answer crucially important questions. Was the 2002 Fumé Blanc ready to release? Had it been given enough time to be sufficiently bottle-aged? Was it still in a state of shock? Were they ready to release it to Meisner, and let him take it out to market to do battle at this most crucial time? It was no exaggeration to say that in the depressed market climate a bad decision—such as they had made two years earlier, when they held the vintage for further aging—could devastate their future. So they had held it back for a couple of extra weeks, seeing no harm in an excess of caution.

This year, when they had put the Fumé Blanc into the bottle and withdrawn the vacuum, the wine had been shocked, and had taken on a muted character. Its oakiness became more apparent than the quality they wanted to emphasize, had worked so long and hard to cultivate, what they called its fruit-forwardness. The shock could subdue the baby wine for a week, or two, or even a couple of months. Had it subsided?

Rhonda was the first to speak. "I always get this cotton candy nose out of it," she said. "It's really changed in the last two weeks. You can tell it's coming together." It was the first time I had seen Rhonda since her surgery, and she looked healthy, and was as hospitable and engaged in her work as always. For all that her cancer frightened them, as Don had told me, "It brings you together, too."

Just a few days earlier Don had assured me they had a great wine, and not only that, I was the reason for the exceptional Fumé Blanc; my being there had kept everybody focused and on their toes.

"This is one of the best Fumé Blancs we ever produced," he had said on the telephone. "And I'm sure it's because of the pressure you put on."

That my presence had sometimes affected what they were doing was probably true, but whether for ill or good was ambiguous, and not the point. They had made their process as transparent as they could manage; allowing me to follow the making of the wine was, at times, uncomfortable for the people at this table. It had led them into questions they had not anticipated and exposed vulnerabilities they were not delighted to have seen. George had said at the outset that it would be a journey, and it had been, just not the one they had anticipated. In May 2002, Don had come close to withdrawing from the project over questions I asked about the conflict between Steve and his predecessor, Barney Fernandez. The story was supposed to be about making a bottle of wine, Don said, so why was I asking personal questions? He was angry—it was the only time I glimpsed his temper. Deep Cork had explained that, "Don is a very, very big eight-hundred-pound gorilla around here. He's just not used to anybody doing anything he doesn't want."

Nor had he wanted me to go to Reno. "I want to keep Reno out of this, to tell the truth," he told me, the sixth or seventh time I tried to arrange a trip there. "It cheapens The Story, so to speak." Don sells booze to people who want to believe their drinking habits are a sign of good taste, and sells the probability of losing their money to people who want to believe they're going to strike it rich.

Then one day, out of the blue, he not only invited me to Reno but also arranged interviews with his grown children and some of his friends and associates. I asked his law partner John Frankovich why Don had changed his mind. "Well," he said, "maybe he was worried you were going to do some *National Enquirer* type of thing about Don Carano. But he thought about it and realized he had nothing to hide up here. So he thought to do it under the best circumstances."

In Reno I had also learned that plans for the new convention and entertainment center were back on track, that the mayor and council members Don had backed had won the election. "They've all come together now," he said, a classic understatement of raw power.

When Don had almost withdrawn his cooperation, I had arranged to drive up and talk to him in person in the Villa on a Friday afternoon. But it was summer, and traffic heading north for the weekend over the Golden Gate Bridge was backed up for miles. I rescheduled. But it had taken Don only a few days to put aside his misgivings and move forward. Don was not someone to hold a grudge. At his core, he was generous, forgiving, and sufficiently satisfied with himself and his accomplishments to have no need for holding on to grievances. So we left that discussion for another day, a day that would never truly arrive. I had explained to him that the wine was made and marketed by people, and that to write about the wine I had to know about the people. *They* were the story, and I didn't understand how their sorrows and joys could *not* be a part of what was in the bottle.

But now, as I sat sipping their delicious wine, I found my mind full of what more I might have said. One reason writers write is to say what we might have, if only we had been quicker. We get the opportunity to reprise and revise life.

I might have said, for instance, that in French there is no word for wine*maker* (nor for that matter in Italian, Spanish, or German, as Karen MacNeil points out). The French use *vigeron*, meaning vine grower, and consider *winemaker* to be reflective of American egoism and our star system. In France the belief is that nature plays the essential role in determining the quality and character of a wine. They focus on *terroir*, a word for which there is no American equivalent; it combines soil, slope, orientation to the sun, elevation, rainfall, wind, fog, sunshine—in short, every nuance of the natural environment.

Our fundamentally different way of looking at this question may have something to do with our expectation in California that by and large the weather will be fine and the land abundant, a belief so far unshaken by earthquakes or drought, global warming or the appearance of the glassy-winged sharpshooter. The yearning for vitalism—the philosophical idea that emotions can be transferred to substances—never entirely dies, no matter how discredited it becomes, and there is nowhere where it is more alive than in grape growing and winemaking. Wine is the lubricant of communion, with our God, with our friends and family, with our melancholy and joy. Less consciously, we are also communing with where it came from, and who made it.

If I had had the wit at the time he was angry to say all I had wanted to say to Don, I would have asked him: Do you believe for a second that, for the people at this table, the spirits of Marlene and Boa are *not* in this bottle? Or your fears and aspirations? And Rhonda's? Meisner's salesmanship? Steve's perfectionism? George's care? When I taste this wine, I would have said, I am aware of all of that, and though most people who drink it will know nothing about you or the others, what I want to do through what I write is to bring many more people into that communion. Everything that's happened in the last year is in this bottle, and if it cannot be tasted, it can at least be known. All of California is in this wine made from grapes that are such chameleons they change to take on the chemical composition of other plants. Life and death, water and air, war and peace—all contained in California's symbolic product, its face to the world.

OF THOSE at the table, George was the most critical of the wine. Creators see the flaws writ large, like parents observing in their children traits they wish weren't so clearly their own.

"We're still battling aggressive vegetative growth," he said. "It's important to have the grapes be reflective of the style of wine that's already popular."

Nonetheless, he liked what he was tasting. "So this is it," he said. "This is everything we talked about. It's going to improve in the next couple of weeks. I think this is a little more fruity than last year."

"This is really fruit driven," Steve agreed. If George wanted to give credit where credit was due—to his fruit, and thank goodness George hadn't messed it up beyond saving—that was okay with him.

"To put all these components together in a lab situation is a really big deal," said George.

Boys, boys, I wanted to say, enough already.

Don asked for my opinion of the wine. Without thinking, I said I thought the 2001 had been sweeter, or fruitier, or something. There followed an eight-hundred-pound silence: After all the risks they had taken in overcoming their mistrust, would the upshot be that I was going to write that they had failed? They still thought of me as a reviewer. The truth was, left to my own devices, I wouldn't have been able to distinguish one vintage from the other, and I liked them both just fine.

"The 2002 has more going on," Rhonda said, finally. "But it's just a baby."

"People like *this*," George said. "This is Ferrari-Carano."

George wasn't quite ready to let the shocked baby wine go to market. But Rhonda had a different agenda.

"I think this is really consistent with our style," she said. "We were going to release this to *Wine Spectator*." She was not about to miss their deadline. That rating was important. "So let's do that," she said.

Some Witty Quality

RINGERS, RINGERS EVERYWHERE, and all of them pre-pared to quaff. My favorite was Mr. Gersh, who, when I asked for his phone number in case I had any further questions, told me: "You're a nice man. A very nice man." Mr. Gersh would not appear, though, until after a clearly worried Bob McGinn, Ferrari-Carano's northeastern states regional sales manager, slipped a folded bill to a server at the Four Seasons, and whispered: "Nobody's ordering the wine."

That nobody had yet ordered the wine at the Four Seasons on this night in May 2003 was a big problem. A problem because I had come to New York specifically to see the corks pulled from the first shipment of the 2002 Fumé. But perhaps a larger problem for McGinn, a hospitable man who used to teach high school chemistry in Worcester, Massachusetts. His boss, Steve Meisner, had told him: "When this guy shows up"—he meant me—"take care of him one hundred percent."

No effort had been spared. A shipment, the first to leave the winery, had been rushed to the New York distributor, Peerless. McGinn had lined up restaurants. Then they sent out some guys, Meisner told me, to make sure that the wine had arrived and that the menus reflected the 2002 vintage. So from beginning to end New York was a setup. This was the wine business as it really was.

By the time we met Mr. Gersh at the Four Seasons, incentives had been piled on incentives. Incentives to the distributor, incentives to the sales guys, the restaurateurs, and now even the customers. Of course, one man's incentive is another man's bribe. Bob McGinn had told me about a maître d' in Boston who let wine salesmen know he had an account at a clothier, where they could show their gratitude. The whole shebang, as Michael Ouellette of Martini House in St. Helena had told me, "is based on a kind of blackmail. Winemail. And a hot winery will say, 'You want our best wine? You need to take something else, that's not selling.'"

WE HAD begun our New York odyssey on Friday night at Chazal, a three-year-old French Mediterranean bistro on Madison Avenue that McGinn said was one of the hottest in the city. Its owner, Mario Carta, wore the pointiest black boots I'd ever seen on a man. His clientele, he told me casually, "are mostly Eurotrash," a category in which he seemed to include himself.

Enter Michael Amar and his girlfriend, the stunning, raven-haired Faith Carroll, a twenty-five-year-old who said she was a retired model. We met them moments after Amar had become the first person in the world to buy a bottle of the 2002 Fumé—if indeed he had purchased it. This was never clear, because he was also one of Mario Carta's best friends.

"Yes, we are trying it," Amar told me. "I drive a Ferrari, so I decided to try it. I know more red wines than white wines. What you like, *chérie?*"

"I always like dry white wines because I'm a champagne drinker," said Faith.

Amar was a dark, handsome Frenchman with a small ponytail. He and Faith were sitting at the bar at Chazal. The bar was backlit. They made a striking picture. There was a disc jockey, Jayson "Jblends" Ayala, spinning music that, in the confines of the bistro, was deafeningly loud. At the moment it was "I Will Survive," by a singer unknown to me and to Bob McGinn, who was fifty-six and listened mostly to NPR in his Lexus, where he spent many a day plying his product.

"I am middle or higher class," Amar was telling me. "I am in ladies' wear."

So this was it—the moment I had waited seventeen months to witness. The very first bottle of a new vintage of a California white wine was being drunk in a Moroccan Eurotrash hangout in New York by a Frenchman who drove an Italian car and was in the rag trade.

When we left Chazal, Jblends followed us into Twenty-sixth Street, pressing on us a gray-on-gray semitransparent plastic business card, saying he hoped we would write about *him.* Jblends and Chazal felt evanescent.

But, god knows, not the Four Seasons, where we went on Saturday. The Four Seasons felt like forever. The chain mail–like curtains, arranged in descending arcs, were supposed to make diners feel safe and secure, regardless of what madness reigned without.

The restaurant is famously elegant. As the seasons change, so do the menu, the waiters' uniforms, and the décor. On this cool evening in May, with rain threatening, the potted plants in the Pool Room, named for the illuminated pool at its center, were petrified cherry trees with pink silk blossoms. Springtime.

Chazal had priced the Fumé at forty-six dollars, a Eurotrash price. But the Four Seasons charged only thirty-four dollars, making it not only the cheapest wine on their 586-bottle list, but also the only 2002 to have arrived there at this early date. It was also listed first among California whites. Coincidence?

Bob McGinn, who favored dark shirts and ties and monogrammed cuffs, was justifiably proud that Ferrari-Carano was one of only two California wineries to have four selections on Julian Niccolini's world-famous wine list—famous not least of all for having been among the earliest advocates for California wines. While we ate Iranian caviar and drank a bottle of the 2002 Fumé, McGinn told us how he had broken through with the discriminating and influential Niccolini.

"I don't want to take a lot of credit," McGinn said, "but it was mostly my effort." After months of trying—every sales rep wants to "taste" Niccolini, very few succeed—McGinn got an appointment. "I brought our TreMonte Sangiovese to Julian. He grabs it from me, brings it to the bartender. Asks the bartender for a different bottle. He's tasting them side by side. He said to the bartender, 'Buy me ten cases.' Then he disappears. I said to the bartender, 'What was he drinking?' il Poggione!"

The other wine was a Brunello di Montalcino il Poggione, a great Tuscan Sangiovese. It went to prove a wine trade adage: The gems sell themselves. But only if you can get in the door—and Bob Mc-Ginn did.

By now we had finished our tuna carpaccio with ginger and coriander and were working on morel ravioli with spring peas, anticipating the arrival of our Peking duck with apple salad and black curry sauce. I asked our waiter about an Oratorio Gigondas from the list.

He scrunched up his face distastefully. "A little tannic," he said. Let me see if I understood right. The Four Seasons chose to put this wine on its list, charged sixty-five dollars for it, and its waiter had just signaled me that it sucked? Perhaps he'd have been more approving if I had gone for something that cost twice as much? But I agreed with Bob's wife Ruth's review when she took her first sip of the Gigondas. "Oh, wow," she said approvingly. "What is this?"

So we're digging into our filet of bison with foie gras and a perigord truffle sauce, and I'm thinking maybe I should have decided to be a food and wine writer after all, and about then was when McGinn, distressed that nobody has ordered the Fumé Blanc, had his tête-à-tête with the server.

Voilà, the Steven Kayes.

Steven Kaye and his wife and friends, the Michael Pressmans, were enjoying an evening at their favorite restaurant. "Money," Kaye told me, "no object." They had asked Lorenz Pretterhoffer, the maître d', for something elegant to drink with their crab cakes. Kaye trusted Lorenz without hesitation—Kaye's phrase—and Lorenz had suggested, also without hesitation, the Fumé Blanc.

Steven Kaye presented his business card. It said he was president of American Economic Planning Group, Inc., in Watchung, New Jersey. After his name were the following initials: CFP, CLU, ChFC, RHU, CEBS, and AAMS. CFP was trademarked. I did not ask what any of it meant for fear he might actually tell me.

"My specialty," he said, "is total wealth management." At thirty-four dollars, the Fumé Blanc was value.

His wife Mindy introduced herself now. "Thirty-six C," said Steven Kaye proudly. Mindy smiled. I looked.

Now he was ready to taste the wine. He swirled it in his stemware. The wine was pale gold, the color of California in early summer. He took a tiny taste. "Mmmm," he said. "Light. Fruity. It's delicious."

"And," said the Kayes' dinner companion Michael Pressman, an attorney, "it has some witty quality."

Perhaps the Kayes were the customers to first buy a bottle of the Ferrari-Carano 2002 Fumé Blanc. Or maybe it had been Michael Amar and Faith Carroll—if indeed they had paid for their wine. Whatever. The Kayes and the Pressmans, happy with their choice and themselves, clinked their glasses as Lorenz beamed. "Cheers," said Mindy Kaye.

And, finally, there was Martin Gersh, sitting alone on the opposite side of the pool, a good long swim away, but we walked around the perimeter.

"Mr. Gersh," the server explained on the way, "he's one of our regulars. He was also, I believe, a wine critic for *Vogue* and *Wine & Spirits*. The guy's drunk three bottles in one sitting. A wonderful guy."

Indeed, Mr. Gersh welcomed us with three bottles' worth of cordiality.

"I don't drink any California Sauvignon Blancs; I drink Loire wines, so this should be interesting," he said. He sniffed. "A slight bit of sweetness." He sipped. "Very agreeable. A fruity wine."

How did he come to order it, I asked.

"Oh, I didn't order it," he said. "It was brought to me. I don't know anything about it."

All those months ago, George had said to me, about success and failure: "We won't really know until that guy in a restaurant pulls that cork."

Apparently, I had witnessed that moment. But was it a success?

Not a Bad Thing to Be

"IT'S DON'S OPINION," says Deep Cork, "that Jim Laube used to love Ferrari-Carano, and doesn't anymore." James Laube is the Napa-based senior editor and columnist for *Wine Spectator,* a gloriously glossy magazine celebrating all things vinified, and jam-packed with gloriously expensive industry ads. It would be hard to overstate its influence. The world of wine is snobbish, faddish, and—for ordinary punters such as me, simply seeking a tasty swallow at an affordable price—obscure, expensive, and intimidating to boot. Faced with bewildering choices, "The average wine consumer takes that publication as gospel," says Amy Kelsey. "Oh, boy, don't get me started on *Wine Spectator.*"

From mass marketers to top-end wine boutiques, many retailers display *Wine Spectator* ratings on shelf tags, and these numbers have an influence on purchases unheard-of in other segments of the food and beverage industry. The commercial power of wine critics is akin to the sway of movie or drama critics; you might even say that in this regard, wine is more like the entertainment industry than it is the grocery business. In the same way that Roger Ebert and a few other crit-ics can make or break a movie at the box office, Jim Laube and a hand-ful of other wine writers can make or break a label, or even a vintage.

Deep Cork first met Laube in 1990, and "thought that he was hon-est and passionate about his job. Through the years, I thought Jim be-came more and more jaded. And why not, when every winery in California is lying in wait for you to try the wines, rate the wines, praise the wines, put the wines on the cover, place the wines in the top 100, etc., etc. Perfectly nice people, after having written for *Wine Spectator* for a couple of years, become insufferable and arrogant."

Wine Spectator, says its executive editor, Tom Matthews, "has a stringent code of ethics . . . We insist on independence from the wine industry, and know that avoiding conflicts of interest is the key to maintaining our credibility." Yet rumors abound of wineries—no matter their view of the ethics involved—at least trying to lavish cases on the critics. Don Carano, for example, frequently wanted me to accept bottles and even cases of wine, not because he wanted to buy me off but because hospitality was essential to the industry, and his own nature was generous. In fact, in the trade *gift* is sometimes used as a verb—*I gift you, you gift me*. I consistently refused Don's largesse, but on several occasions accepted when refusing seemed churlish. I can only imagine the temptations experienced by true, full-time wine writers. Not surprisingly, critics at the leading magazines and newspapers are feared and in some cases reviled.

At Ferrari-Carano, already reeling from the industry-wide slump, and having introduced incentives that transformed their fourteen-dollar Fumé Blanc into, in effect, an $11.99 wine, the summer of 2003 was an anxious time as they awaited the judgment of *Wine Spec-tator*. Of course, Don was not going to get his long-hoped-for 99—not for this wine. It was universally known within the trade—though not, generally, among consumers—that the so-called 100-point scale was applied differently, depending on the variety of wine. A well-reviewed Cabernet Sauvignon, Pinot Noir, or Chardonnay could all get ratings in the high 90s. A top-rated Sauvignon Blanc would get a 90, or even an 89 or 88. Nobody knew why, but that's the way it was.

In Ferrari-Carano's earlier years, after *Wine Spectator* put their new Chardonnay on its cover, the Fumé Blanc also did well with the magazine. An 89 in 1992, followed by an 88 in 1993, and then a 90 in 1994. More recently, though, their ratings had slipped. In 1999, when they had to recall the wine to allow for more bottle aging, they had missed the deadline, and received no rating. In 2000, they had received an 85; in 2001, an 87.

On the face of it, those are good ratings. On a report card, 87 translates into a B-plus. Only that's not true for wine, and the reason is that, as Amy Kelsey pointed out to me, *Wine Spectator* is for the most part not really operating on a 100-point scale, but rather a 20-point scale. It is rare, though not unheard-of, for a wine to receive less than an 80. On a true 100-point scale, a wine that gets a 65 is average, and a wine that gets an 85 is very good indeed. In *Wine Spectator,* 85 is teetering on the fault line for failure. Sauvignon Blancs that get less than 85 do not receive the capsule reviews that accompany the ratings—only the stark, condemnatory numerals.

Of course, these ratings are subjective, literally a matter of taste. Could anybody seriously claim to know the difference between an 87- and an 88-rated wine? Perhaps at the highest and most refined levels—first-growth Bordeaux and such—there is a set of long-established criteria having to do with flavors, aromas, complexity, and resemblance to past vintages that, even if not objective, seems to be agreed upon by a tiny handful of leading oenophiles, all of whom have enough money to afford these thoroughbreds. But even among the elite critics when assessing *grand cru* wines, the equivalent of food fights break out now and again, as when Jancis Robinson, author of

The Oxford Companion to Wine, and Robert Parker, whom some consider to be the single most influential critic in the world, got into it over a bottle of 2003 Château Pavie that Parker said was a wine of "sublime richness," and Robinson called a "ridiculous wine."

At the more pedestrian level of a wine like Ferrari-Carano's 2002 Fumé Blanc, all that remains is personal taste. These preferences are gussied up in the fancy-schmancy language of publications like *Wine Spectator*: "Intense, with tart quince, green pear, fig and grass flavors." Tart quince? There's a flavor always on the tip of my tongue. Or this, from a major newspaper: "Pleasant whiffs of motor oil." Who's fooling whom here? And yet, this kind of emperor's-new-clothes lingo, slung around by critics speaking mostly to each other while intimidating the nouveau, can drive pricing, boost or depress sales, and in the most extreme cases, make or break a winery.

Wine Spectator supports itself both through its $5.95 cover price for the 375,000 copies it sells, and by accepting ads from the very wineries whose products it reviews. So a 2002 Ferrari-Carano Reserve Chardonnay selling for thirty-two dollars ("rich, elegant and seductive") received a 92 rating in the May 31, 2003, issue, and in the very next issue the Caranos placed a full-page ad: "Savor the difference handcrafted wines bring to the table." The busy, glossy ad, featuring bottles of the just-reviewed Reserve Chardonnay and the 2002 Fumé Blanc beside a tray of California figs and local artisanal cheeses, was selling The Story. It hit on every element: Italian, Family, Hospitality. An inset photo of Rhonda sitting on Don's lap with her arm around his shoulder, and the tag line, "Don and Rhonda invite you to visit on your next visit to California wine country," completed the package.

Was there a relationship between the favorable review—the Chardonnay had also been a Selection of the Month—and the full-page ad? One might ask whether any periodical can maintain the necessary impartiality when reviewing the products of its advertisers. This may be everyday commerce in many industries. But it nonetheless raises the question of whether a wine magazine is able to offer objective assessments of wines produced by the very advertisers that help support its existence. *Wine Spectator*'s Tom Matthews denies that advertising has any influence on its reviews, saying that an "independent study of all our reviews found that there is no significant difference between average scores for advertised and nonadvertised wines."

Many vintners hate the game, but feel they have little choice. Don told me that once, a few years back, after receiving ratings from Laube that he thought were unfair, he invited the critic to the Villa Fiore for a tasting—a true, blind tasting—the bottles wrapped in brown paper. According to Don, Laube praised some of the very wines he had written less-than-flattering reviews about. When Don removed the brown paper, Laube chuckled. But he didn't amend his reviews—not where it counted, not on the pages of his magazine.

Another thing that drives some vintners nuts is not knowing the criteria by which their wines are being judged. A lot of effort goes into trying to figure out what someone like Robert Parker likes (*Wine Advocate* has never reviewed a Ferrari-Carano wine), and then making wines that conform to his taste.

"It would be fair if these critics described their aesthetic," says Dr. Mark Matthews, a professor at the U.C. Davis Department of Viticulture and Enology. "They should hold out a model of what they're trying to reach. Parker. Laube. Part of their job should be to bring those along who want to know more. These guys aren't bringing anybody along."

Matthews tried to get a grant to study the critics' tastes, with no success. "The grape and wine industry funds most of what we do," he says. "They will not fund research to find out what these guys believe. They call it market research, and will not fund market research. I don't know what that's about—I have some ideas, though."

And so, when the August 31, 2002, issue of *Wine Spectator* hit the streets, the disappointment at Villa Fiore was palpable:

85: *Ferrari-Carano Fumé Blanc Sonoma County 2002 $15*
Curious, but with good concentration to sweet-sour apple and apricot character framed by vanilla.

You could hear the air go out of the balloon all over the Villa. Don accounted for the disappointing rating by saying that Laube preferred a more varietal style. And indeed, there were certain characteristics the magazine attributed to those 2002 Sauvignon Blancs that got the highest ratings. All were described as "concentrated"—but so was the Ferrari-Carano. All mentioned the word "green"—either green apple (Is that different from "sweet-sour apple?" How can we know?) or green pear. Something "citric" or "tart"—that varietal tang—was attributed to all of the top-rated wines, the four that received 90s, and the one that received a 91. But no matter how you slice the grapefruit, there was no getting around the fact that twenty-nine wines received higher ratings than the Ferrari-Carano, and only eleven had lower ratings—the lowest being an 81.

I felt bad for Don and Rhonda, George and Andrew, Steve and Jeffrey. Except for one brief conversation with Don in a stairwell, I didn't talk to any of them about it. I already knew how they felt—disappointed, angry, perhaps humiliated. Nearly eighteen months of effort, and the upshot was this: 85. In effect, a D-minus.

I wanted to know more about how this judgment was reached, and also more about Laube's views—far more knowledgeable than mine—of Ferrari-Carano's wines, and its place in the industry. The man tastes about three thousand California wines each year. I have never met

Laube, but a photo of him in the magazine showed someone of late-middle years with a thatch of silver hair, a wide brush mustache, a nice tan, and wide-spaced eyes that appeared amused and world-weary. I called to talk to him, but he had his assistant reply that it would not be possible; he was too busy. I asked again a few months later—and again, his assistant said he was too busy. I offered him a two-month period during which I would make myself available at his convenience. And he replied in an e-mail that he had not actually written the rating, someone else had. There was no way for me to determine whether what he said was true or not. So, like the people who made the wine, I was never able to learn what he meant by "curious"—a word I have not otherwise seen in a *Wine Spectator* rating. A curious word, one might almost say.

"I don't know what *he* meant," said Amy Kelsey, who helped to make the wine. "But it makes some sense to me. Over time, it seems to have this odd sweet-and-sour quality that's sort of incongruous in the mouth, compared to what you get in the natural grape. The result of those manipulations of George's. That's my interpretation—I don't know if that's what Laube meant. I learned to take everything he and *Wine Spectator* said with a grain of salt. I saw the blatant favoritism that Jim Laube played with everybody. I know people who looked back twenty years, correlating the ads placed with the scores the wines got. Who even knows if he tastes all the wines? He has a right to his opinion, and he has to give some wines bad reviews. But you pour your whole heart and soul into a wine, and he'll dash out a bad review, and it's heartbreaking.

"I do find the wine to be curious on the palate. I mean, I like it. I think our 2002 came out to be one of our best Fumés. I'm really happy with it. It's a summer sipping wine."

An $11.99 summer sipping wine—because again in 2003, that was the everyday price in larger California retailers. Things had changed a lot since Steve Domenichelli had snapped those sleeping vines, the way his grandfather taught him, on a drizzly day at Keegan Ranch in November 2001. They had taken the journey George Bursick had promised, but when they arrived, it was not at the destination they had anticipated. For all the sleepless nights, the sweat, tears, and care that went into making the wine, and whether or not the people at Ferrari-Carano wanted to acknowledge it, their "friendship wine" as Steve Meisner called it, was no longer positioned as a thing of desire. The alchemy of the shifting market—some combination of the grapes they grew, the wine they made, their position, its reception—had transformed it into a simple backyard pleasure.

Not a bad thing to be, when all is said and done.

Acknowledgments

THIS BOOK BEGAN with a multipart series in the *San Francisco Chronicle*. Many people at the *Chronicle* had a hand in its making, more than I can possibly name here. Phil Bronstein, the editor, gave me that rarest of gifts in the newspaper business—time: some two years from conception to completion. Then Carolyn White, the deputy managing editor for features, encouraged me to expand what had been intended as a magazine story into a 60,000-word series—the longest the newspaper has ever published. Both of them supported the project, and its author, from beginning to end. I am forever grateful.

I was doubly fortunate to be working with two photographers, John Storey and Eric Luse, who also make wine at their own winery, Eric Ross, in Sebastopol. Their hands-on knowledge was incalculably important to me. And I am especially grateful to John King, the newspaper's architecture critic, who took time out of his busy schedule to spend a day at the Villa Fiore and share his observations.

Many others were also generous with their time and expertise, both for the series, and later when I began to expand it into this book.

I especially want to thank Mel Knox, a contributor to *The Oxford Companion to Wine*; Carole Meredith, Linda Bisson, and Mark Matthews, all faculty in the Department of Viticulture and Enology at the University of California, Davis; Nancy Gilbert, for her newsletters written for Simi Winery; Eileen Fredrikson of Gomberg, Fredrikson & Associates; Michael Ouellette; and the extraordinary winemaker and restaurateur Pat Kuleto. Their contributions greatly enhanced my understanding. I, not they, however, must be held accountable for any mistakes in describing the science and craft of winemaking.

Of course, without the cooperation of Don and Rhonda Carano and their talented, energetic, and dedicated staff, there would have been no book. I cannot thank them enough for welcoming me into their business and their lives.

At Gotham Books, I was greatly aided by my editor, Brendan Cahill, and my publisher, Bill Shinker, and their staffs. Thank you. Thanks as well to my agent, David Vigliano. My friend Danelle Morton offered her help, her concern, and her unfailing good humor. All my children gave me a reason to write. My daughter Casey seemed to hover about me throughout, making me feel I was under her protection and that she was my guardian angel.

Among the books I drew upon were three of particular value: *The Wine Bible* by Karen MacNeil, *Through the Grapevine* by Jay Stuller and Glen Martin, and *The Far Side of Eden* by James Conaway.

The idea for this book came from my wife, Carole Rafferty. We were sitting on the deck of our hotel room in Mendocino, drinking a California red wine and watching the sun set into the Pacific, when she asked, "Did you ever think about all that goes into a bottle of wine?" I did no more than seek the answers to her question. To her, more than anyone, I owe this book, and much, much more.